THE 4% SOLUTION

THE 4% SOLUTION

UNLEASHING THE ECONOMIC GROWTH
AMERICA NEEDS

Foreword by George W. Bush
Introduction by James K. Glassman
Edited by Brendan Miniter

CROWN
BUSINESS
NEW YORK

GEORGE W. BUSH
PRESIDENTIAL CENTER
★ ★ ★

Copyright © 2012 by the George W. Bush Foundation

Library of Congress Cataloging-in-Publication Data is available upon request.

ISBN: 978-0-307-98614-6
eISBN: 978-0-307-98615-3

Printed in the United States of America

Book design by Lauren Dong

10 9 8 7 6 5 4 3 2 1

First Edition

Contents

George W. Bush served as the forty-third president of the United States.

James K. Glassman, executive director of the George W. Bush Institute, was formerly undersecretary of State for public diplomacy and public affairs. He is the author of several books on finance.

Brendan Miniter is senior editorial director of the Bush Institute.

W. Michael Cox is director of the William J. O'Neil Center for Global Markets and Freedom at Southern Methodist University.

Richard Alm is writer in residence at the William J. O'Neil Center.

Robert E. Lucas Jr., the John Dewey Distinguished Service Professor of Economics at the University of Chicago, received the Nobel Memorial Prize in Economic Sciences in 1995.

Edward C. Prescott, the W. P. Carey Chaired Professor of Economics at Arizona State University, received the Nobel Memorial Prize in Economic Sciences in 2004.

Steven Gjerstad is a visiting research associate at Chapman University.

Vernon L. Smith, professor of economics at Chapman University, received the Nobel Memorial Prize in Economic Sciences in 2002.

Kevin Hassett is a senior fellow and director of economic policy studies at the American Enterprise Institute. He was formerly a senior economist with the Federal Reserve System.

David Malpass is president of Encima Global LLC, an economic research firm. He served in the administrations of Presidents Ronald Reagan and George H. W. Bush.

Myron Scholes, the Frank E. Buck Professor of Finance, Emeritus, at Stanford University, received the Nobel Memorial Prize in

Economic Sciences in 1997. He is co-originator of the Black-Scholes options pricing model.

Peter G. Klein is associate professor of applied social sciences and director of the McQuinn Center for Entrepreneurial Leadership at the University of Missouri, Columbia, and senior fellow at the Ludwig von Mises Institute.

Robert Litan is vice president for research and policy at the Kauffman Foundation and a senior fellow at the Brookings Institution. He has authored or coauthored more than twenty books.

Nick Schulz is the DeWitt Wallace Fellow and editor of American .com at the American Enterprise Institute. He is the coauthor of *From Poverty to Prosperity* and writes the Economics 2.0 column for *Forbes* online.

Maria Minniti holds the Bobby B. Lyle Endowed Chair of Entrepreneurship at the Cox School of Business at Southern Methodist University. Her chapter draws significantly on her previously published works.

Carlos Gutierrez, vice chairman of the Institutional Clients Group of Citigroup, served as U.S. secretary of Commerce from 2005 to 2009. Born in Havana, Cuba, he was formerly CEO of the Kellogg Company. He thanks Peter Tillman for his assistance with the chapter.

Steven F. Hayward is the F. K. Weyerhaeuser Fellow at the American Enterprise Institute.

Kenneth P. Green is a resident scholar at American Enterprise Institute.

Charles Blahous, a senior research fellow at the Mercatus Center at George Mason University, serves as one of the two public trustees for the Social Security and Medicare programs.

Jason J. Fichtner, also a senior research fellow at the Mercatus, was formerly chief economist at the Social Security Administration. He and Charles Blahous thank Jakina Debnam and Brandon Pizzola for their assistance with the chapter.

Eric A. Hanushek is the Paul and Jean Hanna Senior Fellow at the Hoover Institution of Stanford University. He chairs the executive committee of the Texas Schools Project.

Gary S. Becker, professor of economics and sociology at the University

of Chicago and Jack R. Anderson Senior Fellow at the Hoover Institution, received the Nobel Memorial Prize in Economics in 1992.

Pia M. Orrenius is a senior economist and research officer at the Federal Reserve Bank of Dallas. She is a research fellow at the Institute
for the Study of Labor in Bonn, Germany.

Madeline Zavodny chairs the economics department at Agnes Scott
College. She is a research fellow at the Institute for the Study of
Labor in Bonn, Germany.

Floyd Kvamme, partner emeritus at Kleiner Perkins Caufield & Byers, a
high-technology venture capital firm, helped found National Semiconductor. He served as cochairman of the President's Council of
Advisors on Science and Technology from 2001 to 2008.

Amity Shlaes, senior fellow and director of the Bush Institute's 4%
Growth Project, is the author, among other books, of *The Forgotten
Man: A New History of the Great Depression* (2007) and *Coolidge*
(2012).

Michael Novak, a theologian and author of more than thirty books,
served in various Democratic and Republican administrations since
1972. He was the 1994 recipient of the Templeton Prize for making
an "exceptional contribution to affirming life's spiritual dimension."

The United States economy has long been characterized by periods of strong and sustained growth, interrupted by brief, periodic recessions that ultimately give way to renewed economic expansion. Between 1983 and 2008, America enjoyed twenty-five years of nearly continuous and often explosive economic growth, interrupted only by brief recessions. The downturn that followed the financial crisis in 2008 was more sudden and severe than many recessions, but we have every reason to believe that like every other economic disruption in our history, it can be followed by a return to robust growth.

While the causes of the 2008 crisis will be debated by scholars for decades to come, we can all agree that excessive risk-taking by financial institutions, irresponsible decisions by lenders and borrowers, and market-distorting government policies all played a role. The question now is which policies we should adopt to fix the problems, speed the recovery, and lay the foundation for another long, steady expansion. That is the topic of this book. In the pages that follow, leading economic thinkers offer ideas on how to revive the economy. Guiding their work is the belief that the solution to today's problems is sustained and significant economic growth and that the surest path to that growth is free markets and free people.

To get ourselves on that path, we first need to recognize the power and importance of free enterprise. Every economic system has its shortcomings, but free-market capitalism offers the most efficient and just way to order an economy. At a fundamental level, such a system allows individuals to decide the course of their own lives. By making decisions about where to invest and what to purchase, they help drive our economy. And as they make decisions about what level of education to attain, where to work, and the purpose of their lives, they earn the dignity that comes from using their God-given talents and the pride that comes from contributing to the productivity of our nation.

In a free-market system, individuals from humble beginnings can rise to become leaders in their chosen fields. For an example, consider Vernon Smith, one of the authors in this book. His family moved to a farm when he was a boy during the Great Depression to ensure that they would have enough food to eat. From there he worked hard, got into college, and built a successful career. In 2002 he won the Nobel Prize in Economics.

Looking over the course of history, we can see that free-market capitalism has done more than any other economic system to raise living standards across the globe. Free-market capitalism rebuilt Japan and Western Europe after World War II. It made Hong Kong into a global economic competitor. And it built the United States into the strongest economic power in world history.

At the other end of the spectrum, governments that try to control their markets often face debilitating shortages, or worse. For example, Iran is an oil-rich country. But under the rule of a theocratic government, it struggles to provide refined gasoline to its people. Similarly, Cuba is a fertile island that has historically been rich in sugar cane. Yet, under the rule of the Castro brothers, food—even sugar—is rationed. In North Korea, a country ruled by a backward Stalinist regime, millions starve while their neighbors living under a free-market system in South Korea enjoy the fruits of a thriving, modern economy.

The most successful free-market economies trade freely with other nations. And so the path back to prosperity also requires America to keep its markets open and remain engaged with the world. Isolationism is shortsighted and dangerous. We learned that lesson the hard way during the Great Depression when policy makers imposed the Smoot-Hawley tariffs. The result was that we weakened our economy at a time when events were leading to a world war.

The record is clear. A nation's prosperity depends on where it falls on the spectrum of economic freedom. Capitalist countries have shown that free markets are the surest path to economic growth, opportunity for all, and a just system based on human dignity.

So part of the mission of the George W. Bush Institute, a new policy center in Dallas, is to promote economic growth at home and freedom abroad. All people desire to be free, to have a voice in picking their political leaders, and to determine their own destiny. And when we do well economically, we encourage others to adopt policies that will lead to their own prosperity and enable them to become strong trading partners.

One common theme of *The 4% Solution* is that with the right policies America can be robust again, and the United States can continue to be the strongest economic power in the world. I thank the brilliant economic thinkers who have contributed to this book for providing key insights that policy makers can use to revive our economy. As they spell out in the pages that follow, innovation is the heart of economic growth. We've led the world in developing new technologies and new ideas, and we can continue to do so. Our people are industrious and creative, our universities are the best in the world, and our markets are capable of supporting a resurgent economy. We've seen the resilience of this country before, and we will see it again. Our brightest days reside not in the fading light of past success, but on the horizon of our future.

Introduction: We Can Do It
By James K. Glassman

For the past few years, the United States has been afflicted by some of the worst of economic maladies: a financial crisis followed by recession and stagnation. Now many economic forecasters see sustainable U.S. growth declining by a full percentage point from its trend of the past seven decades. One point may not sound like much, but over the longer term, it has a huge effect. It means that the standard of living of an American born today will be roughly half what it would have been.

Some numbers: Since the end of World War II, the United States has grown at an average rate of 3% annually.[1] That's the increase in real (after inflation) gross domestic product (GDP), the sum of all goods and services. The road has never been smooth. There have been eleven recessions, but after each one a spurt in growth has brought the United States back on track, following the same powerful, upward trend line you can see in Figure 1 of chapter 3. As Robert E. Lucas Jr., one of the five Nobel Prize–winning economists who have contributed chapters to this book, writes of that graph: "The first thing you see . . . is that the U.S. economy is a remarkable growth machine."[2]

But will it continue to be? The Congressional Budget Office, reflecting the views of most economists, predicts that growth, starting in the middle of this decade and extending as far as the eye can see, will level off at only about 2.4%.[3] Even that figure may be optimistic, given our current condition. Kevin Hassett of the American Enterprise Institute writes in chapter 6 that, unless policies change, growth will dip below 2% in 2017 and continue to fall.

There are many reasons for the projected decline. Demographics are unfavorable, with too few workers supporting too many nonworkers, as Charles Blahous and Jason Fichtner show in their analysis of Social Security in chapter 15. The regulatory burden, cited by many of the authors of this book, has affected hiring and entrepreneurship. Education, as Stanford's Eric Hanushek explains in chapter 16, is not keeping pace with global innovation. The debt added in recent years and projected far into the future is a heavy weight that slows down the progress of the economy. And there are intangible and moral reasons for the slowdown as well, as Nick Schulz (chapter 11) and Michael Novak (chapter 21) write, from different perspectives.

Perhaps the most important cause is an abandonment of faith in what got us strong growth in the first place: the free-market system, where government sees its role as establishing an environment for private enterprise to thrive, rather than "creating jobs," choosing industrial winners and losers, narrowing what politicians consider income gaps, and the like. At the very least, policies that have abandoned the free market have caused firms and individuals to worry about making long-term capital and hiring commitments, and the result is a severe dampening of the animal spirits ("a spontaneous urge to action rather than inaction") that John Maynard Keynes himself believed was at the root of progress.[4]

Whatever the causes, the trajectory is clear. Without significant changes in government policies, in business practices, and in moral vision, the robust growth that has characterized America for more than a century could be over.

But we are optimists. We believe those needed changes—if they are laid out clearly and advocated cogently—will come to pass.

In late 2010, as those of us at the brand-new George W. Bush Institute scanned the economic landscape, we came to the conclusion that we could make an important contribution to the well-being of Americans by finding ways to increase growth and then spreading those solutions far and wide. President Bush believes in setting aggressive but achievable goals, and we established a target of 4% average annual sustainable GDP increases. Why 4%? We wanted to reach. To call for a return to 3% would not be so inspirational or aspirational. Four percent: We can get there.

In April 2011 we launched what we called "The 4% Growth Project" with a conference on the campus of Southern Methodist University in Dallas.[5] Among the speakers were leading policy makers, business executives, and economists, including Nobel Prize winners Gary Becker, Edward Prescott, Myron Scholes, and Professor Lucas. We wanted to find out, first, whether 4% growth could actually be achieved and, second, how to do it.

The consensus was that, yes, America can get back to its trend-line growth and even higher, to 4%, but that major changes were needed. At the concluding panel of the conference, James Owens, former CEO of Caterpillar, one of the nation's most successful firms, said of the 4% goal: "I think not only is it a good objective . . . but a realistic aspiration [and] critically important to the performance of our economy and for our citizens."[6]

We asked several of the conference presenters, plus a few others, to put their ideas about 4% growth into chapters for this book. Most of the authors agree with the conclusion of economist and former U.S. Treasury official David Malpass (chapter 7) that a 4% "growth renaissance" is possible. A few see the historic trend as a kind of limit. Even 3% growth would be a significant improvement over what is expected, but we firmly believe that 4%—which has been achieved in 23 of the past 60 calendar years[7]—can become America's New Normal. See Figure 1.

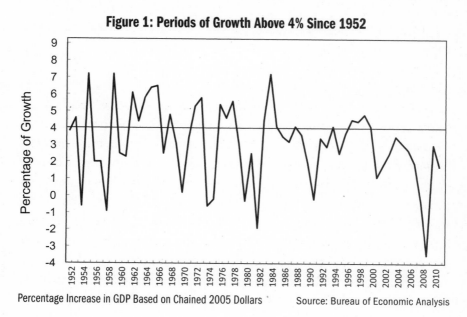

Figure 1: Periods of Growth Above 4% Since 1952

Percentage Increase in GDP Based on Chained 2005 Dollars   Source: Bureau of Economic Analysis

It won't be easy. There is no single antidote. Malpass's own prescription calls for a revival "based on the ageless American principles of sound money, low tax rates, limited federal government, the market-based allocation of capital and labor, and sensible regulatory and trade rules."

■ ■ ■

The objective of economic policy is to allow hardworking individuals, no matter their status at birth, to take advantage of opportunity and achieve a good life. As Brendan Miniter of the Bush Institute writes in chapter 1 of this book, "There is a certain virtue to prosperity. It inspires people, removes pressures that lead to embitterment and division, and allows us all to step back and get a healthy perspective for what is actually important in life."

Policy that encourages growth solves what Lord Keynes in 1930 called "the economic problem." Keynes wrote that "the economic problem may be solved, or be at least within sight of a solution, within a hundred years."[8] Keynes was wrong about many things, but even in the depths of the Great Depression, he got this prediction right. The United States solved the economic problem a while ago, by putting the principles of the free market into practice, but we are now in danger of losing our way for good. A growth rate of little more than 2% does not solve the economic problem. A rate of 4% does.

One goal of the 4% Growth Project is to change America's economic conversation so that it focuses on growth—or, as we like to put it, "growth growth growth." We hear a good deal of talk today about policies that "create jobs" and worry that such a focus is off-track. Of course, employment must rise, and unemployment and underemployment fall. But "job creation" as a goal merely encourages government to engage in counterproductive pursuits. On my first trip to the Soviet Union in the 1960s, for instance, I saw hordes of women sweeping the streets of Moscow with brooms made of twigs. They were employed by the state in a ruinous economic policy that favored job creation and empty production over real sustainable growth. Years ago, I heard an anecdote, attributed to economist Milton Friedman (among others), that illustrates the job creation fallacy well. An American engineer was visiting China decades ago to observe a dam being built. The engineer was surprised to see thousands of workers digging with shovels.

"Why are there no bulldozers?" the engineer asked his Chinese guide.

"The state wants to create jobs," said the guide.

"In that case," said the American engineer, "why not give them all spoons?"

A government can tax its citizens—or borrow from foreigners, as we have been doing recently—and use the proceeds to hire all sorts of workers. But the gains, if any, are fleeting because: a) no government knows how to allocate labor productively, and b) the money used to create the jobs ultimately comes from people and firms that actually do know how to allocate productively. Solid job growth comes from solid economic growth, wrought by private enterprise. When the U.S. economy is growing at 4%, as it was, for example, in 1988, the unemployment rate will necessarily be modest—in that case, 5.3%.

Another worthy goal of policy makers is a lower U.S. debt. The Congressional Budget Office, assuming a plausible projection of key policies, sees the annual budget deficit at a consistent rate of 5.5% of GDP for the long term. That is more than twice the rate that prevailed between 2000 and 2008, the norm for the past forty years.[9] As budget deficits accumulate, they create more and more debt. In the mid-1990s, debt held by the public as a proportion of GDP reached 49%. It fell to an average of 36% during 2000–2008, then soared. It is expected to reach 76% in 2013, the highest rate since 1950, when the effects of borrowing during World War II were still being felt. Total federal debt, including what federal agencies owe one another, is already at 100% of GDP. Several of the authors point out that debt levels this high, by themselves, slow the economy considerably, so it's no wonder that policy makers concentrate on ways to directly reduce the debt.

If debt reduction is our immediate policy focus, however, then the temptation will be to raise taxes or inaugurate a reign of austerity in government spending without thinking of the impact of those policies on growth. Higher tax rates on personal and corporate income might—and I'll emphasize the *might*—reduce the debt in the very short term, but they will certainly have a depressive effect on growth, as technologist Floyd Kvamme (chapter 19) and other authors stress. Similarly, some government spending, such as support of basic research, is essential to growth.

Reducing the debt is critical, but growth comes first. If we devise fiscal policies that promote growth, then the consequence will be a lower ratio of debt to GDP. Several of the authors, including Steven Gjerstad and the Nobel Prize winner Vernon L. Smith in chapter 5, argue for cutting federal spending—and I strongly agree—but the reason for the cuts is increasing growth. Hassett reviews the economic literature (including his own work) and finds that a fiscal policy that stresses spending reductions has been much more successful than one that stresses tax increases. Or take a lesson from history. In chapter 20, Amity Shlaes shows how President Calvin Coolidge relentlessly cut the size of government and, at the same time, boosted GDP growth to well above 4%.

The effect of growth on debt is dramatic. For our conference in 2011, we asked Alex Brill, an American Enterprise Institute economist, to calculate the reduction in expected federal debt from an increase in growth to 4% starting in 2017 (and using projections by the CBO for 2011 to 2016). He found that, under those circumstances, the total debt for 2021 would decline by $3.7 trillion, reducing the projected growth in the debt over the ten years by one-fourth.

Using the CBO's assumptions, he also found that 1% faster growth in only this year would result in a total deficit (and debt) reduction over the next ten years of $756 billion. Again, that's just from one year of increased growth, with rates going back to the lower levels the CBO estimates after that. Why does growth produce lower deficits? By getting higher tax revenues from higher incomes and capital gains and lower government spending from more people working and making more money.

Strong growth interacts with debt to create a virtuous circle. It lowers the drag on the economy that excessive debt causes, and that lowered drag in turn helps create more growth, which lowers the debt and the drag, and so on, as the illustration on the next page indicates.

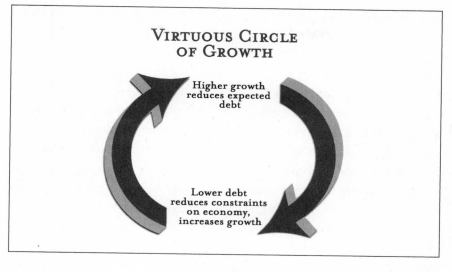

The benefits of 4% growth are clear, but how do we get there? The answers are found throughout this book, but I want to focus on three: taxes, immigration, and entrepreneurship.

A common theme running through these chapters is that government needs to get out of the way of enterprise for growth to take off. Many of the contributors cited the importance of removing government-imposed constraints, one of the most pressing being a corporate tax rate that is higher than that of every industrialized country in the world. While Europe has been cutting tax rates on business, the United States has been raising them.

As a founder of National Semiconductor and a leading venture capitalist, Floyd Kvamme, in chapter 19, shows how elevated taxes on corporate income and capital have pushed high-tech manufacturing to Asia, to the detriment of U.S. growth. Low labor costs are exaggerated as a cause of losing jobs. The real culprits are the lack of skilled engineers, burdensome regulations, and high taxes. "When taxes consume 35% or more of profits, then they also consume a third of the money we needed to keep growing and to continue to create new jobs. . . . CFOs, as a result, are constantly pressured to find ways to preserve cash and lower tax liabilities. Offshore operations have frequently been the answer."[10]

It is not just the level of taxes but the way those taxes are imposed. Kevin Hassett, in chapter 6, argues—as many economists, both of the right and left, do—that taxing *income* discourages investment and thus growth. He cites a 2008 study by economist Jens M. Arnold that shifting "1% of·tax revenues from income taxes to consumption and property taxes would increase GDP per capita by between a quarter of a point and one percentage point in the long run." The same amount of revenues would be collected, but through taxing what people buy and own rather than the returns on what they invest. Hassett also notes a survey of sixty-nine tax economists who concluded that, on average, the 1986 tax reform, which broadened the tax base and lowered rates, boosted growth by a full percentage point over a long period.

Malpass also makes the case for lower tax rates and a broader base through the elimination of special tax preferences, but he adds that a "pro-growth, pro-jobs starting point" for tax reform is to make permanent many of the current annual tax fixes (including the alternative minimum tax patch and the 2001 rate reductions) in a one-time permanent process that would stabilize the tax code and give businesses, both at home and abroad, more certainty—and thus an encouragement to invest here for the long term.

Incentives like certainty are the key to economic growth, write W. Michael Cox and Richard Alm in chapter 2, and smart tax policy can provide incentives to save, invest, innovate, and start businesses. No one explained the effect of higher and higher tax rates better than President Coolidge. In chapter 20, Amity Shlaes, senior fellow and director of the 4% Growth Project at the Bush Institute, quotes Coolidge as saying, "If we had a tax whereby on the first working day the government took five percent, the second day ten percent, the third day thirty, the fourth day forty, the fifth day fifty, the sixth day sixty, how many of you would continue to work on the last days of the week? It is the same with capital." Coolidge discovered the Laffer Curve a half century before Arthur Laffer did. Taxes, because they are such a powerful incentive to mold behavior, are where the leverage is.

During our 2011 conference in Dallas, Gary Becker, who won the Nobel Prize for his work in the field of human capital, said that increasing student achievement by reforming the education system would have a significant impact on growth (Eric Hanushek quantifies that impact in chapter 16), but school reform may take a long time. A route to enhanced human capital that is likely to be quicker, said Becker, is to change our immigration policies to encourage the best and brightest foreigners to come to the United States to live and work, rather than simply getting educated here and then, for lack of a long-term visa, being forced to return home. In chapter 17, Becker writes, "Immigration, especially legal immigration, is good for a country like the United States that has many opportunities for ambitious and hardworking men and women. Immigration increases a country's human capital. That is to say it increases the number of workers available to help businesses expand or innovators make the next big breakthrough."

In chapter 18, Pia M. Orrenius and Madeline Zavodny elaborate on the theme, offering specific ways to reform our immigration system in order to tilt it toward better-educated and capital-contributing foreigners rather than the current tilt toward relatives of those already here. "[O]nly a more rapid increase in productivity growth," the authors write, "will boost U.S. companies' international competitiveness and put the United States on a higher, sustainable growth path." Recent research shows that high-skilled immigration is essential to higher productivity, especially in science, technology, engineering, and math. Other countries, including our neighbor Canada, have already concluded that growth depends on immigration and have fashioned policies accordingly. We need to compete to attract human capital from abroad, or else suffer the consequences.

Immigration is not a zero-sum game. American citizens will benefit. "Immigrants are typically more entrepreneurial than natives in the United States," write Orrenius and Zavodny. In fact, one-quarter of all high-tech start-ups between 1995 and 2005 had at least one immigrant founder. In chapter 10, Robert Litan, fellow of the Kauffman Foundation and a fellow at the Bush Institute, points out that immigrants founded such great American businesses as DuPont, Procter & Gamble, Pfizer, U.S. Steel, Google, Yahoo!, and eBay. More skilled immigrants means more businesses and more native-born American employment.

This book devotes considerable space to entrepreneurship in general.

It is America's great comparative advantage. In chapter 12, Maria Minniti takes a theoretical approach and examines the complex link between entrepreneurship and economic growth to find the best policy changes to boost new-business formation. One of the advantages of concentrating on enhancing the power of what Peter G. Klein (chapter 9) calls "entrepreneurial judgment" is that what's required is small changes in attitude rather than massive changes in policy. Washington doesn't have to pass a law to encourage entrepreneurial activity; it needs to refrain from jumping in. For example, Klein urges that we take seriously Joseph Schumpeter's celebration of "creative destruction." Let businesses fail; don't bail them out. Focus on individuals. Don't try to plan clusters of innovation; let them develop organically.

Litan suggests that universities can play a significant role in reviving economic growth if they change how they handle intellectual property developed by their researchers. By letting their professors keep more of the gains from innovations they develop, the nation will benefit from faster economic growth. He also advocates removing some of the obstacles—many of them of recent vintage—that discourage businesses from going public and thus raising the money needed to grow and hire.

■ ■ ■

This book extends the search for ways to increase growth to energy, where, as Steven F. Hayward and Kenneth P. Green in chapter 14 show, technology has removed some of the physical obstacles to finding new resources in the United States, but obstacles erected by government and radical environmentalism remain. Boosting student achievement, Eric Hanushek writes in chapter 16, could have a spectacular effect on growth. And Carlos Gutierrez, in chapter 13, makes the case for free trade, which "gives exporters access to new markets [while] competition from imports forces firms to become more productive." Consumers benefit from lower prices and more choice, raising their standard of living, and workers gain from higher wages.

In chapter 15, Blahous and Fichtner present a model for a pro-growth Social Security system, which encourages older Americans to choose work over retirement if they're still healthy and directs savings toward real capital investment, in contrast to the current pay-as-you-go model, where dollars come out of the pockets of workers and go directly into the pockets of retirees. This chapter complements chapter 4, in which Edward Prescott, a Nobel Prize winner, writes about how Europe's welfare programs have slowed growth by about one-fifth. Several of the contributors, including, from different perspectives, Gjerstad and Smith in chapter 5 and Malpass in chapter 7, address the role of monetary policy.

While GDP increases are the best single measure of economic growth, they are far from perfect metrics, as another Nobel Prize winner, Myron Scholes, explains in chapter 8. Still, we believe that if America focuses on a single target—sustainable 4% GDP growth—the nation can achieve opportunity and prosperity for all.

■ ■ ■

This book, like all the work of the Bush Institute, begins with the inspiration of President and Mrs. Bush and the principles that have guided their lives: freedom, opportunity, responsibility, and compassion. The concept of 4% growth as a target came from one of the members of the Bush Institute Advisory Board, former Florida governor Jeb Bush. It was nurtured by John Chapman, an economist who fashioned our initial 4% growth conference and persuaded an impressive group of academics, policy makers, and business leaders to participate, both as presenters at that conclave and as contributors to this book. Brendan Miniter, formerly of *The Wall Street Journal*'s editorial page, moved to Dallas in 2011 as the institute's senior editorial director. He deployed not only his editing skill but his organizational prowess in pulling this book together from the minds of nearly two dozen smart and independent contributors. Finally, we offer gratitude to Sean Desmond of Crown and literary agent Rafe Sagalyn for having the imagination to understand that a book of this sort could have a broad and avid audience, and for having the drive to make it a reality.

■ ■ ■

At a dinner meeting between President Barack Obama and Silicon Valley business leaders in February 2011, it came time for Steve Jobs, cofounder and rejuvenator of Apple, to speak. The topic was the sputtering economy, and much of the talk was depressing. Jobs, who would die eight months later at the age of fifty-six, had, as usual, his own opinion. "This country is insanely great," he told the president. "What I'm worried about is that we don't talk enough about solutions."[11]

He was right. Yes, America is insanely great, and, yes, we're talking about solutions.

THE
4%
SOLUTION

Chapter 1

Why We Grow

By Brendan Miniter

Economic growth is not an issue normally associated with the Pentagon. But on January 23, 2006, in a little-noticed ceremony, officials there handed the Defense Department's Distinguished Public Service Award to then outgoing Federal Reserve chairman Alan Greenspan. The reason for the award: He helped unleash tremendous economic growth that had strengthened the country, led to new advances in science and technology, and demonstrated the power of a free and open economic system.

The importance of economic prosperity is hard to overstate. A growing economy produces jobs that allow workers to provide for their families, live comfortable and stable lives, and give back to their communities. A growing economy creates new opportunities for entrepreneurs. And it also creates the capital needed to support innovation and research in science and the arts. America's economy has long produced the types of jobs that have enabled many Americans to enjoy comfortable middle-class lives.

From the end of World War II until our recent "Great Recession," the United States economy grew, on average, at a little more than 3% annually. At that rate the size of the economy doubles roughly every generation. There were, of course, recessions during that period. But nearly every economic downturn was followed by a period of significant growth. Over the past seventy years, the American economy has grown at 4% or greater about two-fifths of the time. The result has been a rapid transformation. Today most Americans have a substantially higher standard of living than previous generations. And they also carry with them an expectation for growth. Americans hold the optimistic view that it is natural for the economy to grow at a rapid pace year in and year out.

But survey the historical data stretching back long before World War II and you may be surprised to see that economic growth is a relatively new phenomenon. In a brilliant essay[1] published in 2004, Nobel Economist Robert Lucas outlined the history of economic growth. His findings show that prior to the industrial revolution in the middle of the 18th century, per capita gross domestic product (GDP) growth had largely been flat around the world. Technological advancement had occurred, but the economic gains that were made were essentially offset by increases in population.

However, with the advent of the industrial revolution, economic growth managed to outrun population (industrialized economies grew, while birthrates declined) and the result was the rise of a middle class. Lucas calculates that the world economy grew at a fraction of 1% annually through the latter half of the 18th century, at about 1% annually on average through the 19th century, at about 2.4% for the first sixty years of the 20th century, and at about 4% annually after that.

Modern growth theory—the theory that looks at innovation and human ingenuity as engines for expanding the economy—is itself relatively new. Robert M. Solow, the economist often credited with advancing modern economic thought in this area, did much of his groundbreaking work in the 1950s and '60s. Others, such as Lucas, have since developed alternative growth models, which have sparked research and debate among economists about the role of human capital, entrepreneurship, and other factors in economic growth. The short of it is that these are exciting times to be thinking about economics, growth, and the outer limits of human potential. There is a lot of cutting-edge work being done now. And it is reshaping what we know to be possible, while also forcing us to realize that much of what we have done in the past may have actually hamstrung the economy.

Consider the work of another economist who hasn't won the Nobel Prize, but likely deserves such high honors: Gordon Tullock. Half a century ago, he worked closely with economist James Buchanan, who went on to win the Nobel for his work on something called public choice theory—a body of ideas that argues that rather than being driven by altruistic motives, government policies are often driven by hidden incentives. For example, government agencies have a strong incentive to spend all the money in their budgets, even if they have to spend it in wasteful ways, because not spending the money can lead lawmakers to cut those agencies' budgets the following year.

The combined contributions of Tullock and Buchanan can be found in an often cited volume, *The Calculus of Consent*, which sorts through incentives that drive democratic systems and offers reasons why, for example, a legislature might back public policies that are not widely popular and may not even serve the greater public good. But perhaps Tullock's most relevant work to discussions of economic growth has to do with what has been called "rent seekers"—those who seek special payment or privilege, usually from the government. His insight, accessible in a volume titled *The Rent-Seeking Society*, is simply that individuals or institutions often seek to profit by tilting the political landscape in their direction, rather than by creating real value.

This concept is critical to understand in today's environment of large federal deficits and a stumbling economy. It's often assumed that federal spending will stimulate the economy—after all, it pumps money into the system. But Tullock's insight offers us an explanation into why government spending can actually be harmful to economic growth. Spending is funded by taxes, which pulls capital out of the productive economy. The destructive power of taxes is something that has been long discussed and seems to be well understood. Collecting taxes, however, is only part of the harm that public policies can cause. Rent seekers, as Tullock discovered, profit through the political process, not by producing a better or cheaper product. Their aim is to receive payment (or privilege) through government policy.

In some cases, rent seekers can look to gain privilege by lobbying for new regulations that, if imposed, would harm their competitors. In other cases, rent seekers can look to profit by receiving government payments or inflated prices thanks to government policies. Donald Boudreaux, an economics professor at George Mason University, brilliantly illustrated Tullock's insight in the *Christian Science Monitor* in late 2008 by looking at Illinois governor Rod Blagojevich. At the time,

Blagojevich was at the center of a corruption story involving naming someone to fill a vacant Senate seat.[2] Boudreaux concluded that when the government can bestow a privilege or profit on someone there is a strong incentive for entrepreneurial people to spend their time figuring out how to profit off the government. "As Tullock first recognized (in a paper published in 1967)," Boudreaux wrote, "enormous amounts of resources—including human talent—are wasted in pursuit of government privileges."

Not all payments or privileges provided by the government are problematic or even wasteful. But since the government uses a political process to decide whom it pays and how much, there is little incentive for rent seekers to push for greater efficiency or innovation. This is a problem in part because the public and the private sectors compete for the same financial and human capital. That is to say, they compete for the same pile of money and the same group of innovative entrepreneurs. So when the government spends a large volume of money, there is that much less money in the system for private entrepreneurs. And when the government has a wide variety of programs that businesses can profit from, without being efficient producers, it drains away talented entrepreneurs who would otherwise put their talents to work in the private economy. Think of it this way: When profits are relatively easy to make in government contract work, there are fewer innovators willing to spend their time and their capital developing the next new innovation that could revolutionize an entire industry.

If we place Tullock's work next to the insights offered by Lucas, Solow, and Buchanan (among others), it is possible to imagine that the era of significant economic growth is only just beginning. If sustained economic growth is relatively new to human history, if many of the theories explaining growth are still being refined, and if public policies can create incentives that hurt economic growth, then we may not yet know our full economic potential. We haven't yet found out how fast the economy can run on a sustained basis if public policy is lined up with the right incentives to grow the economy.

There isn't a clear consensus on the rate of growth that the country should shoot for. As this book came together, Lucas said to me in an email that he didn't support the idea that sustained long-term

4% growth was possible for the United States. I understood his point to be that the world as a whole might grow at 4% or faster and some countries—including China—could far exceed that growth rate. But that was because many countries are racing to catch up to the United States. They are experiencing catch-up growth, which is much easier to achieve because it involves adopting technologies and practices that others have already developed. It's much harder to grow at an accelerated rate when you are leading the pack—when you are the one developing new technologies that everyone else will copy.

And he's right to think so. The United States is much more likely to achieve the average growth rate it maintained from the end of World War II to the most recent economic downturn—a rate of about 3%—than it is to accelerate to a new long-term economic growth rate of 4%. That doesn't mean that in the short run the country won't exceed that annual average—indeed it will have to grow at a rate that exceeds its long-term average rate of growth for a period of time just to return to the trend line it has adhered to for decades. The question is, will the United States be able to grow at a faster rate than its long-term trend? Is 4% sustained annual growth possible?

The difference between the long-term trend of 3% and 4% may not seem very big. As Lucas put it to me, the difference we're talking about is one percentage point, and what's that "among friends"? "A lot, for a growth theorist," he wrote. The safe money, and the evidence he has amassed, is on the long-term trend of 3% (or less) holding steady once the United States recovers from its current recession.

But then innovation is, by its nature, disruptive. As new technologies and new practices come into being, is it possible to know how fast the economy can grow for a sustained period of time if we find new ways to unleash the creative potential of our entrepreneurs? The Bush Institute has set an intentionally provocative target, in part because one way to find out what is actually attainable is to stretch for a goal that is seemingly just beyond one's reach.

In any case, given the state of its economy, the United States needs to push hard and reach for new ways to unleash the creativity of its people. The challenges facing the country today are significant. As this book went to press, unemployment had exceeded 8% for nearly three years, and there was little sign that a new jobs boom was on the horizon. American businesses, unwilling to deploy capital in an uncertain economy, were sitting on approximately $2 trillion in cash on their balance sheets. And an unprecedented wave of federal stimulus spending had washed through the system without doing much to lift the nation's economy.

There is little doubt that the American economy is undergoing a transformation. For decades, the number of jobs in manufacturing has fallen. Textile, assembly-line, and other well-paid manual labor jobs that supported the middle class in years past are simply no longer available to many Americans entering the workforce today. In their place, an information economy—which requires highly skilled, highly educated, and often highly mobile individuals—has taken shape and has become a key driver of economic growth. This new economy offers the prospect of greater prosperity than what it is replacing, but it comes with a catch. To take advantage of the new economy, many Americans will have to retool with new skills and a new approach to their careers.

The result is that today the United States must not only restart its economic engines, it must do so while simultaneously pulling millions of Americans into productive jobs in a new economy. If, instead, it stumbles into a prolonged period of little or no economic growth, it risks allowing millions of Americans who lack skills for the new economy to be pushed permanently to the economic sidelines through unemployment or underemployment. Thus, how to fix the flagging economy is one of the most important social issues the country faces today.

Many of the chapters that follow will offer specific ideas for how to spark immediate and substantial economic growth as well as outline aspects of the economy that are not usually covered in the press. But before we turn to them, let's first consider one important aspect to growth not factored into economic arguments often enough.

Economic growth isn't an end unto itself. Growing the economy is a vital task for this generation because of what economic growth produces: a better life for millions upon millions of Americans and hundreds of millions of people across the globe. There is a certain virtue to prosperity. It inspires people, removes pressures that lead to embitterment and division, and allows us all to step back and get a healthy perspective on what is actually important in life.

Today, there is a vigorous debate over how best to lift people out of poverty. In an era of high unemployment, economic uncertainty, and falling expectations of what is possible in the future, this debate has taken on added significance. This country may be at a crossroads, and what path it takes next could determine whether its future will be dominated by how it has decided to address poverty, unemployment, and economic distress of the middle class.

So let us step, for a moment, beyond the economic arguments and the ramifications of government debt, and address the underlying fundamental question of how we respond when our fellow citizens are being battered by vicious economic trends. Do we turn to government to provide for the people? Or do we turn to the people by empowering them to help themselves and one another?

If we care about poverty and if we care about enlivening the souls of our fellow citizens by freeing them from the economic despair of joblessness, we need to recognize that there is a moral component, and even a moral imperative, to a free economy. It has been said that there is dignity in having a job, but economics is about more than allowing people to have a modicum of dignity and self-worth inside the confines of what we collectively allow them to have. To be successful, economic policy can't be thought of as charity. If it is to achieve its aim, it needs to allow an individual to live up to his potential. To thrive in a free society, people need to form strong bonds that connect them to others. Merchants must build trust among their customers, and individuals must build a community with their neighbors. We can only weaken those bonds when we take away the necessity and the imperative of forming them.

The Pentagon was right in 2006 in believing that a vibrant, strong, and free economy makes for a vibrant, strong, and free nation. Prosperity brings with it material gains, but it also strengthens communities and allows all of us to reach our greatest potential. There is an imperative to grow.

Chapter 2

Incentives

By W. Michael Cox and Richard Alm

Can the U.S. economy grow at 4% or faster? Conventional wisdom says no, even though China, India, and other countries have grown at 10% or more for more than a decade. The doubters say developing nations can sprint forward at a brisk pace as they play catch-up, but mature economies should accept crawling ahead at perhaps 2% a year, maybe doing a little better in good times. The pessimism reflects the experiences of the world around us, where most of the highly developed nations of Western Europe and North America haven't managed to maintain high growth rates.

Before the Great Recession, the United States outperformed the world's other advanced economies. In the quarter century from the end of a deep recession in 1982 to the start of an even deeper one in 2007, the U.S. economy grew at an average of 3.4% a year—tantalizingly close to 4% (Chart 1).[1] We can't re-create the economic conditions of 1982–2007—but such a long period of strong growth in the very recent past suggests 4% isn't some pie-in-the-sky daydream. So it's worth thinking about how the U.S. economy might get there.

Standard prescriptions for boosting economic growth usually focus on macroeconomic policies—for the most part, on government spending—as a way to stimulate demand. These policies rarely work, because they ignore the economy's prime motivating force—incentives.

Rather than going down this *macroeconomics* dead end, we take a *microeconomic* view to focus on the wages, prices, rates of return, and profits that guide the decisions of individuals and firms.

From stockbrokers to panhandlers, all of us spend virtually every

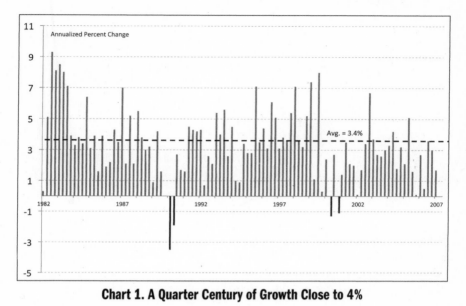

Chart 1. A Quarter Century of Growth Close to 4%

waking moment of our lives making choices based on the costs and benefits of what we do. Incentives rule our behavior.

And they drive economic growth. Through incentives, free markets encourage workers, companies, and investors to undertake productive activities. Growth picks up when people choose to get an education in a field the economy values highly, when they choose to work full time and hone their productivity, when they choose to save, invest, and take business risks, when they choose to start a company and hire workers, when they choose to innovate and create new products, and when they choose to seize the business opportunities around them.

Good economic policy will support these choices, increasing the growth rate. Bad economic policies short-circuit incentives, create barriers to productive activity, and slow growth. Revving up the long-term growth rate isn't a matter of good luck or government largesse. It's a matter of getting the incentives right and unleashing capitalism. The United States won't achieve 4% growth on a consistent basis unless politicians, policy makers, and the public champion the powerful microeconomic forces that propel the economy forward.

INCENTIVES FOR EDUCATION AND CAREER CHOICE

For decades now, an epochal shift has been transforming the U.S. economy, pushing it away from industry and toward services and advanced technology. The new order places a high value on knowledge— making education the right place to begin discussing the incentives that lead to faster growth.

Education is one of life's most important choices. In 2009, workers aged 25–34 who stayed in school, studied hard, and received professional degrees made an average of $126,000 a year working in such fields as law, medicine, pharmacy, and architecture. Members of the same age group who dropped out of school before ninth grade held menial jobs and earned an average of $26,000 a year. Between the two extremes, average income rose as individuals chose to get more education—without exception (Chart 2).

In fact, the link between years of schooling and income is so consistent that the American workforce's education profile provides a good first approximation of the income distribution. Doctors, engineers, lawyers, scientists, accountants, financial analysts, business consul-

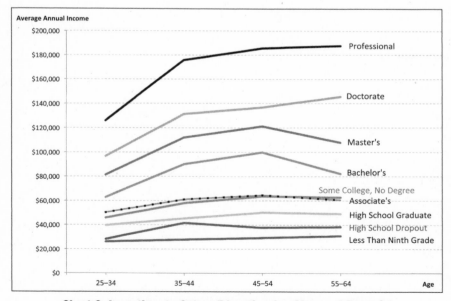

Chart 2. Incentives to Get an Education Are Clear and Powerful

tants, managers, and other highly educated workers—all of them boost GDP as they move up the income ladder. Workers who quit school early provide less benefit to the economy.

Education incentives can be parsed from another angle—what students choose as their field of study. In 2010, graduates with bachelor's degrees in petroleum engineering started work at a median pay of $92,000 a year. Majoring in chemical engineering, computer science, civil engineering, physics, statistics, economics, and finance also led to relatively high starting pay. By contrast, bachelor's degrees in English, music, sociology, journalism, theology, art, and social work commanded median pay of less than $40,000 a year. Think about it this way: A student's decision to switch majors from history to petroleum engineering would raise GDP by $52,000.

Through its wage structure, the labor market sends powerful signals to young people, telling them that it values education in some fields a lot more than others—not for arbitrary reasons but because of the economy's needs and priorities. When students respond to the market's incentives and enter fields in which they'll do better, they also make choices that help the economy grow faster.

The private sector largely determines the demand side of education, and it provides strong incentives to get an education and choose a field of study with a higher economic value. The supply side of education, however, is largely controlled by local, state, and national governments, especially from kindergarten through high school.

Compulsory education and massive subsidies may herd more Americans into school, but the heavy hand of government bureaucracy drags down quality in the classroom. For decades now, the public school monopoly has been spending ever greater amounts of money without improving the quality of education. The inflation-adjusted cost per student has risen from $55,000 in 1970 to about $150,000 in 2010.

Despite the gusher of money, test scores have barely budged. U.S. students lag in international rankings of math, science, and other subjects.[2] Compared with their peers in other countries, Americans fare worse in high school than they did in fourth grade, suggesting educational outcomes deteriorate the longer students are exposed to public schools. Mediocre public schools lead to high dropout rates and graduates with poor basic skills that limit their productivity and earning potential.[3]

Workers often fret about a lack of "good jobs." But companies have a complaint of their own—they can't find qualified workers. In a well-oiled market economy, there will be as many good jobs as there are qualified workers to fill them. Our public education system has largely failed to equip today's workers with the knowledge and skills required for today's knowledge-intensive jobs. Outsourcing provides the proof. American employers are increasingly looking abroad for the educated workers they need.

Better-quality education would boost the economy's performance—but decades of more government spending and dozens of new programs haven't delivered improved student performance. America's public schools are a millstone on economic growth. The best hopes for changing the American education system are consumer choice and competition, the forces that drive markets to lower costs and improve quality.[4]

In all parts of the country, parents are rebelling against the public education monopoly and demanding charter schools, vouchers, and similar competitive programs. Tax dollars may always fund public education, but government need not dictate that those dollars are limited to supporting just one school system—its own. The shift toward market-based educational systems typically pays off in better student performance.[5] In the long run, America will achieve faster growth only if it exploits competition to improve its K–12 education. Competition is what made this country's colleges and universities the world's best.

INCENTIVES TO WORK AND GET AHEAD

A good education gets workers off to a good start. What happens in the years that follow, however, depends on individuals' initiative, their opportunities, and their choices. Striving to get ahead leads to raises, promotions, and moving up to better jobs—all pluses for the economy.

Workers earn more as they gain experience and take advantage of the economy's incentives to work full time, acquire additional knowledge, and bolster their job skills. In 2009, workers aged 45–54 with bachelor's degrees made roughly $38,000 a year more than those with the same education in the age 25–34 cohort (refer to Chart 2). An even bigger payoff from added years of experience comes at the top of the educational ladder, among workers who earned doctoral and professional degrees.

Education and experience are a powerful combination for advancement. Those with the most years of schooling saw the largest and most durable payoff from experience. Earnings peaked for holders of bachelor's and master's degrees by age 54, but average incomes continued to rise into the mid-60s for those with professional degrees and doctorates.

Like starting salaries, income gains tied to on-the-job experience vary by field of study. Through midcareer, income for workers with bachelor's degrees rose the fastest in petroleum engineering, chemical engineering, physics, economics, and computer science. Years of experience added the least in social work, theology, art, music, art history, and sociology.

Even within the same discipline, bachelor's degrees can yield very different incomes. Some workers choose to simply get by on the job, and their paychecks reflect their lack of ambition. The hardest working and most talented rise to the top of their professions, and they reap the rewards of their success.

At midcareer, for example, graduates with bachelor's degrees in economics show a wide dispersion in pay—from about $50,000 at the 10th percentile to $100,000 at the median, to more than $200,000 at the 90th percentile. For math majors, salaries range from $40,000 to $170,000. The gap is smallest in nursing, education, and other fields—but it persists across the board, proving that individual performance matters. Markets provide incentives to excel—for the doctor operating on your spine, for the advisor managing your finances, for just about everyone.

In the United States, governments routinely thwart incentives to work. Federal and state income taxes that combined take as much as 46% off the top reduce the market's rewards for education, work, and striving to get ahead.[6] They punish success—the very thing that stimulates growth. Entitlements reward the decision to not work.

Unemployment compensation,[7] earned income tax credits, rent subsidies, Medicaid, and other direct payments weaken the link between consumption and holding a job. When people live on entitlements for too long, their skills atrophy and reemployment becomes all but impossible.

Governments stymie labor market performance in other ways—by constricting employers' rights to dismiss unwanted workers, by mandating employer-paid benefits, or by encouraging the growth of unions.[8] All these interventions in the labor market misallocate resources, reduce productivity, and slow growth.

Left alone, a free-enterprise economy offers higher incomes as the reward for making good choices about how much to learn (years of schooling), what to learn (field of study), and how much effort to put into work (experience plus initiative). How much different professions pay helps direct our most talented workers to the fields where they are needed the most. A pro-growth strategy, therefore, must center on reducing taxes and other burdens on individuals' choices to work and get ahead. The economy benefits because better-educated and motivated workers become more productive, which in turn stimulates growth rates.

INCENTIVES TO SAVE AND INVEST

In fostering growth, financial markets are just as important as labor markets. Banks, stock exchanges, bond markets, and other financial institutions mobilize the money that households choose to save, transferring it to investors who start new businesses, expand existing companies, introduce new products, and create new jobs. Increasing investment is the holy grail of growth.

Financial markets don't dole out money randomly. They channel it to the most economically valuable uses by offering varied rewards. Using 1925 as the starting point, investing in the private sector has delivered strong annual real rates of return—8.8% for small-company stocks, 6.7% for large-company stocks, and 2.85% for long-term corporate bonds.[9] Even this lower rate of return looks good when compared to the meager rewards offered by government debt—2.4% for long-term bonds, 2.3% for intermediate issues, and 0.6% for short-term Treasury bills. Gold, the investment of choice for iffy times, performs more like government bonds than private-sector stocks.

If left in place, a dollar invested in small-company stocks in 1925 would have the purchasing power of $1,313 in 2011. A similar stake in big companies would have grown to only $243. By comparison, the investment in government bonds and gold would amount to chump change.

Economies grow faster when investors choose to put their money into productive assets rather than government bonds or gold. Some companies may languish or even fail—but that's the risk investors willingly take in exchange for higher expected rates of return. With risk must come reward—or else the risk won't be taken, the businesses won't get started, workers won't get hired, and the economy won't grow.

Government policy influences incentives to save and invest—for good or ill. Income taxes punish success in financial markets, just as they do for education and work. Raising capital gains taxes will chill investment by eroding after-tax rewards. So will higher taxes on profits. Lowering taxes on capital gains and profits will boost investment and the economy.

The staggering losses from Enron's phony accounting and Bernard Madoff's Ponzi scheme remind us of the chilling effects of fraud and the importance of regulators who enforce transparency and honesty. They can't fall asleep on the job. At the same time, while some agencies are charged with keeping the game honest, others steer investment to politically privileged projects—something that leads to lower productivity and therefore lower rates of growth.

In 2010, for example, federal subsidies for renewable energy reached $14.7 billion. Yet alternative energy sources barely make a dent in America's energy consumption. Without subsidies, according to the U.S. Energy Information Administration's 2011 Energy Outlook, growth in solar capacity would slow to less than 1% annually between 2017 and 2035—and wind capacity would fall to nearly 0% growth.[10] Tax credits and subsidies may increase incentives to invest in alternative energy and other favored markets, but they carry an inherent risk of misallocating capital from productive uses to politically favored boondoggles.

When it comes to incentives to save and invest, policy makers can follow no better course than maintaining sound and steady macroeconomic and regulatory policies. It takes time to build a business and hire workers—so productive risk-taking is by its very nature long-term. Investors will make more sensible judgments about the relative risk and reward of particular projects in an environment that's stable and predictable.

Too often, however, government sours the investment climate by adding political risks to the normal uncertainties of doing business. One way government does this is with monetary policy that risks unleashing inflation. Fiscal policies can also hamper growth if they offer little beyond reckless deficit spending, ballooning public debt, and capricious future tax burdens. Regulatory and social policies that threaten to increase costs, taxes, and red tape also press down on our rates of growth. With such burdens coming down the pike, entrepreneurs often think twice about investing their money and their time in new ventures. Such policies all add to uncertainty, make planning more difficult, and discourage investment.

Unfortunately, they also describe the U.S. investment climate as we write. Government policies and pronouncements have sowed the seeds of uncertainty and confusion. Stocks have been seesawing. Gold has been soaring. Investment has been languishing. And that's all bad news for the economy. Government chaos has contributed to growth slowing to a snail's pace.

INCENTIVES TO INNOVATE AND START BUSINESSES

The highest rewards in capitalist economies go to entrepreneurs. The most successful have risen to the top of the *Forbes* list of richest Americans—Bill Gates of Microsoft, Warren Buffett of Berkshire Hathaway, Larry Ellison of Oracle. Among the Forbes 400, more than 80% owe their fortunes to their own efforts in business rather than inheritance.

Most entrepreneurs don't make the Forbes 400, but they all expend great amounts of time and effort to make themselves better off. In doing so, they benefit society as a whole. We say this with complete confidence because all transactions in a capitalist system are voluntary. People don't part with their money unless they feel that what they buy makes them better off. Entrepreneurship and progress go hand in hand.

Nearly every sector of the economy has gained from the creation of new businesses, but the example of the microprocessor and its progeny is among the best. Since the 1970s, increasingly powerful miniature circuits have revolutionized the way we process, store, and transmit information. Entrepreneurs introduced a mind-boggling array of new products based on the microprocessor—computers, the Internet, software, iPhones, digital cameras, DVD players . . . the list is endless. Pierre Omidyar created eBay. Jeff Bezos created Amazon.com. Mark Zuckerberg created Facebook. Larry Page and Sergey Brin created Google. All told, the economic activity based on the computer expanded from $164 billion in 1977 to more than $1.6 trillion three decades later (Chart 3). It added nearly a half percentage point to the nation's annual growth rate.

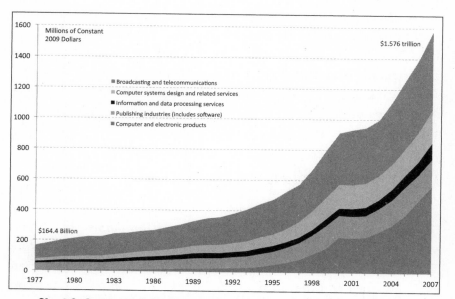

Chart 3. Computer-Related Industries Grew Rapidly over Three Decades

Innovation is a powerful engine for growth because it fuels capitalist progress. Companies emerge to deliver new and better products that satisfy consumers' needs and wants. Shifts in technology and consumer demand mean some firms go out of business, with workers losing their jobs, while other companies rise that provide new jobs.

Two points are important to capitalist progress: First, *profit* isn't a dirty word. Far from it. Profit is the bait that lures entrepreneurs into untested waters. It animates a free-enterprise economy by providing incentives to innovate—without it, there's little economic rejuvenation. Second, higher living standards can't be achieved without the turmoil of bankruptcies and layoffs. This truth gave rise to Joseph Schumpeter's wonderfully apt oxymoron to describe the process of capitalist progress—creative destruction.[11] Technological unemployment, another Schumpeterian coinage, describes an essential feature of creative destruction.[12]

In hindsight, creative destruction is easily accepted. About 97% of Americans worked on farms in 1800, struggling to feed a nation of 5.3 million people. Two centuries of agricultural innovation led to one of history's greatest downsizings, leaving a mere 1.5% of U.S. labor in farming. Yet today's farmers produce food in abundance for a nation of more than 300 million—with enough left to make the United States a leading agricultural exporter.

The descendants of those who left farms are now aerospace engineers, insurance brokers, nurses, gas-well drillers, plant managers, executive chefs, and a whole lot of other things that contribute to growing the nation's GDP. Their move gave us the material abundance we take for granted—cars and airplanes, electronic gadgets, shopping malls, restaurants, drugs that prolong life, and even Hollywood movies. Most important, it all became affordable to the great mass of Americans.

Any effective strategy for maximizing growth must let the churn of progress work its magic. In broadest terms, that entails policies that promote greater economic freedom—allowing people to pursue their own economic objectives without the burden of taxes and regulation. This becomes crystal clear in the *Economic Freedom of the World* report, an annual ranking published by the Fraser Institute. It covers more than 140 countries, finding clear and consistent evidence that countries with low taxes, light regulations, strong property rights, and sound money tend to grow faster than nations that don't pursue these types of policies.

In the here and now, without the detachment of hindsight, the lessons of creative destruction run headlong into political and social realities. Displaced firms and workers call on government to stop the economic dislocations that hurt them, and government often responds with outright handouts or policies designed to protect existing jobs and entrenched business interests. These policies may have popular political appeal, but they favor the status quo over the changes that bring progress. The cost is slower growth.

INCENTIVE TO EXPAND GLOBALLY

In the second half of the 19th century, the U.S. economy took off on its first great growth spurt as railroads spread across the country and drove down the cost of shipping goods. Markets expanded from local to regional to national. Bigger markets always create incentives for growth. The modern equivalent of the railroads is the Internet, which has slashed the cost of moving information, creating opportunities for profit as more markets go from national to global.

Faster domestic growth will strengthen incentives for companies to expand, but global prospects have never been brighter. Over the past two decades, geopolitical upheavals have brought more than 3 billion people into the capitalist realm. Economic freedom has gained ground in parts of the former Soviet Union, South America, and even Africa. Most important, of course, has been the opening up of two Asian giants—China and India. Taken together, they're eight times larger than the United States in population, with economies growing three to four times faster.

As their incomes rise, these big and fast-growing economies are rapidly becoming major consumer markets. Their citizens aspire to the American lifestyle, and they're hungry for American goods. They drink Coke and Pepsi, eat at McDonald's, surf the Web on Apple computers, and shop at their local Wal-Mart or Home Depot.

The profits in global markets have galvanized the U.S. private

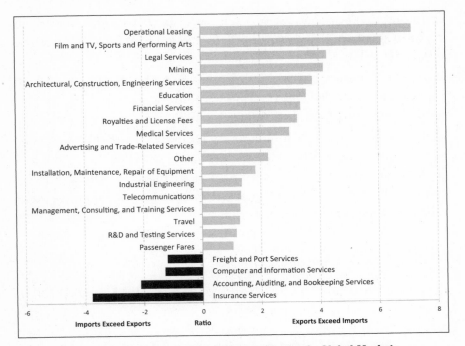

Chart 4. U.S. Services Exporters Are Winning in Global Markets

sector. Since expanding internationally in 1985, Texas Instruments, a Dallas-based semiconductor producer, saw its overseas revenue rise from 68% of total revenue to nearly 90%. On the strength of the iPod, iPhone, and iPad, Apple's foreign sales as a share of total revenues went from 40% in 1998 to 56% in 2010. Google, Amazon, eBay, and Cisco all began the decade with negligible overseas sales and ended it reaping about half of their revenue from foreign customers. Among the Dow 30 companies, the share of foreign business in total revenue rose from 35.3% in 2008 to 46.1% in 2010.

The U.S. economy will grow faster as Caterpillar sells more bull-dozers, Boeing sells more airplanes, Archer Daniels Midland sells more grain, and other firms sell more of the products they make. America's goods producers who sell abroad boost the U.S. economy, no doubt about it. Services exports, however, offer an emerging opportunity, thanks to technology.

In the past decade or so, the Internet has reached critical mass in two key areas. First, data-transmission capacity has become large enough to move vast amounts of information at trivial cost. Second, connectivity has reached nearly every corner of the world, greatly expanding the potential for making business and consumer contacts. The Internet breaks down the physical obstacles that once stifled international trade in services. Companies can now court far-flung customers and deliver services nearly anywhere in the world cheaply and quickly.

American companies sold $549 billion in services abroad in 2010, a gain of 90% since 2000, surpassing the 71% growth rate for goods.[13] Digging deeper into the data, we find the United States has been a top-notch competitor in many of the high-value-added services that support well-paying jobs. Exports exceeded imports by nearly seven to one in operational leasing, a segment of the industry that handles short-term deals on airplanes, vehicles, and other equipment. The edge was six to one in distributing movies and television shows and better than four to one in both legal services and mining services. Architectural, construction, and engineering services came in above three to one, as did education, finance, and royalties and license fees, one of the largest categories in dollar terms (Chart 4).

When it comes to going global, American companies are the best judges of their opportunities and risks. They'll go where they think they can make the sale; they'll invest where they think it makes business sense. Competing globally will encourage companies to use resources efficiently. Bigger markets add to incentives to innovate because the fixed costs of bringing new products to market can be spread across more customers.[14]

Trade is a two-way street. Exports will help the U.S. economy grow—but so will imports. Many domestic companies rely on foreign inputs to their production processes. Access to low-wage foreign labor through outsourcing makes U.S. companies more competitive and productive, helping expand sales at home and abroad. The Internet opens new vistas for Americans to become global entrepreneurs who look outward and see a vast pool of talent and use it to create new enterprises that lower costs with foreign labor and hire U.S. workers highly skilled in managerial and marketing jobs. The furor over out-sourcing is misplaced: We're not outsourcing too many jobs. We're just not creating enough global entrepreneurs.

By championing freer trade and investment flows, governments will help companies make the most of global incentives. Passing the free trade agreements with South Korea, Colombia, and Panama in 2011 was a good step—it signaled Washington can move on policies that promote freer trade. In strictly economic terms, a new global trade deal would be even more important in triggering faster U.S. growth.

The biggest threat comes from misguided policies based on the notion that the U.S. economy will be better off if businesses and jobs stay at home. Unfortunately, slow growth and job losses in recent years have fed the belief that restricting trade and limiting outsourcing will benefit American workers. If protectionist forces prevail in the coming years, the economy will suffer and slip backward. Trade barriers push up prices, shelter inefficiency, slow innovation, and retard growth. The Smoot-Hawley tariffs kicked off the Great Depression of the 1930s and proved that protectionism is the enemy of economic growth.

Government burdens go beyond trade policy. The United States maintains the world's highest corporate income tax—nearly 40%.[15] That encourages firms to produce and profit in other countries. Excessive and capricious regulation will create similar incentives. With heavy taxes and regulation, U.S. policy is driving companies to create jobs overseas, where they boost foreign growth rather than U.S. growth.

INCENTIVES FOR IMMIGRATION

The United States as a nation of immigrants is no mere cliché. From colonial times to today, foreigners have succumbed to the powerful incentives to leave their homelands in pursuit of opportunity and a better life in America, Land of Opportunity. As of 2009, the country had a total of 38.5 million foreign-born residents, or 12.7% of the population.[16]

Immigrants helped build this country. The foreign-born tilled the fields when the United States was a largely agrarian society. They built the railroads, worked the mines, and manned the factories as America forged its industrial power. Today, immigrants are still helping fuel U.S. growth, but critics ignore the lessons of the past and portray the newcomers as a drain on the economy. Nothing could be more wrong.

The U.S. economy benefits from the skills and talents of educated foreign-born workers, who fill gaps left by shortages of native-born graduates in such fields as science, technology, engineering, medicine, and mathematics. These educated immigrants ease the bottlenecks that slow growth and encourage U.S. companies to keep operations at home. Educated immigrants are also significant contributors to research and innovation. More broadly, newcomers help grow the U.S. economy as they work, consume, buy homes, and start new businesses.[17]

Foreigners have ample incentive to seek their place in the United States, but since 1882 the country has put limits on the number of foreigners it will admit.[18] From the start, immigration policy has been muddled—and so it remains today. Humanitarian impulses seek to unite families and provide refuge to victims of war and oppression. Few quarrel with these ends. They epitomize America's traditions and values. Economic impulses seek to admit foreign-born workers who possess skills, talents, and initiative. These ends embody the tradition of America as an immigrant nation, drawing the huddled masses yearning to breathe free, eager for the chance to work hard and make a better life for themselves and their families.

Immigration's humanitarian side has enjoyed more public support than its economic side. Domestic interests fear added competition for jobs, and they frustrate most attempts to expand the number of work visas. The opposition persists despite studies showing that immigration spurs economic growth without depressing wages for most workers.

The result is that immigration debates become a heated political cauldron that produces a policy that has failed the U.S. economy. It admits too many foreign-born workers in sectors that already struggle with excess labor supply. High unemployment rates indicate the United States has plenty of painters, cashiers, carpenters, dishwashers, cooks, and maids. Yet a large number of workers still come from overseas in pursuit of these jobs.

At the same time, the policy admits too few immigrants in

industries in which employers have difficulty finding enough work-ers.[19] Low unemployment rates signal shortages of computer scientists, engineers, and medical personnel. Foreign penetration has been low in these professions, however, largely because of restrictions imposed by immigration laws.

Elements of U.S. immigration policy range to the absurd: Doors swing wide open for foreigners to study at American universities, some of them even receiving financial aid. When these students graduate ready to make a contribution to the economy, the immigration laws deny them the right to work in the United States, so they have little choice but to take their newly learned skills and return home.

If we are to increase growth, we'll need an immigration policy that puts the needs of the economy first. Such a policy would entail admit-ting more foreign workers who have the types of skills we need most. This would involve giving preferences to applicants with education or business and financial resources. Individuals with these attributes will make the biggest contribution to the nation's livelihood.[20]

GETTING INCENTIVES RIGHT

Markets are powerful motivators. They push students to become better educated. They pull students toward fields of study that the economy values highly. They drive workers to build their job skills and strive to get ahead. They steer savings and investment to uses that provide the most economic benefit. They rouse innovators who create new products and entrepreneurs who start new companies. They encour-age companies to expand businesses—both at home and abroad. And markets lure immigrants who can help us expand our economy.

Best of all, people respond to incentives willingly in pursuit of their own self-interests. No cudgels are needed to make people produce. No calls for patriotism or public service are needed. No grand master plans are needed. If underlying realities change, then labor, finance, and product markets adjust incentives automatically—no act of Congress is needed. The market's inherent incentives give individuals and compa-nies reason to choose productive activities that strengthen and expand the economy, which also creates a flexible and dynamic society capable of adapting to changing needs. If the United States wants to raise its long-term growth rate to 4%, it must get incentives right.

The United States hasn't been doing that as well as it used to. The *Economic Freedom of the World* report shows a disappointing drift away from free-market policies in the past decade. The country's absolute scores have ebbed and its ranking fell from third in the world in 2000 to tenth in the 2010 report. Not surprisingly, economic growth is languishing. Further declines in economic freedom will only hurt economic growth.

It would seem that faster economic growth would give government plenty of incentive to embrace market incentives. So why doesn't it?

In part, it's ignorance of the ways that policies can destroy incentives and hurt economic growth. In part, it's the perverse incentive created by rent-seeking behavior, where some individuals or companies seize the chance to gain from policies that are, overall, harmful to the country, to incentives, and to our economic prospects.[21]

If incentives are powerful, so is government. Government can do a lot of damage by interfering with the market's orderly and consistent incentives. Higher income taxes, for example, send all the wrong messages. They say don't get educated, don't choose a higher-valued field of study, don't work hard and strive to get ahead, don't save and invest, don't innovate or start a company, don't seek to profit by growing the business. Government handouts send a similar message—working and pursuing success aren't necessary.

Onerous regulations divert money and manpower from productive activities. Over the past decade, Congress has passed two sets of financial reform regulations—Sarbanes-Oxley and Dodd-Frank—that cost individual businesses millions of dollars every year in additional insurance, accounting, legal, and compliance expenses. Many regulations are blatantly antigrowth. The health-care law enacted in 2009—which some have dubbed Obamacare—creates an incentive for small companies to limit their total number of employees to fewer than fifty. Why? The law requires businesses that cross that threshold to take on the added expense of paying for health insurance for their employees.

Market incentives are potent, but current policies largely shunt them aside. Accelerating the pace of U.S. growth will require fundamental changes in government—a wholesale revision of policy away from demand-side stimulus and toward supply-side incentives. And if actions speak louder than words, the American people have already rendered a clear verdict on which set of policies they prefer. One study by the O'Neil Center, a research institute at Southern Methodist University, looked at why Americans move from one state to another, using data from 2004 to 2008. It turns out that lower income taxes, smaller growth in government spending, decline in union power, and cheaper housing are among the key factors in decisions to move.[22] In other words, when Americans move from, say, California to Texas, they are essentially voting with their feet for the kinds of policies they prefer.

It's now up to our national leaders to recognize that and to take a dispassionate look at what policies will, in fact, lead to significant economic growth in this country. We've experienced significant economic growth in the past, and it has brought us new innovations that have improved our quality of life and provided good-paying jobs for tens of millions of Americans. If public policy is lined up with the right incentives, we can do that again. When America unleashes capitalism, the United States will be on its way to long-term growth of 4% or better.

Chapter 3

The History and Future
of Economic Growth

By Robert E. Lucas Jr.

To think about the possibilities for future economic growth in the United States we need to know something about the varieties of economic growth that have been observed in the past, in the United States and elsewhere. Instead of telling you what I know about the history of economic growth and what I think are the growth possibilities for the future that this history suggests, I thought it would be more useful just to show you some of the evidence that has influenced me and let you draw your own conclusions about our future options.

All the evidence I will present is in the form of graphs of production (real gross domestic product) in various years in the United States and elsewhere. There is more to life than production, I know, but real GDP per person is the best single measure of an economy's ability to produce goods and services, largely because a lot of thought has been given to how to make measures of GDP comparable across both time and space. The postscript at the end of this chapter describes the data sources I used for the graphics.

■ ■ ■

Figures 1 and 2 show the history of U.S. economic growth from 1870 through 2008, charting per capita gross domestic product. Figure 1 plots the evolution of GDP per person since 1870, expressed in thousands of 1990 U.S. dollars. For example, the hash mark at 20 on the vertical axis means $20,000 in 1990 prices, so the figure shows that GDP per person was about $20,000 in 1985, or about $80,000 for the near-mythical family of four. This may seem too high, but remember

Figure 1: GDP per Person in the United States, 1870–2008

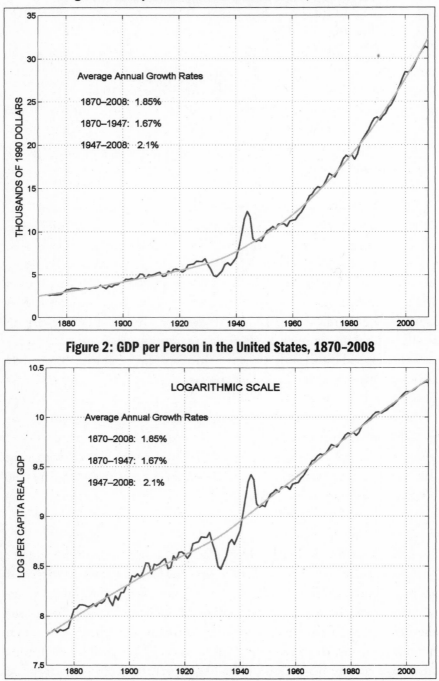

Figure 2: GDP per Person in the United States, 1870–2008

that this is production per person, which is a lot larger than take-home pay. The wiggly curve on the figure is data. The smooth curve is a fitted trend line that I will call "potential" or "normal" GDP.

Figure 2 shows the same data and trend line, but here with a logarithmic scale. In this variation, the vertical axis needs translation to show dollar values, but the *differences* between hash marks are constant in percentage terms: going from 8.5 to 9 means a 50% increase in GDP; so does going from 9 to 9.5. On a log scale, a constant growth rate will show up on the figure as a straight line. The log scale also makes comparisons, across countries and over time, easier to interpret.

The first thing you see on either of these figures is that the U.S. economy is a remarkable growth machine. Our growth history is not quite a constant 2% per capita rate—the Great Depression and the war years are obvious exceptions—but even after these shocks the economy returned to the old trend line and stayed pretty close to it. Add in a 1% growth rate in population and you get 3% growth in *total* GDP. A 2% per capita growth rate means a doubling of real incomes every 35 years—almost once in a generation. In my lifetime, living standards have multiplied by a factor of four—so far. Over the entire 1870–2008 period shown here, living standards have multiplied by 13, from $2,500 per person in 1870 to more than $32,000 today.

This achievement—for that is what it is—owes much to the background provided by stable government and, especially in the United States, to the provision of good-quality schooling to an ever-increasing fraction of the population. But it is not the result of five-year plans, of job creation programs, or of any miracles of social engineering. It is the product of free-market capitalism facilitated by, but not created or directed by, government.

To be sure, the deviations of actual GDP from the trend line are the products of capitalism, too. For the most part, these have been minor wrinkles and can be viewed as natural consequences of the fact that technological change does not occur at a perfectly steady pace. But the depression of the 1930s cannot be explained in this way, nor, in my opinion, can the recession we are in now. These are serious problems that deserve our attention, and I will return to them later in the chapter. But it will add perspective to look first at the growth experiences of some other successful economies.

■ ■ ■

Figure 3, again using a logarithmic scale, compares the 1870–2008 growth experience of the United States to the experience of the United Kingdom, which is where the industrial revolution began. Until the start of World War II, the economies of both nations grew at a similar pace. But around 1940, America's GDP began outpacing Britain's—and it has remained ahead ever since.

Not surprisingly, the immediate beneficiaries of the U.K.-led industrial revolution included North America, Australia, and New Zealand, areas that had been settled by British immigrants and had remained culturally close to the United Kingdom itself. From about 1880 until say, 1940, the United States and the United Kingdom had similar

Figure 3: GDP Growth in the United States and the United Kingdom

GDP growth and income levels, exchanging leadership several times. The American war mobilization far exceeded the British, however, and at the war's end the United States returned to the old prewar, pre-depression trend line. The United Kingdom followed a parallel trend on which British GDP remained about 30% lower than America's or than its own prewar trend line. The per capita growth rates in both countries settled back to a common 2% and held there, but the difference in income *levels* persisted because of the U.K.'s drop nearly seventy years ago.

Why the large, persistent difference in income levels between the United States and the United Kingdom, countries that had shared economic leadership in earlier years? The Labour government that took power in 1945 nationalized many important industries, established socialized medicine, and in general undertook a dramatic expansion in the role of government in the economy. In the postwar United States, conservative hopes for reversing parts of the New Deal of the 1930s were not realized, but the expansion of government here was much less dramatic than in the United Kingdom. How much of the 30% GDP gap that emerged after the war can be attributed to these policy differences? I'll come back to this question, but let us first take a look at the experiences of some other successful economies.

Figure 4 adds three more countries to those in Figure 3: Germany, Italy, and Japan. Again, per capita GDP is charted on a logarithmic scale from 1870 to 2008. The economic effects of the defeat these countries shared in 1945 are clear on the graph, but the prewar situations of these three had important differences. By 1870 a newly united Germany had already industrialized, but German GDP then lagged behind the United States and the United Kingdom (another 30% gap!) and fell back further in World War I. War mobilization in the 1930s probably contributed to reducing the GDP gap, but World War II was another economic disaster. Then after the war came the "West German miracle": an episode of rapid growth that brought GDP in defeated Germany to the level of victorious Britain by the 1960s. The Marshall Plan? It might have been a minor factor, but the United Kingdom got more than twice the Marshall funds that went to West

Figure 4: GDP Growth, Five Large Countries

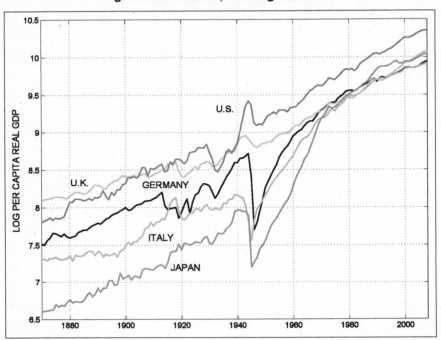

Germany, and the U.K. produced no economic miracle. The main factors were surely the German focus on free markets and the free trade regime established by the Common Market.

Italy in 1870 had perhaps half the per capita GDP of the United States and the United Kingdom, and this gap had not closed up to 1940. Economically, southern Europe was a poor relation to the north. The gap widened still further in the war and then—another postwar miracle—there was not merely a recovery from the war but a nearly complete elimination of the gap between Italy and northern Europe by 1970. As did Germany, Italy benefited enormously from the free trade established by the European Common Market.

But for the largest miracle of all—really, two of them—we need to look at the history of Japan. In 1871, Japan was a typical East Asian agricultural economy, with per capita GDP of about $700 in current U.S. dollars, or something like a quarter of GDP in the United Kingdom. By 1940 Japan had become the first non-European economy to industrialize, leaving the rest of Asia far behind, though it remained much poorer than the United States and the United Kingdom. World War II set Japan back to pre–World War I levels of production. After 1945, Japan grew rapidly, far surpassing prewar levels, equaling European levels by 1970, and reducing the gap with the United States to only 20% by 1990.

The economic performances shown in Figure 4 all reflect the successes of the capitalist democracies of the postwar world, and, of course, many countries not shown on these graphs enjoyed similar success. But it would be a mistake to rank these performances by the countries' average growth rates. The postwar United States and the United Kingdom have both continued to grow at something close to the 2% annual per capita rate they have enjoyed since the middle of the 19th century. The only miracle—or episode of very rapid growth—for the United States was during the war mobilization in the early 1940s. The most impressive miracles we do see on the figure are of two kinds: the postwar recoveries of Italy, Germany, and Japan, and the industrialization/modernization of the backward economies of Italy and Japan. Both of these—I will call them *recovery* growth and *catch-up* growth—are welcome events, but they are symptoms of earlier economic failure, not of success. I will call the 2% rate shared by all the successful economies in the postwar era the *maintainable* growth rate.

Although the five economies shown in Figure 4 share a common growth rate, they do not share common levels of GDP per person. I remarked earlier on the 30% gap between real incomes in the United States and the United Kingdom. Roughly this same gap or a larger one also separates the United States from Germany, Italy, and Japan, and although they are not on the figure, from Spain, France, Scandinavia, and the Low Countries. Research by Edward Prescott[1] and others has shown that most or all of the gap between Western Europe and the United States can be accounted for by much lower employment rates in Europe. This in turn can be viewed as a reflection of the higher marginal tax rates paid by workers in Europe as compared to the United States. Of course, European families get some real benefits from their larger welfare programs, but a 30% loss in production is a very stiff price to pay.

■ ■ ■

In Figure 4, you can see the catch-up growth in the history of Japan, beginning when Japan—alone among Asian economies—introduced European technology and policies in the 1870s and began to grow. But the most striking instances of catch-up growth took place after the end of the European colonial age, in the 1950s and 1960s. Figure 5 plots the average growth rates over the forty years from 1960 to 2000 for all the countries in the world against each country's 1960 per capita GDP level. You can see that the initially rich countries, the ones to the right of the figure, enjoyed average growth around 2%—the rate I referred to earlier as maintainable. But as we move to the left, to the poor former colonies, much higher growth rates—up to a 6% average over forty years—can be observed as well as much lower, even negative rates. Where is the catch-up growth effect?

To answer this question, Jeffrey Sachs and Andrew Warner classified countries into two categories: the "open" economies—those with relatively liberal, free-market internal institutions and relatively free trade policies toward the rest of the world—and the remaining "closed" economies. This classification necessarily involved many judgment calls, described in detail in their 1995 paper.

This work is highlighted in Figure 6, which repeats the pattern of income levels and growth rates shown in Figure 5, but the countries classified by Sachs and Warner as "open" are shown as black dots and "non-open" as shaded dots. They found that the countries with the fastest growth rates were all "open," with relatively free-market economies. There were a handful of open economies with slower growth rates, but these countries have large, illiterate agricultural populations. In other words, freedom helps, but it is not the only factor in economic growth.

I like the Sachs-Warner study because it illustrates two opposing facets of economic growth so well. One is the bewildering variety in the growth experiences we can see in the world. There are many countries that were actually poorer in 2000 than they were in 1960 (including one that was rich in 1960: poor Venezuela!). Then there are others— South Korea, Hong Kong, Singapore, Taiwan—that were among the poorest in the world in 1960 and that now have living standards com-

Figure 5: Income Levels and Growth Rates, 112 Countries

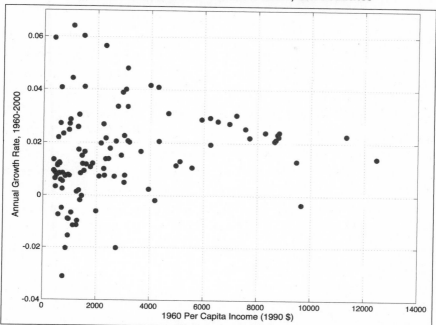

Figure 6: Income Levels and Growth Rates, 112 Countries

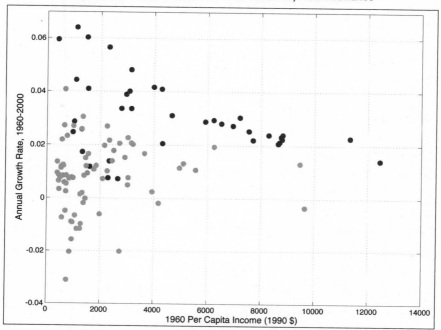

parable to Europe and North America. We are very far from a complete understanding of economic development. On the other hand, among the open, decently governed, literate economies, rich and poor, there is a very clear curve describing catch-up growth: The poorer you are, the faster you can grow.

For those of us in the United States, Japan, or Western Europe, though, all the catch-up growth we will ever have is already behind us. Our average per capita growth rates are about 2%, and the most optimistic long-run forecast we can make is that this pace will be maintained. The implied maintainable growth rate for *total* GDP is 3% for the United States, adding in our 1% population growth rate. As Figure 1 shows, there is no reason to be discouraged by this. We can look at China today and envy their 8% growth rate, but be assured that people in China look at our living standards and envy our $32,000 incomes compared to their $6,700 average. It is this second comparison, a comparison of income *levels*, not of growth rates, that best reflects the economic well-being of people in a society.

If you want your country to grow at 8%, establish a dictatorial regime, initiate a suicidal war, and reduce your economy to poverty. Then establish a peaceful liberal democracy, open up to trade, and take off. If your country is already poor, you can skip the war, keep your labor force in a communist prison camp for decades while the rest of the world grows and prospers, then release your workforce, open up to trade, and take off. Better late than never, certainly, but these are not models that the successful economies should envy or try to follow!

To sum up the growth prospects for the United States that I see in these figures, maintainable growth for our economy is about 2% for GDP per person and 3% for total GDP. The prospect for catch-up growth is nil: We have had the highest living standard of any economy in the world for seventy years, and there is no successor in sight. There is no one to catch up to, except us.

■ ■ ■

That being said, I must also note that the 4% growth target used in this book seems to me an entirely reasonable, even modest, goal for the U.S. economy today. We are in a recession situation, producing at a level that is far below our potential. The only way to realize this potential is to have a period of *recovery growth*. Only growth at a faster rate than the maintainable per capita 2% (or 3% overall) will restore our production *level* to where it should be. I think that Figure 7 is a perfect illustration of this.

Figure 7 uses quarterly data on U.S. real GDP (total in this figure, not per person), plotted as dots. The dotted line reflects the actual ups and downs of U.S. GDP since 2005; the plotted trend line grows at 2.95% annually, which is the historical norm for the U.S. economy. The contrast between expected and actual U.S. GDP growth illustrates the economic consequences of the recent recession.

Both scales are in logs, so that the hash marks describe percentage differences. The two big declines are the fourth quarter of 2008, immediately following the Lehman Brothers failure, and the first quarter of 2009. Before these events, the figure shows a shortfall (relative to the trend line) of 3–4%: a typically modest postwar recession. The

Figure 7: U.S. Recession of 2006–2011

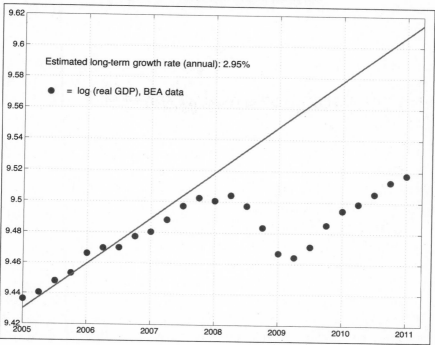

financial crisis changed all that, despite what I see as timely responses by the Fed and the Treasury, and production fell to 8% or 9% below trend. Since then, the growth rate has returned to something close to what I have called its maintainable rate and stayed there. One can see that without some quarters of growth at a faster rate, the economy will *never* get back to the trend line.

Figure 8 shows how atypical this recovery is. It is one of many illuminating figures made available online recently by Thomas Cooley and Peter Rupert in what they call a "snapshot" of the current recession. Figure 8 provides a comparison of the behavior of total real GDP in five recessions: those beginning in 1973, 1981, 1990, 2001, and the current one, dated as 2007. Each of the five curves gives the percentage difference between actual GDP and what it had been in the year that is taken as the beginning of the recession. The chart illustrates the GDP drop from the previous peak as each recession set in and tracks the eventual recovery to normal economic growth. As in my earlier figure, the two largest drops in GDP in the current recession are the fourth quarter of 2008 and the quarter following, here identified as the

Figure 8: Real Gross Domestic Product

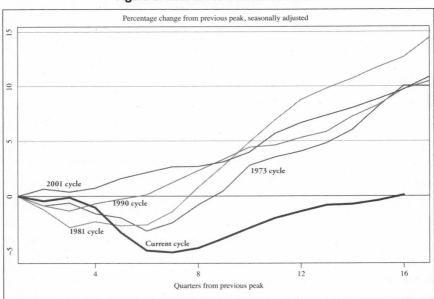

fourth and fifth quarters of the recession. At this point, the economy is 5% below its previous peak. (My 8–9% shortfall is larger because my benchmark is potential output, growing at 3% per year, and not the previous peak. The data used are the same in the two figures.)

Compared to the four earlier recessions, the current one is the deepest by a good margin, but what is even more striking is the slowness—almost the invisibility—of the recovery. The relatively fast recoveries and return to normal growth reflected in all four earlier recessions on Figure 8 are the norm in the United States. These recoveries were not the result of bold stimulus packages or job creation programs. They were representative of the natural resilience of the private economy. This is clear enough from Figures 1 and 2. Recovery from recession is typically something that governments permit to happen, not something governments need to make happen.

■ ■ ■

But if resilience is the norm, where is it now? And where was it during the entire decade of the 1930s? Some interesting research has been directed at the 1930s by Hal Cole and Lee Ohanian.[2] Amity Shlaes's *The Forgotten Man*[3] offers many insights on the way New Deal programs and attitudes affected investment decisions. I think the work of these authors also illuminates the present slow recovery, but the effects they emphasize are hard to quantify. We can get a quantitative sense of what is at stake by thinking of the 30% GDP gaps that we saw in Figures 3 and 4.

When I use the term *recovery* in discussing Figure 7, I mean a return of U.S. GDP to the trend line on the figure. When Cooley and Rupert use it in Figure 8, they mean a return of GDP to a preceding peak. The idea of a "return" in either case presupposes a norm to which the economy, if displaced, will come back. But what if the economic parameters that define the norm—the tax structure, the scope of government, the structure of international trade—change? Then there is no reason to assume that GDP will recover in the sense of returning to some older norm. We observed that the postwar recovery in the United Kingdom returned to a new GDP norm, relative to the United States, after the Labour government elected in 1945 carried out major changes in the role of government in the economy. The norm that prevailed in prewar Britain no longer existed in the postwar period.

Nothing like this has taken place in the United States, but imagine that households and businesses were somehow convinced that the United States would soon move toward a European-level welfare state, financed by a European tax structure. These beliefs would naturally be translated into beliefs that labor costs would soon increase and returns on investment decrease. Beliefs of a future GDP reduction of 30% would be brought forward into the present even before these beliefs could be realized (or refuted).

This is just hypothetical, of course, but it is a hypothesis that is entirely consistent with the way that we know economies work, everyone basing current decisions on expectations about future returns. What I have called *recovery growth* has happened after previous U.S. recessions and depressions and is certainly a worthy and attainable objective for economic policy today, but it would be foolish to take it as a foregone conclusion.

Postscript: Data Sources

Figures 1–6 all use an international data set assembled by the economic historian Angus Maddison. These data (which go back to AD 1!) are made available in very convenient Excel files by the Organisation for Economic Co-operation and Development, which has continued to maintain and update the data series since Maddison's death in 2010. I would be glad to email the data I used here to anyone who asks for it: Email me at relucas@uchicago.edu.

I got the idea of Figures 5 and 6 from figures in Jeffrey Sachs and Andrew Warner's "Economic Reform and the Process of Global Integration," *Brookings Papers on Economic Activity*, 1995, and took the classification into "open" and "closed" economies directly from their paper. But my figure is drawn using Maddison's data from 1960 to 2000 while Sachs and Warner used another data source and only for 1970–90. I simply applied their classification to the longer period, a practice that can certainly be improved on.

I based Figure 7 on data from the U.S. Bureau of Economic Analysis. It is easier to download from the narrower but well-selected statistical tables at the back of the *Economic Report of the President.* The 2011 tables can be found at http://www.gpoaccess.gov/eop/tables11.html.

Figure 8 is taken from the Cooley-Rupert Snapshot, available at http://econsnapshot.wordpress.com. Their pictures cover a very wide selection of time series on employment, consumption, investment, etc., all from well-documented U.S. government sources and all in the same comparative format. They plan to update the snapshot quarterly as new data come available. You will be seeing their graphics everywhere before long.

Chapter 4

More Time on the Job

By Edward C. Prescott

Today, the United States is 40% more prosperous than Western Europe, or, put another way, Western Europe is depressed 30% relative to the United States.[1]

Why? The answer is not that Western Europeans are less productive than Americans. After creating what became the European Union with the signing of the Treaty of Rome in 1957, European workers caught up to American workers in terms of output produced per hour worked—that is, in productivity. But beginning in the 1970s and '80s, Europeans also reduced the amount they worked in the market sector and, as a result, output and income per person did not catch up to the United States even though productivity did.

The primary reason for the fall in market hours per adult was that Europe increased tax rates in the 1970s and '80s. These tax increases created an effective marginal tax rate of about 60%. So when a European works more and produces an extra 100 euros of output, he or she gets only 40 euros' worth of additional consumption. In the United States and most other advanced industrial countries the effective marginal tax rates are closer to 40%. This means an average American gets $60 of additional consumption for each $100 of additional output he or she produces.

■ ■ ■

Over the past forty years or so there has been a revolution in macroeconomics. Today it is a hard, quantitative science, like physics. This allows us to gain a precise quantitative accounting of what's happening in the economy and why. It allows us to refine economic theories based on real-world observations. It allowed us to figure out why Europe is depressed relative to the United States, and what Americans should do now to avoid making the same mistakes Europeans have.

One of the most interesting things economists have observed is that one factor accounts for most of the large differences in income across countries at a point in time and for the large growth in the per capita income of countries over time. This factor is productivity—that is, how much output is produced per unit of input. The reason for the long-term growth in productivity is growth of the stock of knowledge useful in production. The reason for differences in productivity across countries is the nature of policy regimes—that is, the nature of the legal and regulatory system. Generally speaking, policy regimes that result in groups of people producing more with the same amount of inputs make that country richer. In other words, the more efficient and productive we become, the more income we create for ourselves.

For two centuries, the increase in the efficiency of the U.S. economy has made the United States substantially better off. Today we are 25 times richer than we were in 1810, because we are 25 times more productive. Today we are 10 times wealthier than India, because American workers are 10 times more productive than Indian workers now are. The only way to get higher income is to produce more output—because income is, by definition, claims against output. And it is clear that our output has increased at a healthy rate over our history. If this continues, and almost surely it will because of the continual growth in the stock of knowledge useful in production, our grandchildren will be four times richer than we are, just as we are four times richer than our grandparents were.

If, however, there is a shift to a bad regime, the U.S. economy will become depressed and remain so until there is a shift to a better policy regime. It's important to note that what people expect policies to be in the future determines what happens now. Bad policies can and often do depress the economy even before they are implemented. People's actions now depend on what they think policy will be—not what it was.

There was a shift to a bad policy regime in 1930, and as a result the U.S. economy became depressed by about 23%, as measured by the number of hours worked in the market sector per working-age person. This depression persisted for nine years, before the economy began its recovery back to a long-term-trend growth path. Currently the U.S. economy is depressed about 10% relative to its pre-2008 trend growth path. This estimate is based upon the behavior of the fraction of the population sixteen years and older that is employed, a statistic reported by the Bureau of Labor Statistics monthly. I emphasize that depression and prosperity are relative concepts and when I say, "We are experiencing a depression," I am saying the economy is depressed relative to trend.

Surveying the economic data, we can see that weathering depressions and producing an economy that is experiencing healthy growth along a high path is something the United States is good at. Following the Great Depression, the United States rebounded back to the secular growth path. Likewise, in the first half of the 1960s, the country experienced a big expansion with the economy moving above trend. We know the driver of that boom was advancements in technology. Innovations in air travel, mainframe computing, chemicals, and other industries made America a more productive country.

The interstate highway system also contributed greatly to the rapid growth in productivity in the late 1950s and '60s. It contributed by increasing the efficiency of the transportation sector. An important aspect of this increase was the resulting competition between rail and truck transportation, which led both transportation modes to become more efficient. This greater transportation efficiency lowered the cost of transportation, which in turn increased competition among businesses across regions of the United States; moreover, this increased competition led to greater productivity in other sectors of the economy. The increase in productivity did not lead to less employment. Rather, it led to more output and higher incomes.

The standard measure of productivity is GDP per hour worked in the market sector. However, in looking over the historical data, we should be careful not to rely too heavily on GDP numbers. There are significant investments that aren't included in the GDP, even though these investments pay dividends to the economy in the form of greater output and income in the future. One of these is investments in human capital. When young or new workers (such as mothers reentering the workforce) land a job, they often are paid only a modest wage. But, in fact, they are earning more than their wage before they started working. They are acquiring human capital through on-the-job training, and this increase in their human capital results in higher future wages. This important component of output is hard to measure and is not included in GDP. These and other unmeasured investments are an important part of output. One very important component of unmeasured investments is associated with developing new products and improving business organizations.

One implication of human capital investment is that the booms of the 1980s and '90s were bigger than suggested by the GDP statistics. The cut in the marginal tax rate fueled the boom of the 1980s. Many married women entered the workforce, and, with their on-the-job acquisition of skills, their wages relative to married men subsequently increased significantly.

Similarly, GDP numbers don't show the true size of the boom in the 1990s. A big unmeasured investment is needed to build a successful new business, and there was an explosion in the number of new businesses in this period associated with the information technology revolution. It's nearly impossible to capture in GDP numbers all the investments a new business requires. Beyond start-up capital, there is also a lot of "sweat equity"—the intangible value created by hard work of those with an equity position in the business for which they work. The time and effort an entrepreneur puts in are substantial, and the knowledge he or she acquires along the way is tremendously valuable. These entrepreneurs develop new products, build a customer base, and train workers—a huge unmeasured investment that is certainly part of economic output, but not part of GDP, which is the *measured* part of output.

The people who are financing these unmeasured investments are not compensated at the time they produce their capital. Rather, they are rewarded when they sell their equity in their business and realize a capital gain. The intangible investments of starting a business and developing new products is as big as the investments in tangible capital, such as factories, vehicles, buildings, computers, office desks, and other producer durables.

To get a better handle on economic trends, I therefore pay a lot of attention to the number of hours worked. And by my calculations in 2011, the United States economy is depressed by about 10% relative to the pre-2008 trend. The so-called Great Recession, from the second quarter of 2008 to the third quarter of 2009, saw a 10% decline in output and employment relative to trend. Things had been going along nicely before the decline.

The disturbing fact is that, as of the beginning of 2012, the economy has not even partially recovered from this recession. When it will recover is a political and not an economic question. Only if the Americans making personal economic decisions knew what future policy would be could economists predict when recovery would occur.

I call this current decline the Not-So-Great Recession because it's not in the same class as the Great Depression. During the 1930s, the hours worked per working-age person was depressed by nearly one-fourth for nine years. Things didn't start to turn around in a real way until 1939. We can pray that the current recession won't last that long, or we can come to a consensus as to what reforms are needed and commit to implementing them. The most-needed reforms to restore prosperity are 1) to cut marginal tax rates, which will increase the number of hours people work in the market sector, and 2) to adopt pro-productivity growth policies that will increase output and income per hour worked in the market sector.

One of the more troubling statistics in the current depression is the extremely high underemployment numbers for younger Americans, ages 16–24. This is troubling because, when we hire young Americans, we are making an investment in human capital. Part of that investment is made by employers, who hire workers who need significant training. And part of the investment is made by the employees themselves, who put in long hours at relatively low pay to learn new valuable skills. Put those two investments together and you will see that the human capital investment decline is a very big number.

Not making this investment doesn't bode well for the future. The young are the ones who are suffering now as they struggle to find work. In the long run, this lack of investment in human capital will almost certainly dent our future economic progress. There are data that show that Americans who graduate from college during a recession earn less than peers who graduate during boom times, a trend that lasts beyond a single business cycle.[2] And there is plenty of reason to believe that losing this capital will lead to a prolonged period of time when the nation as a whole is less productive than it should be. In other words, millions of young Americans will spend the years ahead scrambling to make up for the ground they are losing now or face the prospect of never earning what they could have earned.

Japan is the classic modern example of a country that had been thriving (and many predicted would own the future) but then saw its economy get bogged down. Beginning about 1950, Japan caught up and became one of the advanced industrialized countries. Everything was seemingly going great for the country—its automakers and electronic companies were leading the world, its influence was expanding, and its economy was growing rapidly—until 1992. Then its growth dropped to almost zero for a decade. The problem was that the productivity growth rate fell to almost zero. I suspect that Japan's problem was that it subsidized inefficient businesses through the government-banking complex, which depressed the expansion of the productive businesses and thwarted the birth of more efficient enterprises. In any case, since 2002 Japan's productivity growth has resumed, and its output per working-age person has stopped falling relative to the other industrial countries. The reason for its slow growth in aggregate output stems from the fact that its working-age population is falling.

■ ■ ■

So what can the United States do to avoid Japan's fate or end up resembling Western Europe, with slow growth and lower productivity?

I mentioned the importance of unmeasured investment for a simple reason: Policy makers would do well to find ways to encourage such investments. They could start by cutting marginal tax rates. This would give workers a greater incentive to work longer, innovate more, and find ways to produce. Having a system where people move quickly from where they are less productive to where they are more productive increases productivity and living standards. Policy makers must also cut government expenditures. Milton Friedman reminded us that to spend is to tax—meaning that every dollar spent by the government today has to be financed by taxes paid today or in the future.

One negative drag on the economy often talked about, but not well understood, comes in legal and regulatory systems. They can be reformed to foster higher productivity. Cutting back needless or wasteful regulations is one way to encourage the workforce to be more productive. Another way is to make the labor force as flexible as possible. We need workers to be able to jump from one job to the next or one industry to the next—if they are jumping to a job that makes them more productive than the one they are leaving. Raising productivity in this way raises the output and income of the economy.

Some countries in Europe have flexible labor markets—such as Switzerland and Denmark—and they are doing well economically. Others have incredibly inflexible markets—such as Spain and Italy—and these countries have been teetering on the edge of insolvency. That inflexibility is socially wasteful. In the long run, it leaves the population poorer. No country can afford to subsidize inefficiencies in order to preserve the status quo of its industries. Innovation and new blood are essential to economic health. Each job you save with new mandates or other government controls costs about two jobs that would have been created in growing or new companies.

Take a look at the approaches of two Latin American countries that stumbled in 1981: Chile and Mexico. Chile embraced market-based reform, including privatizing its national pension system. It didn't simply recover from its recession—it experienced a growth miracle. It moved significantly above its old trend line to put itself on a higher economic growth path. Mexico, on the other hand, lost fifteen years of growth before reforming. In the end, it did create a sound banking system and cut corporate taxes. And over the past few years, Mexico has started to improve. I hope and expect this improvement will continue as Mexico develops better political and economic institutions. If so, in time the United States will have a rich southern neighbor.

We can learn from these examples and enact policies now that encourage more innovation and more investments in human capital. In the end, policies matter. The wrong policies can discourage growth. But the right policy regime will encourage Americans to work harder and build the next great surge in our economy. We can't know where the next innovations will come from, but we do have some idea of who will develop them: those individuals who see it as worthwhile to burn the midnight oil, work harder, and create the wealth that will benefit us all.

Chapter 5

At Home in the Great Recession

By Steven Gjerstad and Vernon L. Smith

This chapter examines three closely related problems: the usual impact of monetary policy on the economy, its limitations in the aftermath of the Great Recession, and a proposed course of action to support a stronger recovery. We first describe the course of the typical postwar economic cycle in the United States. This allows us to determine the usual impact of monetary policy on key sectors of the economy. We then consider differences between today's Great Recession and the typical downturn. And we conclude by evaluating financial crises and their associated economic downturns in other countries to determine how much of an impact fiscal policy (government spending) can have on reviving economic growth.

Our evaluation of postwar cycles and our comparison of them to the Great Recession indicates why monetary policy has been so ineffective and has failed to stimulate aggregate output even with extreme growth of the monetary base; our assessment of financial crises in other countries strongly suggests that it is fiscal discipline rather than fiscal stimulus that is capable of generating robust recoveries. Cutting government spending, as opposed to cutting interest rates or spending more government money, could be a critical step to recovering from a financial crisis.

■ ■ ■

The United States has just experienced one of the largest real estate bubbles in history, and it is now facing the aftermath of a financial crisis and coping with a stumbling economy. To understand how the Great Recession differed from more typical recessions, we compared it to every downturn the country has experienced since the 1920–21 recession.

What we found may surprise many economists and policy makers. Except in its magnitude and its impact on the financial sector, what we've experienced with the housing crash isn't an anomaly. For the past eighty-five years changes in spending on new housing units have led us both into and out of nearly every recession, and the evidence suggests that there were mitigating factors for the few exceptions. We found that, more than business investments, spending on new housing units is a leading indicator of whether a recession is likely to occur, how deep it could be, and how long it may last. We also found that monetary policy typically has its greatest effect on mortgage lending, residential construction, consumer credit, and the purchase of durable goods when monetary policy is tightened just before and in the early stages of a recession, and when monetary policy is relaxed during and after a recession.

We will describe the evidence for this claim in a minute, but above all its implications are far-reaching. Monetary policy normally stimulates mortgage lending, and that lending leads quickly to new residential construction because consumers suddenly gain the means to buy new houses, which increases demand for new housing. However, a relaxed monetary policy of low interest rates has not been stimulating new housing construction or new housing demand now, and for a few important reasons. Many Americans are currently encumbered with an unusually high level of mortgage debt. What's more, the housing market is saturated with an inventory of unsold homes. Banks are also acting cautiously due to their weak balance sheets. So it will likely be a long time before monetary easing generates a significant increase in mortgage borrowing and residential construction.

Despite the fact that spending on new housing units is a small portion of the economy, its movements are sufficient to account for a large portion of GDP changes during contractions, even before taking account of how the decline of income from housing construction or the decline of household wealth from loss of housing equity affects demand in other sectors. Since changes in how much Americans spend on new housing units and on durable goods precede and exceed changes in nonresidential investment, we believe that "business cycle" is a poor description for the economic fluctuations in the United States over the past eighty-five years. We found evidence that a *household expenditure cycle* generates a *business investment cycle* and that combined the two make up an *economic cycle*. In short, our economic cycles are heavily influenced by how much (or how little) Americans are spending on new housing units and durable goods.

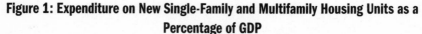

There have been fourteen recessions since 1929. Some of these have been severe and long lasting (such as the Great Depression), while others have been short or mild (such as the shallow 1960–61 and 1969–70 recessions, which preceded the deep 1973–75 recession, or the mild 1990–91 and 2001 recessions, which preceded today's Great Recession). To get an overview of how housing is connected to each, we looked at how much Americans spent on single-family or multifamily housing units as a percentage of GDP over the past ninety years.

Figure 1: Expenditure on New Single-Family and Multifamily Housing Units as a Percentage of GDP

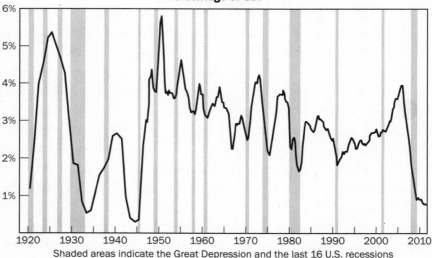

Shaded areas indicate the Great Depression and the last 16 U.S. recessions

In plotting those figures on the graph above, we can see that housing was a leading indicator that a recession was coming in 11 of the most recent 14 economic downturns because housing expenditures declined shortly before the recessions began. And one of the three exceptions doesn't support the notion that declining business investment causes recessions, because it was caused by a drop-off of government spending that came with the end of World War II. From 1945 to 1946, national defense expenditures fell from 36.7% of GDP to 11.3% of GDP. All major components of private expenditure rose in 1946, but GDP fell by 10.9%. Moreover, households' consumption of durable goods and expenditures on new housing units increased 2.35 times as much in 1946 as business investment, so households contributed substantially to the recovery in private expenditures. The other two recessions that were not led by declines in expenditures on new housing units and on consumer durables—in 1937–38 and 2001—resulted primarily from declines in nonresidential fixed investment.

Mortgage credit and consumer credit extended to households declined sharply in every recession between the 1953–54 recession and the 1990–91 recession. The average change in the net flow of mortgage and consumer credit between the peak of the economic cycle and the end of the recession for the eight recessions between 1953–54 and 1990–91 was a 33.7% decline, with a minimum decline among them of 21.2%, but in the 2001 recession, new credit to households increased 8.8% between the peak of the economic cycle in the first quarter of 2001 and the end of the recession in the fourth quarter of 2001.[1] While the 2001 recession differed from the typical postwar recession in that expenditures on new housing units and on consumer durable goods both rose, the reason appears to be an unusual pattern of rising mortgage and consumer credit that supported household expenditures.[2]

In 10 of the 11 postwar recessions, the fall in spending on new housing units and consumer durables preceded declines in every other major component of GDP; their declines in percentage terms exceeded declines in other major components of GDP. The dollar value of the decline in the sum of housing and durable goods expenditures has been larger in 8 of the 11 postwar recessions than the dollar value of the decline in business investment.

Housing is often overlooked in macroeconomic analysis, probably because it is not a large component of GDP. Nonetheless, housing is volatile, declining before the Great Depression and nearly every reces- sion since, and has rarely declined substantially without a recession following soon afterward.[3] What's more, the extent of its decline is a good indicator of the depth and duration of the recession that follows.

In addition to its role as a leading indicator, and its volatility over the economic cycle, expenditure on new housing units has recovered faster than any other major sector of the economy after *every* recession between 1929 and 2001, including even the abortive recovery from the 1980 recession, when the housing recovery faltered after two quarters and a new recession began two quarters later.

In short, housing fluctuates more over the economic cycle than any other major component of GDP, so it is natural to consider what causes its movements. Monetary policy is one important factor. Nearly five decades ago Milton Friedman and Anna J. Schwartz argued in their now-classic book, *A Monetary History of the United States,* that mon- etary policy has a clear impact on the course of the real economy. For decades much of the economics community has agreed with this analy- sis. By lowering short-term interest rates or using other tools to increase the money supply, the Fed can typically provide a boost to the rate of economic growth. We take this argument one step forward and find that mortgage lending and residential construction are primary trans- mission channels for monetary policy. The Federal Reserve's efforts to combat inflation, stimulate economic growth, or regulate the flow of credit often have the most impact on mortgage credit and residential construction. Housing responds first to tightened monetary policy and typically recovers first when monetary policy is relaxed. If we trace through the effects of open market purchases of Treasury securities by the Federal Reserve System, we can see why.

Since the Treasury–Federal Reserve Accord of March 1951, open market purchases of Treasury securities have been the primary policy instrument employed by the Fed. When the Federal Reserve increases its purchases of short-term Treasury securities, that pushes their price up, which is another way of saying that it pushes down short-term interest rates. This has two effects on depository institutions. It brings down their cost of funds, since Treasury bills, which are a close substi- tute for demand and time deposits, have a low yield and banks can pay a low interest rate and still attract deposits. At the same time, mortgage and other interest rates fall much more slowly, so open market purchases by the Federal Reserve open up a gap between the lending and borrowing rates of depository institutions. Consequently, open market purchases by the Federal Reserve encourage lending, primarily to households and small businesses that rely on depository institutions.

We began by asking how residential construction influenced and was influenced by other recessions during the past century. To address this question, we examined movements in four key GDP components from the National Income and Product Accounts (NIPA): consumers' spending on nondurable goods and services (C), their expenditures on durable goods (D), their expenditures on new single-family and multi-family housing units (H), and nonresidential fixed investment (I) by businesses.[4] These four elements of private expenditure have accounted for an average of 79.8% of GDP between 1947 and the second quarter of 2011.[5] Government spending absorbed most of the remaining 20.2% of output.

We find that changes in households' expenditure on new housing units and changes in business investment differ systematically prior to and during recessions, and in recoveries.[6] In the typical postwar economic cycle, inflation remained low while expenditures on new housing units expanded. Then inflation began as housing slowed. In response to developing inflation, monetary policy was tightened and housing began a sharper decline. The resulting downturn in the household expenditure cycle reduced inflationary pressure, but also led to a turn in the investment cycle as firms encountered reduced demand for consumer durable goods. The combination of this household expenditure cycle and the investment cycle form an economic cycle.

The Great Recession and all seven recessions between the 1957–58 recession and the 1990–91 recession fit this pattern closely. The 1948–49 and 1953–54 recessions fit it in most respects, but elimination of wage and price controls after World War II and large defense expenditures prior to the 1953–54 recession disrupted the usual patterns somewhat. The 2001 recession deviates from this pattern, but there is substantial evidence that the pattern was disrupted by the huge influx of foreign investment into the United States and a correspondingly large influx of mortgage credit into the housing market. We now examine these patterns by reviewing five of the past six U.S. recessions. The 1973–75, 1980, and 1981–82 recessions conform to the common patterns that we've identified. The 2001 and 2007–2009 recessions deviate in important respects, but these deviations provide insights into why the 2001 recession was so shallow and why the 2007–2009 recession was so deep and the recovery from it has been so weak.

THE 1973–75 RECESSION

The 1973–75 recession, displayed in Figure 2, was the third-largest recession in the postwar era. It demonstrates all of the most frequent patterns that we've observed in postwar U.S. recessions. Housing peaked in the first quarter of 1973, three quarters before the peak of the economic cycle. From its peak until the peak of the economic cycle, housing fell 14.9%. The sharp rise in the inflation rate began just as the housing market began to decline. This apparent puzzle has a natural explanation: In another common pattern, mortgage finance peaked just after housing peaked. Mortgage finance peaked one quarter after the peak in residential construction, and mortgage finance fell much more slowly than construction. When mortgage finance dropped sharply in the first quarter of 1975, the inflation rate finally began to decline.

In terms of the magnitude of declines by sector, the $103.8 billion housing decline was more than two and a half times as large as the $40.7 billion investment decline. The decline in housing plus consumer durable goods, at $177.2 billion, was 4.35 times as large as the investment decline. This evidence suggests not only that housing was a leading indicator, but also that the decline in housing and durable goods played a much larger role in the recession than the decline in investments.

The housing decline lasted into 1975, about two quarters after monetary policy was eased at the end of 1974. Once the federal funds rate was reduced to a level comparable to where it stood in 1972, a rapid recovery in housing and in the economy began. In the first two years of the recovery, from the second quarter of 1975 until the second quarter of 1977, housing increased 116%, consumer durable goods increased 38.4%, and investment increased 31%.

We'll see all of these patterns repeated in the 1980 and 1981–82 double-dip recessions, but those two recessions also included two sharp monetary policy reversals in quick succession, with corresponding contractions and expansions in housing. These policy reversals provide a very clear demonstration of the effect of monetary policy on economic activity in general, as well as its transmission through mortgage finance and residential construction.

Figure 2: Percentage Changes to GDP and Its Major Components Before, During, and After the 1973–75 Recession

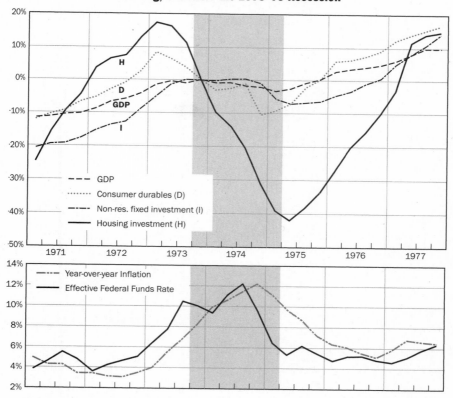

The housing decline was the second-largest of the postwar era, as was the decline in durables, while the investment decline was delayed and moderate. In a common pattern, inflation rose sharply after housing peaked and inflation peaked during the recession. Values are relative to their levels at the start of the recession in Q4 1973. For example, housing construction was 17.5% higher in Q1 1973 than it was in Q4 1973 when the recession began; housing was 41.9% lower when it bottomed out in Q2 1975 than it was in Q4 1973. Other series are interpreted similarly.

THE 1980 AND 1981–82 "DOUBLE-DIP" RECESSIONS

Our analysis of the 1980 and 1981–82 "double-dip" recessions (Figure 3) demonstrates the sharp impact that monetary policy has on mortgage lending and residential construction. In those recessions, monetary policy was tightened and relaxed twice in quick succession. With each shift in monetary policy, expenditures on new housing units responded most quickly and with the largest magnitude to the policy change. The fact that monetary policy largely impacts the economy through the housing market is an important insight that helps bring the broader economic story of the United States into focus. It explains why the Fed's efforts to combat inflation can accelerate a decline in the housing market, why a rising housing market can lead to increases in other areas of the economy, and why today the Fed's policy of low interest rates isn't reigniting significant economic growth in our economy.

As in the 1973–75 recession, the two recessions of the early 1980s once again demonstrate that housing is a reliable leading indicator of a coming downturn. From its peak in the second quarter of 1978 until the peak of the economic cycle, housing fell 21.7%. When housing reached its first trough in the third quarter of 1980, it had fallen 40.6% from its peak. Soon after monetary policy was relaxed toward the end of the second quarter of 1980, the housing collapse slowed and then reversed. However, just as housing began to recover, monetary policy was tightened again toward the end of 1980. In the second housing decline, which lasted from the first quarter of 1981 to the second quarter of 1982, housing fell 36.0%. Over almost a four-year period, from the third quarter of 1978 to the second quarter of 1982, housing fell 55.2%. Each shift in monetary policy quickly had a corresponding impact on residential construction, and each foreshadowed what followed in the overall economy.

What's more, declines in housing and durables came before investment declines and exceeded the size of investment declines over the same period. In the 1980 recession, housing fell $88.7 billion, whereas investment fell only $29.6 billion. Over the course of the two combined recessions, housing fell $120.9 billion, the sum of housing and durables fell $201.7 billion, and investment fell $131.5 billion. House-

Figure 3: Percentage Changes to GDP and Its Major Components Before, During, and After the 2001 Recession

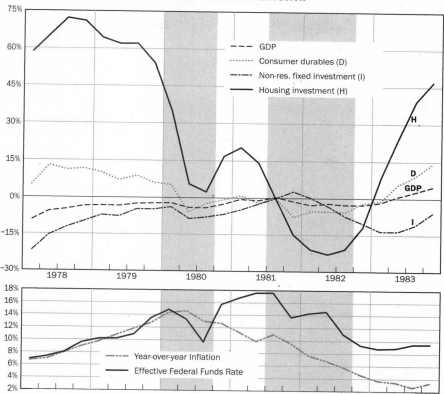

Monetary policy was tightened and relaxed twice in succession between late 1979 and late 1982; each shift produced a corresponding shift in mortgage finance and residential construction. The series is interpreted in the same way as those in Figure 2.

holds' interest-rate-sensitive components of consumption therefore had a stronger impact on the development of this downturn than nonresidential fixed investment: Housing plus durables peaked twelve quarters before investment, and the dollar amount of their decline exceeded the investment decline by 53.4%. The timing and the magnitude of these events aren't coincidental; they reveal that housing and other interest-rate-sensitive items play a key role in economic cycles.

This double-dip recessionary period illustrates another point that is relevant today: Not only does monetary policy have a clear impact on the economy, but also it does so primarily through mortgage and consumer credit and their effects on construction of new homes and households' purchases of durable goods. We will reinforce this point later in the chapter, but in brief here is the evidence for this point from the double-dip recessionary period.

President Jimmy Carter appointed Paul Volcker as chairman of the Federal Reserve in August 1979. In its meeting on October 6, 1979, the Federal Open Market Committee (FOMC) voted to increase the federal funds rate sharply. By early April 1980, the federal funds rate reached 19.4%, up from 10.6% when Volcker arrived at the Fed. In April 1980, many bank managers faced with the choice of making a mortgage loan at 16.3% or purchasing a three-month Treasury bill with a yield of 19.4% chose to limit their mortgage lending.

The demand for loans, too, must have been seriously diminished by such high interest rates, but the rapid decline in mortgage borrowing and the rapid increase in the cost of borrowing suggest that the supply reduction dominated the demand reduction.[7] The decline in mortgage lending in the second quarter of 1980 was the sharpest of the postwar era up to that time. In response to the fall in lending that resulted from the tightened monetary policy, construction of new housing fell 34.8% from the last quarter of 1979 to the second quarter of 1980. By April 1980, the money supply was contracting rapidly, but the Fed had only sought to reduce its growth rate. So Volcker cut the federal funds rate from 19.4% in early April 1980 to 9.5% eight weeks later, in late May; he then kept the rate below 10% until the end of August.

The effect of the monetary policy reversal on housing was sharp, and operated with only a one- to two-quarter lag. The housing decline ended in the third quarter of 1980 and turned up in the following quarter. But that didn't last as Volcker again raised the federal funds rate. Between September 1980 and January 1981, the rate went from 11% to 20%. The increase sparked another housing collapse starting in the second quarter of 1981. Over five quarters, housing fell another 36.0% to a new postwar low of less than 1.7% of GDP in the second quarter of 1982.

In the first two quarters of 1980, when Volcker's tightened monetary policy first began to have a strong effect on housing, the inflation rate averaged 14.4%. By the end of 1982, when the recovery began, inflation averaged 4.7%. Monetary policy had been tight in 10 of 11 quarters from the end of 1979 to the second quarter of 1982, bringing inflation under control. When monetary policy was finally eased sharply in the third quarter of 1982, housing again responded almost immediately, increasing 92% between the third quarter of 1982 and the second quarter of 1984. The fact that housing followed monetary policy so closely in this period demonstrates that housing is a key component of the Fed's ability to wring inflation out of the system. In other words, housing is a vital transmission channel for monetary policy.

■ ■ ■

There are two conditions that deprive monetary policy of much of its power, and both are present in the Great Recession. First, accommodative monetary policy (such as low interest rates) primarily affects new residential construction. And when there is a glut in housing, as there is today, lower interest rates won't spur residential construction even if it entices new buyers into the market. Builders will want to wait until homes currently on the market are sold before they hire new workers, and start building homes again. Second, ten million Americans owe more on their homes than their homes are worth, and even more households have suffered large declines in their home equity, so we can expect many homeowners to focus on shedding mortgage debt rather than on consumption.

In rare cases, a saturated housing market leads to a decline in the amount of mortgage credit outstanding. Such a contraction will reverberate throughout the economy as Americans have less money to spend on homes, durable goods, and other items. We've seen reductions in the amount of mortgage credit outstanding just three times. The first was during the Great Depression. The second came in World War II and was the result of government controls on new residential construction. The third came recently in the Great Recession.

The collapse of mortgage lending itself resulted from the extreme buildup of mortgage debt that households accumulated during the housing bubble. Before we describe the course of the Great Recession, we begin by examining the course of the 2001 recession and the growth of foreign investment and mortgage credit that contributed to the bubble.

THE 2001 RECESSION

The sluggish recovery from the 2001 recession (Figure 4) generated responses that fostered the large buildups of mortgage and consumer credit that fed the housing bubble. The credit buildup itself led to an unusual pattern in the 2001 recession, seen only once before in the past ninety years in the United States. As noted in note 2, in the 1923–24 recession and the 2001 recession, households' consumption of nondurable goods and services, their consumption of durable goods, and new residential units all increased through the recession. Unusual as these recessions were, they are more concordant than the typical recession with the common belief that business investment drives the economic cycle.

Investment reached a plateau between the second and fourth quarters of 2000 and started to decline in the first quarter of 2001. (The crash of the dot-com stock bubble started in the first quarter of 2000 and extended through the fourth quarter of 2002.) The investment decline continued much longer than it typically does, and in another unusual pattern, residential construction and consumer durable goods both continued to rise through the recession. The prolonged decline in investment prompted the Federal Reserve to pursue an expansionary monetary policy at a time when funds were flowing into the mortgage market from abroad at an unprecedented rate.

In spite of both the large capital inflow and the expansionary monetary policy, the housing recovery failed to deliver its usual stimulation to the recession recovery. In the four quarters following the end of the recession, it increased only 7.8%, far below its 28.3% average increase in the four quarters after the previous nine postwar recessions.

A full year after the end of the recession, in its November 2002 meeting, the FOMC lowered the federal funds target rate to 1.25% because "the generally disappointing data since the previous meeting . . . pointed to a longer-lasting spell of subpar economic performance than they had anticipated earlier," and the FOMC concluded that "a relatively aggressive easing action could help to ensure that the current soft spot in the economy would prove to be temporary and enhance the odds of a robust rebound in economic activity next year."

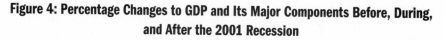

Figure 4: Percentage Changes to GDP and Its Major Components Before, During, and After the 2001 Recession

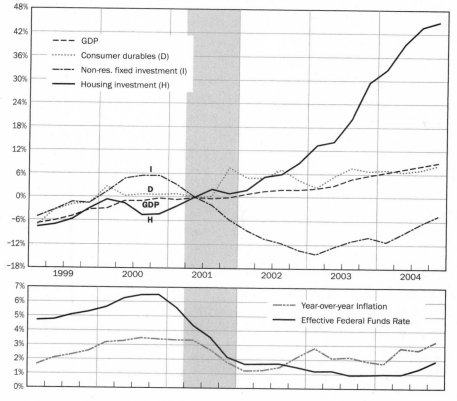

While investment declined, housing had been growing modestly, though not enough to offset reduced investment. On June 25, 2003, the FOMC lowered the fed funds target rate to 1%, noting in its press release that the economy "has yet to exhibit sustainable growth," and "with inflationary expectations subdued, the Committee judged that a slightly more expansive monetary policy would add further support for an economy which it expects to improve over time." In the second quarter of 2003, investment turned the corner and began to increase, but the federal funds rate remained at 1% for the next year. Investment growth was slow, even with the expansionary monetary policy, but the net flow of mortgage funds had already surged above 7% of GDP. Supported by the unprecedented level of mortgage finance, residential construction grew 21.9% in the four quarters when the federal funds rate was 1%, from the second quarter of 2003 to the second quarter of 2004. However, even in this recession evidence supports the general rule: The investment recovery was delayed until the robust housing recovery in 2003.

Although this 21.9% increase was large, it was well below the 28.3% average increase in housing during the first four quarters following the nine postwar recessions between 1948–49 and 1990–91, and this 21.9% increase came between the sixth and the tenth quarters after the recovery began. Except for the abortive housing recovery in 1980, the increase in housing construction in the four quarters after the 2001 recession was the slowest of the postwar era.

Even when the delayed recovery came, it wasn't unusually large. For example, residential construction as a percentage of GDP was higher every quarter between the first quarter of 1972 and the third quarter of 1973 than it was in any quarter during the housing bubble. Yet the growth in mortgage finance was fast, and it reached an unprecedented level of 8.8% of GDP in the second quarter of 2006. Since the extremely high level of mortgage credit was supporting only a modest level of new residential construction, there was a great deal of credit available to support rapid house price appreciation. That combination left households and the financial services sectors in a precarious situation when house prices fell.

Where did the money come from for such a large increase in mortgage debt? In part, it came from overseas. As Figure 5 illustrates, in 1997, the current account deficit (the amount of money flowing into the country minus what was flowing out) stood at $152.8 billion, or 1.55% of GDP. By 2006 the current account deficit had ballooned to $772.9 billion, or 5.97% of GDP.[8] Foreign capital was flowing into the country, inflating our housing bubble. Of course, this arrangement couldn't last indefinitely.

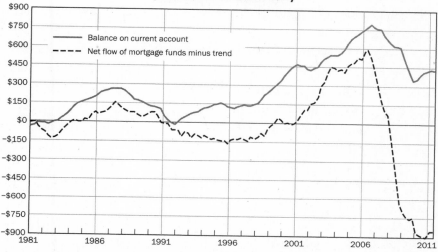

**Figure 5: Net Flow of Real Mortgage Funds
(in billions of 2005 dollars)**

This graph shows the current account balance over the past thirty years. It also shows the flow of mortgage funds minus its trend growth, where the trend is calculated based on the growth of mortgage lending between 1952 and 1997. The deviation from the trend is close to the inflow of capital into the United States during the housing bubble. During the tech sector bubble, much of the capital inflow went into the stock market rather than mortgage finance.

In January 2010, Federal Reserve chairman Ben Bernanke reported evidence that in recent decades countries with large current account deficits typically have had high house price appreciation.[9] A country finances a current account deficit largely by issuing or selling financial instruments; during the U.S. housing bubble, mortgage securities formed a large portion of the instruments issued to finance our trade deficits. A significant portion of the funds that supported our housing bubble came—either directly or indirectly—from foreign investors, and many of the mortgages that formed these securities were issued to borrowers in weak financial condition who eventually were unable to meet the terms of their loans. Thus the large flow of foreign investment into the mortgage market and a lack of regulatory oversight of mortgage underwriting practices combined as significant factors in the formation of the housing bubble.

THE GREAT RECESSION

The recent recession is widely attributed to the housing bubble that began in about 1997 and culminated with huge house price increases between 2003 and 2005. During the period of most rapid price increases—between July 2003 and July 2005—the Case-Shiller composite index of housing prices in twenty U.S. cities increased 35%.[10] It's worth noting that the period of the most rapid housing price increases was also a period with a historically high level of mortgage finance. Much of the price increase was driven by people who, for a variety of reasons, purchased homes that they could only afford (even temporarily) if they were able to refinance relatively quickly as the house increased in value.

A large increase in mortgage lending provided the impetus to the rapid rise in home prices. Between the first quarter of 2002 and the first quarter of 2006 the real mortgage debt of U.S. households increased from $5.97 trillion to $8.97 trillion, an increase of just over 50%.[11] Figure 6 shows mortgage lending as a percentage of GDP. Excessive lending that combined lax underwriting standards and low down payments pushed house prices well above sustainable levels. When the bubble burst, many mortgages became delinquent as a result of lax

Figure 6: The Flow of Household Mortgage Credit as a Percentage of GDP

underwriting standards, and a substantial part of the loan principal for defaulting borrowers was lost by lenders and investors because of the low down payments.

In 2006 house prices leveled off, putting many homeowners in a bind. Those who relied on rising home prices in order to refinance their loans were suddenly unable to refinance. What followed was a rapid rise toward the end of 2006 in the number of people who fell behind on their mortgage payments. Delinquencies increased between the third quarter of 2006 and the second quarter of 2007 by factors of 3.02 in Arizona, 2.75 in California, and 2.68 in Nevada.[12] The states with the highest house price appreciation were also among the states with the most subprime loans and subprime ARM (adjustable-rate mortgage) loans. Those loans created additional demand by facilitating entrance into the market by buyers who otherwise would most likely have remained renters. These buyers pushed prices up, but were also among the first to default.

Across the country, the rapid increase in serious delinquency in late 2006 and early 2007 frightened investors and further reduced the flow of funds into the mortgage market, which led to falling home prices. Between the second quarter of 2006 and the second quarter of 2007, the net flow of mortgage funds fell by one-third. Three quarters later the net flow of mortgage funds turned negative for the first time in the postwar era. By the third quarter of 2011, after declining in thirteen of the past fourteen quarters, nominal home mortgage credit outstanding had fallen $729.9 billion, from its peak level of $10.61 trillion in the first quarter of 2008 to $9.88 trillion in the third quarter of 2011.

The decline in the flow of mortgage funds accelerated the price collapse: When the money started to run out, home prices started to fall rapidly. And since many mortgages had been written with slender down payments, the collapse in home prices impacted lenders. Many homeowners stopped paying their mortgages, and lenders couldn't recoup their losses by foreclosing on homes that were suddenly worth less than what was owed on them. As a result, the value of mortgage securities fell, dragging financial stocks down with them.

The impact of these developments on housing is apparent in Figure 7:

Figure 7: Percentage Changes to GDP and Its Major Components Before, During, and After the Great Recession

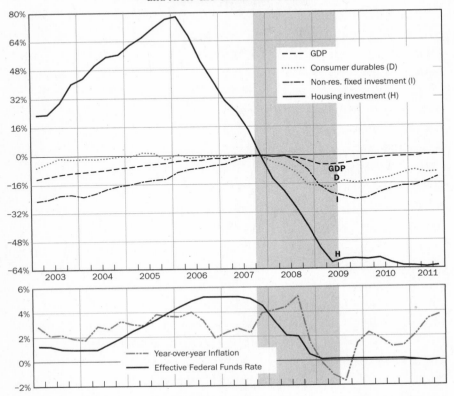

Housing (H) represents the percentage difference between real expenditures on new housing units in the indicated quarter and its level at the start of the recession in the fourth quarter of 2007. For example, housing was 78.2% higher in Q1 2006 than it was in Q4 2007; it was 63.0% lower in Q2 2011 than it was in Q4 2007.

Residential construction began to collapse in the second quarter of 2006. When investment peaked in the first quarter of 2008, housing plus durables had been falling for seven quarters and had already fallen $230.9 billion. The damage eventually spread from a large fraction of the nearly six million subprime loans to the broader economy.

The gray area in Figure 7 shows the recession. It was only in the third quarter of 2011 that GDP recovered to its peak level from the first quarter of 2008. This is the longest downturn in GDP in the United States since World War II. The recoveries to investment and consumer durables have been weak, and there has been no recovery in housing, as Figure 7 shows.

Lost home equity led to financial distress among homeowners. Their distress reduced the flow of mortgage payments to lenders, which created financial sector losses. Pressure on households' and financial firms' balance sheets reinforced residential construction declines, and eventually led to declines in sales of durable goods and in nonresidential investment. Each of these problems led to declining employment, which fed back to generate distress among more homeowners and further consumption declines.

Figure 8 shows the collapse of home equity. The figure shows three lines that seem to move in rough proportion to one another from 1997 through the first quarter of 2006.[13] Afterward, home value began to decline, mortgage debt held steady, and home equity plunged. The decline in home equity has been very large. The fact that only two-thirds of homes have mortgages, and that many of the most recent home buyers had large loan-to-value ratios when their loans were issued, indicates

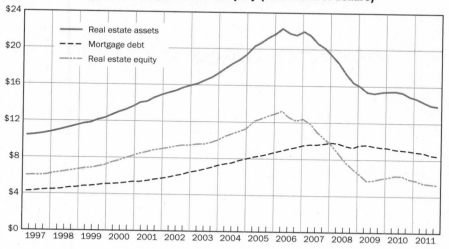

Figure 8: Collapse in Home Equity (in trillions of dollars)

Housing value, mortgage debt, and housing equity (value minus debt) grew steadily during the bubble, but after the bubble collapsed, households were left with high mortgage debt loads and diminished equity. Although real estate assets are only 30% of households' assets, unlike financial assets, they are widely distributed across households and for many households they are highly leveraged.

the extent of the balance sheet problems faced by many homeowners. In nominal terms (unadjusted for inflation), the total value of homes owned by households is $16.2 trillion. If the two-thirds of homeowners who have a mortgage also own two-thirds of the housing value, their houses are worth $10.8 trillion. The homeowners with mortgages have all $9.9 trillion of the household mortgage debt, so about 50 million homeowners with mortgages have about $900 billion of home equity. The average homeowner with a mortgage has $18,000 of home equity. Looked at another way, the average equity position for homeowners with a mortgage is about 8% of the value of the home. Until American homeowners increase the amount of equity they have in their homes, the housing market will suffer. For Americans saddled with a lot of mortgage debt, it is hard to retire, or move for a new job, or make other life decisions if they can't sell their home for at least what they owe on it.

The banks are on the other side of this household balance sheet stress. They hold the mortgages that have been issued on homes that have plummeted in value. Banks are now cautious about mortgage lending because when housing prices fall, the number of foreclosures tends to rise. And banks are also cautious about lending more generally because they want to build up capital reserves against the possibility of future credit market disruptions. The reluctance of households to spend is mirrored by a reluctance of banks to lend.

■ ■ ■

The Great Recession and every recession between 1957–58 and 1990–91 conformed to our description of the onset of economic cycles. Housing peaked well before downturns, inflation developed as housing leveled off or declined, and tightening of monetary policy in response to developing inflation led to a sharp contraction of mortgage lending, accelerated the housing downturn, and initiated a sharp decline in inflation.[14] In all postwar recessions between 1948–49 and 1990–91, as inflation subsided, monetary policy was eased and housing responded with a sharp increase.

The 2001 and 2007–2009 recessions were both unusual, but we believe that their atypical patterns were both connected to the unusual pattern of mortgage and consumer credit that prevailed from 2001 to 2006. The 2001 recession was short, shallow, and dominated by the prolonged downturn in business investment that continued long after the recession ended. Spending on new housing and consumer durable goods was hardly affected, even though these categories of expenditures fell most in percentage terms in every recession between 1948–49 and 1990–91. The 2007–2009 recession was also unusual for its depth, its duration, and the slow recovery from it. The unusual household credit buildup between 2001 and 2006 impacted both recessions, first by preventing the downturn in household expenditures in the 2001 recession and then by creating high household debt levels that have suppressed household expenditures since 2007.

Table 1

Recession	GDP	Housing	Durables	Housing + Durables	Investment
1948-49	−$29.5	−$11.8	−$5.8	−$14.4	−$27.2
1953-54	−$59.8	−$37.0	−$70.2	−$105.9	−$5.1
1957-58	−$97.7	−$35.1	−$41.3	−$73.8	−$43.9
1960-61	−$45.1	−$23.3	−$27.0	−$47.3	−$17.9
1969-70	−$26.8	−$26.8	−$43.0	−$59.0	−$23.3
1973-75	−$157.8	−$103.8	−$84.1	−$177.2	−$40.7
1980	−$131.9	−$88.7	−$90.8	−$168.7	−$29.6
1981-82	−$163.8	−$55.0	−$42.8	−$86.3	−$131.5
1990-91	−$109.4	−$77.4	−$92.4	−$148.0	−$119.5
2001	−$31.2	−$12.0	−$30.4	−$23.4	−$275.4
2007-09	−$489.7	−$392.3	−$202.0	−$579.6	−$358.2
TOTALS	−$1342.7	−$863.3	−$721.8	−$1482.6	−$1072.3

This table shows total GDP declines (in billions of 2005 dollars) during the eleven postwar recessions. It also shows declines in housing, durables, and investment. The decline in housing plus durables is slightly lower than the decline in housing plus the decline in durables in each recession, because the peaks and troughs of the declines in these two series differ slightly.

In ten of our past eleven recessions, housing has declined before any other major sector of the economy. Its declines have been substantially greater in percentage terms than investment declines. Housing recovered more rapidly than investment after all downturns since the Great Depression. The average growth of housing in the first four quarters of recovery has been 24.6%, whereas the growth of investment has been only 4.7%. Housing is a much smaller percentage of GDP than investment. Between the first quarter of 1947 and the third quarter of 2011, it has averaged only 3.0% of GDP, whereas investment has averaged 10.7% of GDP. Yet in 6 of the 11 postwar recessions, the dollar decline in housing has exceeded the investment decline and in 8 of the 11 the dollar decline in the sum of housing and consumer durables has exceeded investment declines.

In the combined double-dip recessions in 1980 and 1981–82, the sum of housing and durables declined $255 billion, substantially more than the $161.1 billion decline in investment (see Table 1). This leaves two postwar recessions, 1948–49 and 2001, in which investment declines dominated the downturn. We've already seen that in the 2001 recession, the normal pattern of declining household expenditures was interrupted by an unusual growth of household credit. So that leaves the 1948–49 recession as the only postwar recession that doesn't fit our usual pattern of decline; even in that one, the housing downturn preceded the downturn in investment, and the housing recovery led the general recovery and its recovery, and was stronger than any other major sector.

In the first quarter of 2006, residential construction reached $4,446 per household; by the second quarter of 2009 it had fallen 78.0%, to $979 per household. In earlier economic cycles, large changes also occurred. In the first quarter of 1973 residential construction reached $3,031 per household, then fell 52.9%, to $1,429, in the second quarter of 1975. A new cycle began almost immediately, with an increase to $2,839 per household in the fourth quarter of 1978, and a long 68.7% decline, to $1,173, in the second quarter of 1982. As we've seen, monetary policy stimulates housing construction and adds temporarily to output, in amounts that add meaningfully to household income, even before considering multiplier effects.

■ ■ ■

Since monetary policy typically has its most pronounced effect on mortgage lending and consumer finance, and since these are both unresponsive due to households' excessive debt burdens and concerns about the prospect of further house price declines, an expansionary monetary policy today is unlikely to generate a recovery, regardless of its size.

Other direct evidence reinforces this view. Lending and economic performance changed little when the Federal Reserve embarked on its second quantitative easing program (QE2). Between November 17, 2010, and July 6, 2011, the Federal Reserve increased its holdings of U.S. Treasury securities by $750.9 billion. We've shown that in past recessions, when the Federal Reserve drives down short-term interest rates, banks have an incentive to lend. But during the seven and a half months of QE2, total lending of commercial banks in the United States declined from $6.92 trillion to $6.56 trillion.[15] Although it's possible that bank lending would have fallen more without the QE2 program, its ineffectiveness strongly suggests that monetary policy alone cannot rekindle investment and growth in the current environment.

Neither fiscal stimulus nor exceptionally easy monetary policy has been effective in generating a robust recovery. We believe this poor performance relates directly to the severe household and bank balance sheet damage caused by the housing boom and bust. Until that damage is repaired we are unlikely to see robust economic growth. The challenge, then, is to determine what, if anything, can facilitate balance sheet repair. Our examination of past financial crises indicates that greater fiscal discipline has been strongly associated with recoveries in other countries.

THE FINNISH AND THAI CRISES

The course of the Finnish and Thai bubbles and collapses in the 1990s and their financial crises were similar in many ways to our own experience. Both of these episodes included large declines in real estate prices. Both of them also included significant overinvestment in industry (if changes in equity prices can be relied on as indicators of the value of those investments).[16] The declines in investment in Finland and

Thailand were extremely deep, yet growth rates during the recovery period in those countries were considerably higher than in the United States since the second quarter of 2009. The annual growth rate in the United States since the bottom of the recession has been 2.4%. In Finland the annual growth rate over the first nine quarters after the recession was 3.8% and in Thailand it was 6.8%.

Our hypothesis is that export-driven growth is the most effective course when the collapse of an investment boom leads to losses on assets, a financial crisis, a severe downturn, and damaged balance sheets.

During those first nine quarters of the recovery in Finland, investment contributed 14.7% of the increase in GDP, whereas net exports contributed 71.8%. In a pattern that we've seen following financial crises in many countries, when government expenditures were brought under control, the currency depreciated significantly and the growth rate of exports moved sharply ahead of the growth rate of imports, as Figure 9 shows. Notably, government expenditures contributed minus 1.4% of the recovery. The turnaround in government expenditures came at the middle of the depression, but even after the recession ended there was a modest decline in government expenditures that continued until the recovery was well under way.

One important question to examine is why contraction of government expenditures, or at least a sharp reduction in their rate of growth, should lead to depreciation. In the aftermath of an investment boom, private investment is sharply reduced, and capital inflows from abroad will either fall or be redirected to support government expenditures. But if government expenditures are curtailed, then there are few investments left to absorb foreign capital inflows. When those inflows cease or decline, that requires either a sharp reduction in a current account deficit or even a shift from deficits to a current account surplus, and that can only be achieved by a shift that leads to more exports relative to imports. Currency depreciation facilitates that shift from imports to exports because it reduces the cost of exports in their destination market and increases the cost of imports in the domestic market.

Soon after government expenditures began to fall in the first quarter of 1992, the value of the Finnish markka fell 33.3% between August 1992 and March 1993. By the time the sharp depreciation ended,

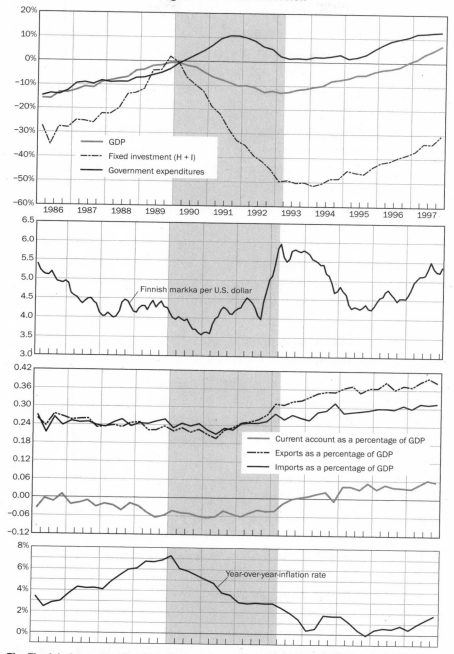

Figure 9: Finnish Recession

GDP
Fixed investment (H + I)
Government expenditures

Finnish markka per U.S. dollar

Current account as a percentage of GDP
Exports as a percentage of GDP
Imports as a percentage of GDP

Year-over-year-inflation rate

The Finnish depression in 1990–93 was nearly two and a half times as deep as the U.S. downturn, and Finland's fixed investment collapse, at 46.1%, was substantially larger than the maximum fixed investment decline of 32.5% in the United States.

a gap had already opened up between exports and imports. That gap grew over time, and by the end of 1993, Finland had entered a current account surplus. (The fact that net exports were almost 4% of GDP in the third quarter of 1993 and the current account was still negative indicates that service costs on external debt were high in Finland after the large capital inflows in the 1980s.) In the middle of their recession, before depreciation of the markka, Finnish exports fell below 20% of GDP. In 1997, four and a half years into the recovery, they exceeded 40% of GDP. Investment, too, was recovering by that time, but surely the export boom was contributing to that recovery as well. In fact, the investment decline ended when the depreciation came about and the growth rate of exports increased.

In Thailand, a similar pattern occurred (Figure 10). As in the United States over the decade from 1997 to 2006, Thailand went through a long period of large current account deficits. Also as in the United States, as investment grew and current account deficits accumulated, investors eventually grew skittish and withdrew. After asset values fell and international capital inflows ceased, the financial crisis developed and International Monetary Fund (IMF) assistance was sought. Loan funds from the IMF were provided with the stipulation that government finances remain on a solid foundation. Restricted access to foreign capital meant that capital was scarce, and that a reversal of the current account from deficit to surplus was the only way to improve liquidity.

In Thailand, the collapses in construction and in investment were very pronounced, as was the 16.0% decline in real GDP. Reversal of the current account deficits came early in the Thai depression, and the improvement was extremely rapid and then subsided, but if we examine the changes in output from the peak of the economic cycle in the third quarter of 1996 to output nine quarters into the recovery, we find that household consumption declined by 1.6% of GDP, investment declined by 19.6% of GDP, and net exports increased by 14.6% of GDP. When we consider that over that entire period, Thai GDP fell by 2.8%, we see that growth of net exports carried all the weight of recovery.

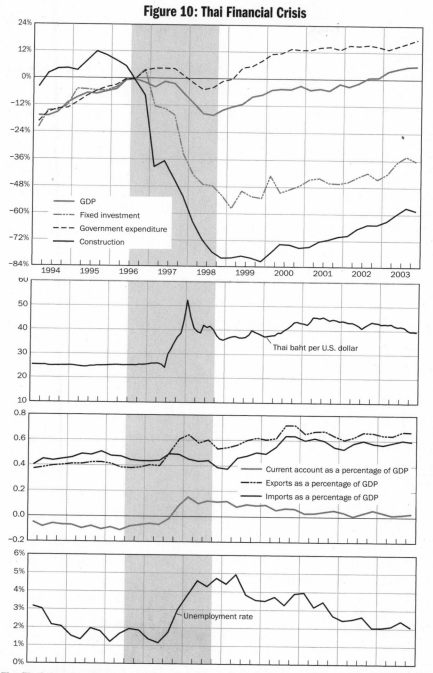

Figure 10: Thai Financial Crisis

GDP
Fixed investment
Government expenditure
Construction

Thai baht per U.S. dollar

Current account as a percentage of GDP
Exports as a percentage of GDP
Imports as a percentage of GDP

Unemployment rate

The Thai downturn was deep, but the quick recovery of the current account facilitated balance sheet repair. The lack of foreign capital investment after the crisis forced devaluation on Thailand because that was the only way to obtain needed funds.

CONCLUSIONS

Because households and banks suffer from widespread continuing balance sheet damage, the economy's response to both monetary and fiscal stimulus has been much muted relative to what would normally be expected if the household and bank equity positions were strong. In these circumstances, the experience of other countries strongly suggests that fiscal austerity triggers a mechanism—currency depreciation—that works favorably for a recovery.

A comprehensive discussion of policies that might help restore broken balance sheets is beyond the scope of this chapter, but we see the current trend toward austerity policies as a positive sign and one that is likely to help the economy recover.

The austerity-depreciation mechanism is remarkable;[17] it offers a subtle end run around the failure of monetary policy to stimulate the demand for housing and durable goods via the normal route of lowering their financing cost. And until demand for these goods rises, there is little incentive for firms to increase investment. In terms of monetary theory, the stock of money has gone up but its turnover velocity is not increasing.

But currency depreciation directly impacts export revenue and earnings, increases output and GDP, and this operates directly to activate idle reserve balances that are plentiful due to the eased monetary policy, but dormant. The effect of depreciation is to immediately increase the solvency and improve the balance sheets in export-related industries and households. It will also tend to be inflationary and—if it does not get out of hand—serves to initiate a mechanism for reducing the burden of debt and improving balance sheets generally in the economy. For the United States, the effect may not be as dramatic as we have shown for Finland and Thailand, but it is working in the right direction and aids rather than impedes recovery.

Although the export increases in Finland and Thailand were very large, comparable increases are not required in the United States, and for at least two reasons. In Finland, fixed investment fell from 30.4% of GDP just before the peak of their economic cycle to only 16.0% four years later. In the United States, fixed investment (including residential construction) fell from a peak of 17.3% of GDP to 11.6% of GDP. The fixed investment decline in Finland was thus more than two and a half times as large relative to GDP as it was in the United States. In the third quarter of 2011, investment in the United States was $380 billion below its peak level. In Finland most of the adjustment took the form of a shift from fixed investment toward a greater emphasis on exports. For the United States to replace that investment gap with exports, we would need to see an increase in exports from 13.9% of GDP to 16.4% of GDP. An increase in exports of this magnitude is feasible. Even if the effect is not that large, it would work in the right direction, aiding recovery.

We do not have much choice. In an environment of stressed household-bank-balance sheets, monetary policy is ineffective, and fiscal policy has been blunted for the same reason. The political economy now favors government austerity and frugality. In our reading of international economic experience this offers a mechanism of hope in which exports lead the process of balance sheet repair, and a sustainable recovery in output and employment.

Chapter 6

Spending, Taxes, and Certainty: A Road Map to 4%

By Kevin Hassett

Economic growth is often portrayed as an elusive concept. Every country yearns for it, but it is not immediately obvious how to achieve it. To a nonexpert it may seem that certain countries are simply lucky and grow faster while others have not been blessed with the gift of high growth. Countries in East Asia have received substantial attention from the media and academics for their astonishing growth rates from the 1960s to the 1990s, which reached as high as 7% as these nations "converged" to the living standards of developed nations. But the benefits of increased growth are so significant that the cause should not be attributed to coincidence without careful consideration.

Consider that with a consistent annual growth rate of 4%, gross domestic product (GDP) doubles every 18 years. For comparison, the United States has grown at an average annual rate of 3.3% since 1948. With annual growth of 3.3%, the GDP level doubles in approximately 22 years. If the U.S. economy had grown at a rate of 4% instead of 3.3% since 1948, GDP would be about 50% larger today. Thus even seemingly small differences in growth rates can have a significant impact in the long run.

Unfortunately, from 2009 to 2012, the United States was stuck in a slow recovery that is consistent with the history of financial crises. As documented by Carmen Reinhart and Kenneth Rogoff, the average decline in real GDP following a banking crisis is 9.3% over a period of two years.[1] The increase in unemployment is equally disheartening—on average unemployment rises by about 7 percentage points for a period of almost five years. Consequently, the average growth of real

GDP in the past five years has been a meager 0.8%. Given these facts, it may appear naïve to imagine growth at the rate of 4% in the coming years. Yet no matter how daunting, the task is not impossible. A review of the relevant economic literature suggests policy prescriptions that, if implemented, would contribute to a significant medium-term surge in economic growth. Here is a road map of these policy prescriptions in the form of several stops on the path to a decade of economic growth.

Figure 1: Historical Growth Rates in the United States

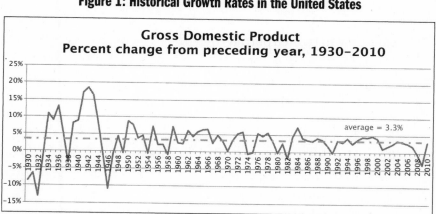

Source: Bureau of Economic Analysis

FIRST STOP: DEBT REDUCTION

To improve the prospects for long-run growth in the United States, the first issue that must be addressed is the level of indebtedness. America's gross debt-to-GDP ratio is not as high as some other countries'. However, what is most disconcerting is not necessarily the level, but the trend the country appears to be following. The level of gross federal debt in the United States was 102% of GDP in 2010, and according to the latest Congressional Budget Office (CBO) projections, it will reach 118% by 2021. If nothing is done about the worsening situation now, the United States could find itself in the unfortunate situation of Greece or Portugal by the end of the decade.

Recent research supports the intuition that government debt

Figure 2: Projections for the Level of Gross Federal Debt in the United States

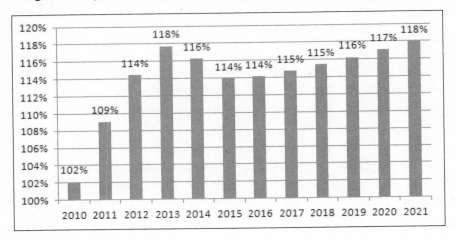

Source: Congressional Budget Office

commonly soars in the wake of a financial crisis, and that this debt surge has a significant impact on growth. Reinhart and Rogoff have documented the striking increase in government debt by analyzing the systemic financial crises that have occurred over the course of the past century. They find that "the deterioration in government finances is striking, with an average debt rise of over 86 percent."[2]

The skyrocketing debt-to-GDP ratio has also been shown to significantly impede economic growth. In a widely cited study, Reinhart and Rogoff document a strong relationship between high debt levels and slow growth. For twenty advanced countries they separate their observations into four groups: years with low debt (below 30% of GDP), medium debt (30–60%), high debt (60–90%), and very high debt (above 90%). They observe that there is no obvious link between gross public debt and growth until the debt level reaches 90% of GDP, at which point the debt effect becomes large and negative (see Figure 3 on page 84).[3] Thus, they conclude that a gross debt-to-GDP level above 90% causes average growth to fall significantly. Since the U.S. gross federal debt currently exceeds 100% of GDP, this evidence, taken at face value, would offer a pessimistic outlook for U.S. economic growth, absent policy change.

Reinhart and Rogoff's work has received some criticism, for example, no evidence of causality is presented[4] and their findings are unlikely to be relevant to the U.S. economy of today since they rely on historical data of many different countries.[5] In response to these observations, economists Manmohan S. Kumar and Jaejoon Woo extend the empirical work by Reinhart and Rogoff in useful directions. Their analysis controls for other growth determinants and suggests an inverse relationship between the initial debt level and subsequent growth—on average, a 10 percentage point increase in the initial debt-to-GDP ratio is associated with a slowdown in annual real per capita GDP growth of around 0.2 percentage points per year. Moreover, they also present evidence that much higher levels of debt (above the 90% threshold established by Reinhart and Rogoff) have a significantly larger negative effect on growth.[6]

Reinhart and Rogoff's conclusions are further supported by the recent work of Mehmet Caner, Thomas Grennes, and Fritzi Koehler-Geib.[7] They are mostly concerned with the existence of an identifiable threshold or a "tipping point." Moreover, they focus on the long-term effects, and their data set includes 99 developed and developing countries, a much larger sample than Reinhart and Rogoff's original data. Their results establish a threshold of 77% public debt-to-GDP ratio. If public debt is above this threshold, each percentage point of debt costs 0.017 percentage points of annual real growth. Finally, Caner and other researchers replicate Reinhart and Rogoff's research for developed countries and arrive at the same conclusion: that debt-to-GDP ratios above 90% are linked to slower growth.[8]

Taken together, these results make a compelling case for the detrimental effects of high levels of public debt. Using the result of Caner et al. as the benchmark and assuming that gross debt exceeding 77% undermines growth, the expected level of public debt in the United States would reduce expected growth by about half a percentage point per year over the next decade. Figure 4 adjusts the current CBO growth baseline to account for this effect and suggests a fairly grim picture of the next decade.

The findings of studies initiated by Reinhart and Rogoff in 2010 highlight the need for timely and decisive action to lower the debt level,

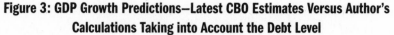

Figure 3: GDP Growth Predictions—Latest CBO Estimates Versus Author's Calculations Taking into Account the Debt Level

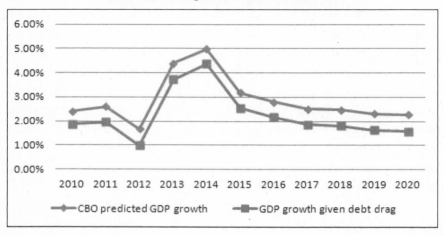

Source: Congressional Budget Office

which is the first step on our journey to 4% economic growth over the next decade. The key insight is that reducing debt relative to the baseline could provide growth benefits, since the United States is already in the high debt range that undermines growth.

How should that debt reduction be structured? Based on a review of the economics literature and an analysis of twenty-one member countries of the Organisation for Economic Co-operation and Development (OECD), Andrew Biggs, Matthew Jensen, and I found that cutting expenditures is more likely to produce a lasting reduction in debt than increasing revenues. It is also true that the more aggressively a country cuts expenditures, the more likely it is to successfully reduce debt in the long term. Biggs, Jensen, and I analyzed successful and unsuccessful fiscal consolidation efforts,[9] using postconsolidation debt reduction as the metric of success. Averaging across a range of methodologies, the typical unsuccessful fiscal consolidation consisted of 53% tax increases and 47% spending cuts.[10] The typical successful fiscal consolidation consisted of 85% spending cuts. In particular, cuts to social transfers, largely entitlement spending and the government wage bill, are more likely to reduce debt and deficits than cuts to other expenditures, as shown by Alberto Alesina and Roberto Perotti in a 1996 paper.[11]

The evidence clearly shows that cutting spending is a more effective way to lower government debt levels than increasing taxes. However, there is an open debate about which aspects of fiscal consolidation lead to macroeconomic expansion. That debate hinges on the balance between two economic effects of fiscal consolidation, the expectational effect and the Keynesian effect. Specifically, the question is whether the first effect outweighs the second. The expectational effect refers to what happens when the government stops spending recklessly. The effect is usually that consumers and investors are willing to spend more because they no longer expect that high government spending will

Figure 4 : Short-Term Growth Effects of Consolidation

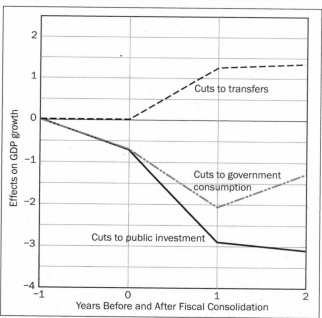

Note: Results based on 5% of GDP fiscal consolidation where the expenditure cuts are primarily to transfers, government consumption, or public investment.

Source: International Monetary Fund, "Will It Hurt? Macroeconomic Effects of Fiscal Consolidation," chapter 3 in World Economic Outlook (IMF, October 2010), http://www.imf.org/external/pubs/ft/weo/2010/02/

lead to higher taxes down the road. The traditional Keynesian effect is similarly straightforward. Cutting government spending reduces GDP growth in the short run, even though it increases the likelihood of economic growth in the long run.

Some authors believe that the expectational effect dominates and therefore a consolidation aimed at spending cuts can lead to immediate growth,[12] while others disagree, saying that fiscal consolidations typically have a contractionary effect; that is, the Keynesian effect prevails. The second view is espoused by a 2010 IMF study.[13] Coincidentally, this study finds that cutting government spending, especially transfer payments (entitlement programs), could produce positive near-term growth effects. Accordingly, one might conclude that expectational effects seem to dominate when entitlements are cut, which suggests that consumers have very little faith that generous but unfunded government benefits will eventually be paid, and thus feel little or no wealth reduction when unsustainable policies are cut.

An additional expansive branch of the literature has found that the size of government may present an impediment to economic growth.[14] Typical of the literature is the work of Andreas Bergh and Martin Karlsson, who find a robust negative correlation between government size, measured through total public revenue and expenditure, and economic growth. They analyze a sample of OECD countries and find that increasing taxes by 11 percentage points reduces annual growth by 1.1 percentage points.[15] Focusing on European Union (EU) countries, Diego Romero-Avila and Rolf Strauch also find a negative effect of total government revenue and expenditures. Their detailed examination identifies a significant depressive effect on growth of direct taxes as well as government consumption and transfers.[16] Economists Antonio Afonso and Davide Furceri have documented that both the share and volatility of government revenue and spending are detrimental for growth.[17] Stefan Fölster and Magnus Henrekson observe a robust (true under varying specifications and assumptions) and significant negative effect from government expenditure and a less robust negative effect for total tax revenue.[18]

These studies support the view that reducing debt by reducing the size of government would help lead to higher medium-term growth.

Since each of the studies measures government size with government expenditures, the reported findings support the point that an expenditure-based fiscal consolidation would successfully address the debt problems of the country and contribute to the journey toward sustainable 4% growth. In other words, if we cut spending and reduce the size of government, we are more likely to experience significant and sustained economic growth. As the various strands of the literature are independent, it is difficult to assess the total growth effect that one might reasonably expect after accounting for each of these policy channels. But given the range identified in each study, it seems quite plausible that a fiscal consolidation through lower spending could easily increase medium-term growth by about 1% per year. This would be a major increase.

SECOND STOP: TAX REFORM

The discussion of the literature on government size leads us to our second stop—the importance of tax reform. Tax reform provides perhaps the best—and most broadly agreed-upon—opportunity to improve the health of the economy in the long run while also encouraging growth in the medium run.

There have been numerous exhaustive surveys of the likely benefits of tax reform. In 2005, economist Alan J. Auerbach and I assembled a number of tax reform proposals that were crafted by economists of varying political persuasions. We identified a wide (if not unanimous) consensus that tax reforms should have a number of specific goals. First, reform should reduce the marginal tax rate on corporate investment. Second, tax reform should improve incentives to save. Third, the reform should smooth out variable treatment of different industries and assets while seeking to distort economic activity as little as possible. And finally, reform should improve incentives to work.[19]

What might such a reform accomplish? One way to know is to take a look at the 1986 tax reform, which aimed at simplifying the tax code, broadening the tax base, and reducing tax rates. In a survey of sixty-nine public finance economists, Victor Fuchs, Alan Krueger, and James Poterba found in 1998 that, at the median, respondents believed that the 1986 tax reform produced about one percentage point higher growth over a long period.[20] This intuition is supported by the review of the literature conducted by Auerbach and me.

Several other economists analyzed the potential effects in the light of the 1986 tax reform. For example, Paul Pecorino estimated the effect on the growth rate of replacing the 1985 U.S. income tax structure with a consumption tax to be of the order of 1% per capita per year.[21] Over the course of several years, this result would closely correspond with the estimates found in other studies that mostly focus on long-run increases in output. Research on the effects of tax reform is not limited to analyzing the 1986 tax code changes. In 2001, economists David Altig, Alan J. Auerbach, Laurence J. Kotlikoff, Kent A. Smetters, and Jan Walliser simulated a variety of different approaches, including a proportional income tax, a proportional consumption tax, a standard flat tax, a flat tax with transition relief, and the X-tax (a form of a value-added tax with deductions made for wages).[22] They find that fundamental tax reform could raise long-run output—by over 9% in the specific case of a proportional consumption tax. On the whole, they conclude that fundamental tax reform provides a significant opportunity for macroeconomic expansion; however, all the scenarios create some small groups that may be made worse off by an overall improvement, and near-term growth effects can be negative as saving increases and consumption declines in response to a consumption tax.

A 2008 OECD study by economist Jens M. Arnold provides an empirical analysis of the effect of the tax structure on long-run GDP. The main findings include:

- "Property taxes, and particularly recurrent taxes on immovable property, seem to be the most growth-friendly, followed by consumption taxes and then by personal income taxes. Corporate income taxes appear to have the most negative effect on GDP per capita."

- Estimates of the effect on GDP per capita of changing the tax structure while keeping the overall tax-to-GDP ratio constant indicate that a shift of 1% of tax revenues from income taxes to consumption and property taxes would increase GDP per capita by between a quarter of a percentage point and one percentage point in the long run.

• A reduction in corporate income taxes (financed by an increase in consumption and property taxes) has a stronger positive effect on GDP per capita than a similar decrease in personal income taxation.[23]

There is also some reason to believe that the growth effects of tax reform in the literature may understate the potential benefits to the United States of fundamental reform, since the United States is currently a worldwide outlier with respect to the corporate tax rate. There is broad consensus that the high statutory corporate tax rate impedes investment in the United States. According to the OECD tax database, the national statutory corporate tax rates in 2011 among the thirty-four members of the OECD ranged from 8.5% in Switzerland and 12.5% in Ireland to 35% for the United States. Within the OECD countries, the United States has the highest statutory rate of taxation at the level of the central government.

The picture changes only marginally when we add the subnational corporate tax rates to the top national rate. In the case of the United States, the average top statutory rate imposed by states in 2010 added just over 4% (after accounting for the fact that state taxes are deducted from federal taxable income)—for a combined top statutory rate of 39.2%. Among all OECD countries in 2011, the United States' top statutory combined corporate tax rate was the second highest, after Japan's 39.5% rate. Top combined statutory rates among OECD countries have fallen from an average of about 48% in the early 1980s to 25.5% in 2011. The main wave of reforms occurred in the mid to late 1980s but has continued in the 1990s and through the 2000s. In fact, the OECD average fell almost 9% in the first decade of the 21st century. The United States, on the other hand, has not reduced its top statutory rate since 1993. In the 1980s and '90s, the U.S. tax rate was close to the average for the bulk of OECD countries, differing by only a couple of percentage points. However, in 2011, with no change in the top rate since the 1990s, the United States is now one of only five OECD countries (the others being Belgium, Germany, France, and Japan) that have tax rates above 30%. Thus the gap between U.S. and OECD corporate tax rates has opened up since the 1990s primarily because of widespread and substantial rate reductions abroad, rather than any significant corporate tax increase in the United States.

For new investments, it is not the statutory rate but the "effective rate" that influences decisions. The United States ranks little better when looking at the effective rates than when looking at statutory rates. The literature, outlined in a 1999 paper by economists Michael Devereux and Rachel Griffith, introduces two measures of effective tax rates. First, there is the *effective marginal tax rate* (EMTR), which applies to marginal investment projects where the last unit invested provides just enough pretax return to cause the project to break even after taxes. In other words, the marginal investment equates the net present value of the income stream to the net present value of the investment costs. The second measure is the *effective average tax rate* (EATR), which summarizes the distribution of tax rates for an investment project over the range of possible profitability levels. The EATR computes, simply, a firm's tax liability as a fraction of pretax economic profits in a particular country. This rate differs from the statutory rate because it reflects the lower rate that the firm actually pays once the other features of the tax code such as depreciation allowances or interest rate deductions are accounted for.[24]

A 2011 study that I conducted with Aparna Mathur computed the EATR and the EMTR for all countries in the sample and for each time period using the methodology outlined by Devereux and Griffith assuming fixed parameter values for the economic depreciation rates, the inflation rate, and the annual discount rate.[25] Their results suggest that the United States is relatively high by these measures as well. While in 1996 the U.S. EATR was slightly below the OECD average, 29.2% versus 30.2%, the OECD average excluding the United States has fallen to 20.5% in 2010 while the U.S. EATR remained largely constant—in 2010 it was 29%. The United States fares slightly better when looking at the EMTR, but remains above the average. In 2010, the U.S. EMTR was 23.6%, compared to the non-U.S. OECD average of 17.3%.

These results are not the sole example of the uncompetitive position of the United States relative to other countries. Considering effective rates, the World Bank Doing Business Report ranks the U.S. tax climate for incorporation worse than all but two industrialized countries. Similarly, a 2010 paper by tax experts Kevin S. Markle and Douglas A. Shackelford also concludes that from 1988 to 2007, U.S. firms faced the second-highest effective rates in the developed world.[26]

Since the United States has high corporate taxes by any measure, and since capital is highly mobile, it is safe to conclude that the potential benefits of tax reform are significant. Moreover, estimates of the benefits of tax reform typically ignore international concerns, so adopting the view that tax reform could deliver annual growth that is about one percentage point higher per year than the baseline for an extended period would be conservative.

THIRD STOP: ELIMINATING POLICY UNCERTAINTY

Lastly, it follows intuitively that uncertainty can have a negative effect on the economy. If businesses cannot reasonably predict future policy changes, they may hold off making large investments. Similarly, consumers may hold off making large purchases if uncertainty about future tax policy makes their wealth highly uncertain. The high level of government debt, and generally unsustainable entitlement programs, create a high level of policy uncertainty, which would be partially reduced by fiscal consolidation. Recent research suggests that the effects of uncertainty may be very large.

The channels through which uncertainty can negatively affect growth were explored extensively in the pathbreaking work of Avinash K. Dixit and Robert S. Pindyck in 1994. They found that when projects are irreversible, uncertainty can depress current investment by making delay in the interest of information acquisition more attractive.[27] This observation ignited a vast literature that has documented the negative effects of uncertainty. In one recent example, Simon Gilchrist and colleagues show that it is possible to link the fluctuation in economic uncertainty and frictions in financial markets to the aggregate investment cycle by exploiting the implication of uncertainty for the price of credit risk in general equilibrium.[28] Joshua Aizenman and Nancy Marion confirm the mostly negative correlation between uncertainty and economic growth and conclude that if macroeconomic policies are persistent, higher policy uncertainty will depress economic growth in the long run.[29]

More recently, some emphasis has shifted from analyzing the channel to investigating the effects in the current policy climate. Probably the greatest source of uncertainty is linked to the level of public debt in the United States. As discussed earlier, the fiscal deficit and government debt have risen dramatically since the 2008–2009 financial crisis. Businesses and individuals know that the country cannot run huge deficits indefinitely, and therefore might expect future spending cuts or tax increases. However, even with this knowledge, questions remain: When will policy changes be put in effect? What form will they take? Will reforms be instituted mainly through cuts in expenditure or will taxes be raised? If so, which ones?

Recent studies support the conclusion that the current high level of policy uncertainty is negatively affecting the country's economic performance. Scott Baker, Nicholas Bloom, and Steven Davis constructed an uncertainty index composed of newspaper coverage of policy-related economic uncertainty, expiring tax code provisions, and disagreement among economic forecasters in surveys. They were able to calculate their index for the years 1985 through 2011. They conclude that greater policy uncertainty sharply reduces GDP. Most important, the authors found that policy uncertainty in the United States was the highest on record in 2011, likely reducing GDP by about 1.4% in that year.[30] Another recent study by Jesús Fernandez-Villaverde and colleagues uses the changes in volatility of different fiscal instruments as an intuitive representation of the variations in fiscal policy uncertainty. They find that fiscal volatility shocks have an adverse effect on economic activity—aggregate output, consumption, investment, and hours worked drop on impact and stay low for several quarters. They estimate this to be comparable to the effects of a 25-basis-point increase in the federal funds rate.[31]

It is important to note, once again, that there is little reason to believe that these effects are independent of earlier results. Fiscal consolidations may well boost economic growth precisely because they reduce economic uncertainty. But taken together, these results increase the confidence with which one can say that significant policy moves could, precisely at this time in the United States, provide a significant boost to economic growth.

FINAL DESTINATION

The outlook for economic growth in the United States is currently quite bleak. The Congressional Budget Office estimates that growth will average about 2.87% over the next decade, but this forecast does not adequately incorporate the negative effects of high government debt. The debt-growth adjustment would reduce that CBO growth estimate to 2.23% over the next decade. Even starting from that lower growth rate, however, estimates of the benefits of fiscal consolidation, uncertainty elimination, and tax reform are large enough that one could easily support the view that the United States could experience 4% growth over the next decade given the right fiscal policies.

Chapter 7

Sound Money, Sound Policy

By David Malpass

Fast growth isn't rocket science. Countries achieve it by creating an environment of stable currencies, low tax rates, sensible trade and regulatory policies, a market-based allocation of labor, and limited government in terms of spending, debt, and federal control of the economy. The United States doesn't have a pro-growth environment now, which explains our slow growth.

By creating the right environment, countries throughout history have transformed themselves from weak economies with low living standards into strong ones with rising living standards. The transformation can be done quickly. People want to produce more and earn more each year. In a free society, they invent and innovate. They get encouragement from their community, from their competitors, and, in theory, from a supportive government structure that provides security and promotes market-based economic principles.

In the United States, we can build on our strong traditions and principles—the rule of law, the Constitution, a history of fast growth, a confident culture. We have a huge store of accumulated wealth and innovation from previous generations that is much bigger than our debt burden. These advantages can help us jump-start a 4% growth renaissance. But right now we are moving in an antigrowth direction.

- The dollar is weak and unstable, the result of harmful policy decisions in the executive branch and the Federal Reserve.
- Tax rates are high and complex, slowing growth substan-

tially. The congressional budgeting system, based on a fictional "current law" baseline, adds a major obstacle to growth-oriented tax reform.

- Government spending is growing so fast it discourages private sector investment and hiring.
- Through regulatory incompetence, the government regularly blocks growth, fuels litigiousness, and imposes tremendous costs on the economy for marginal or nonexistent benefits.

The challenge is to renew the dormant American foundation for fast 4% GDP growth. The necessary transformations are well known but at odds with the current political establishment and incentives.

The starting point for 4% growth is a commitment to a sound dollar. In very simple terms, that means creating the expectation that the dollar will retain the value it has now for the next twenty or fifty years. Currently, we don't have that assurance.

The president, Fed chairman, and Treasury secretary should reverse the current dollar policy, which has caused severe losses in the value of the dollar for more than a decade. The current policy is based on the view that the value of the dollar should be set by markets over an unlimited range of values with the expectation that the dollar will trade up and down with U.S. economic fundamentals. This is very far away from the stable-dollar policy that we need, because it creates tremendous uncertainty, discouraging investment and jobs.

Prolonged currency weakness creates a multitude of problems. Companies have to devote an increasing portion of their time and energy to currencies rather than operating their businesses. Foreigners with more attractive currencies gain wealth relative to Americans. Rather than making the United States more competitive, the dollar's weakness makes it harder to justify investing in this country. The investment killer is that assets in the United States keep losing value in foreign-currency terms, so potential U.S. investments start with a big rate-of-return disadvantage relative to other countries with better currency policies.

The current dollar policy creates a circular growth crisis in which dollar weakness discourages investment in dollars, which weakens America's economic fundamentals, which then in turn encourages further dollar weakness. There's no natural bottom in this game. It costs the government nothing to create new dollars to offset dollar weakness, and there's no competitiveness gain because of the reduced investment, so the theoretical endpoint is hyperinflation. Since 1971, when the United States completely abandoned the gold standard, the M0 money supply—the most liquid measure of the money supply, as it solely combines cash and liquid assets—has been increased 37-fold, causing a 98% reduction in the dollar's value against gold.

Instead of the current weak-dollar policy, which hurts growth by driving investment away from the United States, we need a strong and stable dollar policy. To create such a policy, the president should state that a strong and stable dollar is a part of U.S. growth policy and will be implemented by the Treasury and Fed. The White House should then insist that the policy be evaluated regularly by measuring the dollar against the price of gold.

The Fed should follow up by using each Federal Open Market Committee statement to reinforce the policy of a strong and stable dollar. It can do that by using FOMC statements to measure the dollar against the value of gold and other currencies and also to discuss any inflation implications. The Fed needs to create confidence through word and deed that it believes in a policy that causes the dollar to hold a stable value for decades.

To help create a sound dollar and fast economic growth, the Treasury Department would need to reverse its G7 and G20 positions that downplay the importance of stable currencies. To do that, the Treasury should state in a G7 communiqué that the U.S. policy is for the dollar to be strong and stable. The communiqué should also encourage other countries to support a policy of stable currencies. To emphasize its intention of putting a long-term floor on the value of the dollar, the Treasury should issue debt payable in dollars and payable in gold, as economist Judy Shelton has proposed.

Countries around the world grow faster when they implement sound money. This offers a turnaround path for the United States.

Brazil's economic boom dates from early 2003, when President Luiz Inacio Lula da Silva decided to stop the real's collapse. Since then, the real has risen from 3.6 per dollar to 1.8 per dollar with commensurate gains in Brazil's per capita income. As the currency strengthened, it attracted investment, creating jobs.

Russia's frenzied economic collapse ended almost overnight in 2000 when Vladimir Putin took power and stabilized the ruble. Australia's per capita income has more than doubled since the Aussie dollar started its climb in 2002—a period in which U.S. per capita income declined. Most important for world growth, China's economic surge started in mid-1993 after then–vice premier Zhu Rongji—trained as an engineer like many other senior Chinese leaders—moved his office to the central bank to stop the communist-era black market weakness in the renminbi. As China's currency stabilized, it encouraged investment. China's boom started immediately and has continued to the present, softening the recessions the United States suffered in 2001 and 2008 and adding rapidly to China's per capita income.

Shifting to a policy of a strong and stable dollar would dramatically benefit the United States by creating jobs and raising median incomes. But imposing such a policy is difficult, in part because it would hurt entrenched economic and political interests that are banking on continued dollar weakness. These interests include Wall Street's currency and interest rate trading and derivatives businesses; agriculture and commodity production; select large exporters with access to low-rate loans from banks and the government; and businesses providing Wall Street with Washington-based information on Fed policy and government thinking on the value of the dollar. Currency markets—now $4 trillion per day—trade on currency instability and generate immense profits for a relative few, so they would loudly oppose a U.S. policy change.

The United States is practically alone in the world in pursuing a near-zero interest rate and letting its central bank borrow short-term to buy up the national debt. No fast-growing country does what the United States is doing now. The combination of superlow interest rates and trillions in leveraged Federal Reserve debt constitutes a semiofficial weak-dollar policy. By choosing to pay savers nearly nothing, the Fed's policy discourages thrift and contributes to the weakness in personal income growth.

The zero-rate policy only benefits mega-borrowers like federal and state governments, big banks, and big corporations—a group that does not create many private-sector jobs. And the policy imposes costs on savers and small businesses, whose access to capital is reduced. For those who can borrow cheaply, corporate proceeds often go abroad while most of the subsidized government borrowing turns into extra deficit spending. To protect themselves from the weakening dollar, investors and corporations are shifting growth capital from U.S. businesses to foreign infrastructure and jobs, a process that is dismantling decades of U.S. wealth creation.

Weak monetary policy isn't providing monetary stimulus. Under the 2010 QE2 (Quantitative Easing) Fed bond-buying scheme, the more the Fed intervened in markets, the weaker GDP growth was each quarter. Banks are overflowing with liquidity already, but their lending is rationed by armies of federal regulators sitting rent-free in their offices. The interbank market—which normally moves large sums from cash-rich banks to the growing banks that lend to new and small businesses—isn't functioning properly with rates at zero since there's no benefit to offset the risk of lending to another bank. Monetary policy's goal of promoting the market-based allocation of capital has morphed into manipulating the dollar downward and subsidizing debt through low interest rates and direct buying of debt.

Proponents of the devastating weak-dollar policy have promised for years that devaluations would make us more competitive, yet jobs, capital spending, and innovation keep moving abroad to avoid the shrinking dollar. Near-zero interest rates tag the dollar as the flight currency of choice for world markets.

Thus one of the fastest, most decisive ways to restart U.S. private-sector job growth would be to end the weak-dollar policy and gradually increase the Fed's near-zero interest rate in order to restore short-term credit markets. Presidents Ronald Reagan and Bill Clinton showed that sound money is a core growth strategy that provides a fast and effective way to signal world capital that the United States is aggressively inviting investment. It may take years to fully unwind the federal government's debt buildup and the entrenched tax-and-spend culture driving it. But the president or his deputies could stop the monetary-policy half of the U.S. growth crisis tomorrow, renewing America's spirit and job growth and increasing living standards. The historical evidence is irrefutable—investment floods to strong and stable currencies.

■ ■ ■

In addition to an ironclad commitment to sound money, another hallmark of structural reform and fast growth is a government's resolve to restrain government spending. The federal government is happily spending over $300 billion per month. Of that, $120 billion is borrowed and added to a national debt backed only by the full faith and credit of our children and grandchildren.

While some are still arguing that more deficit spending is needed—to help people consume and to subsidize small businesses through Washington bureaucracies, for example—the reality is that federal spending and debt are now so large that they discourage private-sector hiring and investment. And the country simply can't afford it.

In President Barack Obama's February 2011 budget for fiscal 2012–2021, he proposed $39 trillion in taxes from the private sector and $46 trillion in federal spending, leaving a $7 trillion fiscal deficit. His budget assumed that the statutory debt limit would grow to over $26 trillion, more than double the level when he took office.

What to cut? Washington keeps trying to tackle the big categories of spending such as Social Security and Medicare. The problem is that the public isn't convinced that those programs should be the first to suffer, so Washington politics, loosely representing the national will, rarely agrees on entitlement restraint. Instead, Washington often uses commissions and special committees to shift responsibility.

I suggest a different approach to cutting federal spending. Start with small budget cuts that mostly hurt Washington, not the rest of the country. Abraham Lincoln said he learned "by littles." Washington has to get in the habit of making frequent, small cuts so that the public sees that it's possible.

The president should call his cabinet together and request plans for a thousand cuts in each department, totaling 20% of their budgets—budgets that are enormous, out of control, and filled with programs that are not necessary to the federal government's powers under the Constitution.

The same presidential call for spending cuts should be made for the nearly two hundred independent agencies that extend Washington's power. Many are "independent" precisely to avoid the budget and accountability process, so the president will be setting a healthy example by personally demanding restraint and overseeing reductions.

The goal of this downsizing process is to create a very clear signal for the public that Washington intends to shrink itself, allowing more room in the economy for the private sector to thrive. The ideal is for the president to move front and center in proposing spending reductions and a process for continuous future reductions. His staff has the detailed knowledge to find hundreds of billions of dollars in reductions every year. Cabinet secretaries who balk should be replaced. The intent is to break out of the big-government rut and create an upheaval in the budget starting with Washington itself.

The public and financial markets want deep spending cuts. This means cutting Washington's countless commissions and special committees, idle TARP funds, earmarks, unused stimulus, the costly Jones Act (which by restricting maritime commerce through protectionism, blocked oil cleanup), multibillion-dollar ethanol subsidies, cars, staff, planes, long vacations, above-average salaries, unbuilt buildings, open purchase orders—all the stuff members of Congress approve in order to expand government and win reelection but that isn't affordable during a financial crisis.

Once Washington demonstrates a technique to cut close to home, politicians will be able to use their improved moral position to consider cuts in entitlements. Many good approaches have already been proposed and would have more traction if Washington worked to downsize itself first.

Congress may not be able to create smaller budgets on its first attempt. Congressional rules are set up so that they cause automatic spending increases, not cuts. For example, in 2010, Congress spent $26 billion on "aid to the states." It passed this law on the pretense that it was "deficit neutral," because it promised to cut food stamps and other aid to the poor starting in 2014. No one believed those cuts will actually materialize.

Congress urgently needs to take up budget-process reform in order to make it possible to cut spending. That reform will likely require zero-based budgeting rules or a pay-as-you-go system that truly matches spending increases with immediate spending cuts. It will also likely require timely budgets and appropriations.

That's going to be a heavy lift inside the Beltway. However, to achieve 4% growth, it might be sufficient for now if the president proposed sweeping spending cuts. That would be a dramatic enough improvement in the U.S. fiscal direction to boost private-sector investment, raise equity prices, encourage small-business hiring, and win more investment back from foreign economies.

To be an effective, fast-growing, market-oriented nation, the United States has to restrain federal spending in the long run, which is now more than 24% of GDP, and reverse the growth in the national debt. We're so deep in the fiscal hole it will take a concerted multi-decade national effort to bring debt down to tolerable levels.

The marketable debt-to-GDP ratio stands at 70%—based on $10.5 trillion in marketable federal debt divided by the $15 trillion GDP—and is forecast to exceed 100% of GDP in the spending path set in the Obama administration's ten-year budget. That's a debt level that's well above sustainability. And, although already mind-bogglingly large and growing fast, the $10.5 trillion in marketable debt doesn't include any of the unfunded spending promises—Social Security, Medicare, the constantly risky losses of Fannie Mae and Freddie Mac, and the layers of fast-growing new entitlements and mandates Washington keeps imposing. Counting just the existing trust fund balances as debt, the gross national debt is now over $15 trillion.

■ ■ ■

The Constitution was amazingly farsighted, but it didn't limit debt. Article I, Section 8 reads: "The Congress shall have power to lay and collect taxes . . . and to borrow money on the credit of the United States." But there are no boundaries on this borrowing power in

Section 9, which puts many other limits on congressional power. If the Founding Fathers had realized that a future Congress would borrow $15 trillion, much less plan a $26 trillion national debt as President Obama did in his fiscal 2012 budget, they would surely have installed a debt limitation.

For example, Article 9 states, "No money shall be drawn from the Treasury, but in consequence of appropriations made by law." In that vein, Article 9 should probably also have said: "Accumulated borrowings shall not exceed one-third of the nation's annual output except in time of war."

To restrain federal debt consistent with the Tenth Amendment's restraints on other federal powers, we need an explicit statutory restraint and, if it can be achieved, a new constitutional amendment.

Currently, there is in theory a debt limit in the form of a debt ceiling. Congress can spend (and borrow) below the ceiling without consequence. And when it reaches the ceiling, Congress simply needs to vote to raise its debt limit. We clearly need a more effective mechanism. Indeed, the current system is set up to make it easier to spend borrowed money—before it was in place, Congress had the nettlesome task of having to vote on each bond issuance.

We need a federal debt limit that creates confidence that the government might break the spending rules in one year but will then have to make up for it with extra cuts in future years. The upside is huge. If the United States shows that it has a mechanism to control federal spending and debt, it will create private-sector confidence, a key step in job creation. Financial markets will help by bidding up asset prices and strengthening the dollar.

The current law is fatally flawed because it threatens government shutdowns and debt default but doesn't cause any restraint on spending or debt. The federal government is on a cash-basis accounting system, meaning spending is recorded when bills are paid, not when spending commitments are made or the bill is presented for payment. By the time the debt limit is used up, hundreds of billions of dollars of extra spending is already in the pipeline.

Under the current debt limit, even if Congress and the president agreed to enact a fully balanced ten-year budget tomorrow, the national debt would still have to go up by trillions of dollars in the next few years as the government pays old bills and makes the required contributions to Social Security and Medicare trust funds (which are counted in the debt but aren't included in the deficit or in Treasury auctions).

As a result, the current debt limit presents impossible choices to fiscal conservatives—either approve a debt limit increase to cover spending that has already occurred or shut down the government or risk defaulting on debt. Every time this choice has been presented to Congress, the result has been more debt and more federal spending.

Thus a critical step in achieving 4% GDP growth is to replace the current debt limit with a law (and over time a constitutional amendment) that forces spending reductions when debt is excessive. The current debt limit doesn't control or limit the government's ability to run deficits or incur obligations, only controlling obligations already incurred. I favor a debt-to-GDP ceiling, but it could also be a dollar limit that increases at a slower rate than the economy. Rather than enforcing the new debt ceiling with the harmful and ineffective threat of a debt default or government shutdown, it should be enforced with escalating penalties on the executive branch and Congress when debt is above the ceiling.

When it is over the debt ceiling, the president should be required to submit budgets with lower spending and Congress should be required to vote on reduced spending. The president should be required to submit proposals to reduce entitlement spending growth and Congress should be required to vote on them.

When over the debt ceiling, the administration should be required to make quarterly proposals to Congress on spending cuts and could be given impoundment authority to underspend the budget, a power that all presidents before Gerald Ford had, and which was used to control congressional spending excesses. When over the debt ceiling, benefits for congressmen, senators, the president, the cabinet, and the senior executives in government service should be reduced. It's their job to make the decisions needed to limit government debt. If they don't, they should give up their automatic raises, free parking spots, extra staff, free day care, travel, and an escalating array of power and other perks.

Senior executive branch and congressional leaders should face the equivalent of wearing a hair shirt—prohibitions on naming public works after themselves, or mandatory monthly letters to the public explaining how they will reduce debt. The president should be required to meet weekly in public with his cabinet when the debt is over the limit for more than six months.

Because the debt-to-GDP ratio is too high now, there should be a glide path during a transition period. For example, in 2013, penalties should be imposed on Congress and the executive branch if the marketable debt-to-GDP ratio is over 70%; in 2014, when over 68%; and so on. The most growth-oriented outcome would be an agreement now to an eventual peacetime debt-to-GDP ceiling at, say, one-third of GDP. It could be achieved through spending cuts and fast economic growth. Some of the penalties for exceeding the ceiling could be waived during a national emergency, perhaps with a two-thirds vote in Congress and the president's signature. But giving up perks in a time of crisis isn't too much to ask of our national leaders.

There's another aspect of U.S. debt that should be brought under better control as a step in achieving 4% growth. State and local debt reached $2.7 trillion in 2009, doubling in just ten years. This doesn't count the state and local commitments to lifetime pensions and expensive health benefits for millions of workers. While most state and local governments have balanced-budget requirements, these often do not constrain promises of future benefits. To enhance U.S. growth prospects, the federal government should encourage a shift in state and local government pensions from defined benefit plans (where the potential liability to taxpayers is open-ended) toward a 401(k) system patterned on the federal employee system. This provides government workers with more flexibility in their careers and more assurance of income in retirement. Under current policy, the federal government facilitates costly and unstable state and local pension systems through accounting rules and tolerance of underfunded pensions.

■ ■ ■

In addition to sound money, spending cuts, and an operable debt limit that forces spending restraint, we desperately need sweeping tax reform in order to sustain 4% GDP growth.

On the corporate side, the United States has the second-highest marginal tax rate in the developed world. A lower rate on a broader base would significantly increase our attractiveness to global investment. On the personal income tax side, high rates, extreme complexity, and staggering compliance costs hold down U.S. growth while supporting Washington's tax industry at the expense of the rest of the economy.

The U.S. personal income tax outlook is unraveling fast. An increasing number of existing tax rates are temporary. To keep them from rising automatically, Congress and the president have to agree annually on complicated, hard-to-pass legislation. As that negotiation unfolds, the suspense is killing job creation.

Washington's inclination is to add additional taxes to pay for the theoretical "cost" of keeping expiring tax rates at their current level. As more of the tax system falls into this trap—adding permanent new taxes in order to extend other tax rates for a year—it has created a strong upward ratchet in tax rates and tax complexity. Adding to the artificiality of the current budget process, the budget baseline assumes the temporary tax rates are allowed to expire. This creates large increases in tax receipts on paper, and it assumes that economic growth, stock prices, and home prices will be unaffected by rate hikes.

The logic is strong for new tax-writing procedures to stop the upward tax ratchet. However, with each short-term tax credit or rate reduction that has been added to the tax code—kept short-term in order to hold down the budget cost even though the intention is permanency—the gap between current tax rates and the scoring baseline used by CBO has widened too much to allow for tax reform.

One pro-growth, pro-jobs starting point to address this problem would be to make permanent many of the current annual tax fixes—the alternative minimum tax patch, the research and experimentation credit, the George W. Bush tax rates, some of the energy tax, the "doc fix" that wreaks annual havoc in the Medicare system. Since they are extended regularly, it would greatly enhance the prospects of tax reform for these annual tax cuts to be set aside and fixed in a one-time process that would stabilize the tax code. The surprise step toward tax reform would make clear to global investors that the United States is serious about making its economy more competitive. So even though deficit and debt estimates would increase as a result of the change, the net effect would be to make the United States more attractive for investment.

If the temporary provisions in the code can't be made permanent prior to tax reform, the budget committees need to guide the scoring baseline during tax reform so that it correctly recognizes that many of the temporary tax provisions are extended annually and are, in fact, permanent features of the tax code.

Sweeping tax reform that lowers individual and corporate rates while broadening the tax base is vital. It would simplify the code, add to economic growth and employment, and raise asset prices. The benefits of tax reform should be taken into account in congressional consideration of tax reform legislation. To facilitate tax reform, there should be a one-time negotiated dynamic scoring of tax reform to recognize that the purpose of updating the tax code is to add to economic growth. For example, both parties might agree that a tax reform agreement, if approved by Congress, would add 1% to average annual GDP growth over ten years. That growth dividend would become part of the tax reform scoring process. It doesn't predispose the contents of tax reform, but it brings the scoring system closer to reality and addresses the scoring obstacle that has been blocking any recent attempt at tax reform.

With these two procedures—making temporary tax provisions permanent or adding them to the baseline, and recognizing that a successful tax reform will increase growth and asset prices—a massively pro-growth tax reform process could be carried out through the budget reconciliation process, the approach used in the 1986 tax act on which I worked for Secretary of the Treasury James Baker. It lowered tax rates, broadened the tax base, and contributed to growth rates of 3.2%, 4.1%, and 3.6% in 1987 to 1989 for three years of 4% average growth.

■ ■ ■

The United States is suffering a government-spending and debt crisis, compounded by an investment exodus caused by Washington's weak-dollar policy. First-order U.S. growth solutions rest on clear decisions by the president to end the weak-dollar policy, substantially reduce current and projected federal spending, replace the current debt limit, and immediately undertake sweeping tax reforms to rebuild U.S. competitiveness.

The list of other necessary pro-growth reforms is long. The new health-care and financial reform laws are filled with anti-growth provisions. Regulatory reform and reduced litigiousness need to be a priority if the United States is to sustain 4% growth. The government has taken over the mortgage system, reducing the growth potential of one more major sector of the economy. There's no plan to stop the financial hemorrhage at Fannie Mae and Freddie Mac, both under government conservatorship.

There's time to fix our national problems. Long-term interest rates are low, which will allow us to amortize past spending excesses over several decades. But Washington keeps reinforcing current policies rather than reversing them, creating bigger problems and slower growth.

Countries are in constant competition with each other every year for hundreds of billions of dollars' worth of jobs and global capital. The United States has been losing this competition, with severe consequences for future innovation and living standards.

The solution is a 4% growth renaissance based on the ageless American principles of sound money, low tax rates, limited federal government, the market-based allocation of capital and labor, and sensible regulatory and trade rules. We should start on this agenda today.

Chapter 8

Not All Growth Is Good

By Myron Scholes

he United States has just experienced one of the largest asset bubbles in history. After peaking in 2006 and 2007 at prices that had more than doubled in some markets, in just a few years, home values crashed. The result was a financial panic that sunk storied Wall Street firms and erased the home equity of tens of millions of Americans. Those hit the hardest included Americans who suddenly owed more on their homes than those homes were worth.

It would seem that not all economic "growth" actually adds value to the national economy.

In truth, there are two kinds of growth. One kind is artificial and often driven by misguided policies that aim to increase GDP without regard to adding fundamental value to the economy. For example, monetary policy—through cheap credit—likely contributed to the housing bubble. For a time, this appeared to buoy the economy, even as it was setting the stage for millions of Americans to lose their life savings. Tax and fiscal policies can also create artificial growth. Building a road might create temporary jobs, but does it really create wealth if it doesn't also shorten commute times or otherwise make society better off? Tax incentives might spur hiring in the short run, but how lasting are those gains if the jobs expire with the tax credits and they come at the expense of investing in the new technologies of the future?

The other kind of growth actually increases our net wealth and is usually driven by progress in human or physical capital or advances in technology. This second kind of growth leads to long-term economic expansion by improving education, drawing in new high-skilled immigrants, freeing capital, or developing new technologies that make us more productive. Building that road could produce wealth, if it connects businesses in ways they were not connected before. Similarly, raising student achievement can make workers more productive, and changing tax and fiscal policies to allow entrepreneurs to invest in promising ventures can lead to innovation and to new jobs.

So how do we spur this second kind of growth?

In my view, the economy is facing a unique set of headwinds. The United States has sustained a housing crash of tremendous proportions. The policy response in Washington to this crash has not addressed fundamental underlying problems, even while it has created new problems of its own. And the United States has to survive in an increasingly competitive global marketplace where capital (both human and financial) can shift from one place to another. Any of these three issues would pose significant challenges by themselves. But add them together and you will see that over the past few years the United States has suffered a shock to its economic system that warrants a considered response.

First, let's review a few missteps. Many of Washington's policies over the past few years have created uncertainty among individuals and businesses. And uncertainty has an underappreciated negative effect on the economy. Why? Because people and businesses react to it in an understandable way—they hold on to their money rather than investing in ventures that might lead to innovations. The net result is that there is less money available for investing in technologies or other items that will lead to higher productivity down the road.

Policy makers have fed uncertainty by trying to steer the economy from Washington. The reason that this creates uncertainty is that Washington tends to support the first kind of economic growth— the kind that artificially inflates GDP, but which can actually reduce value to society. Inflating a housing bubble is one example of this. But there are others that range from wasting funds on unnecessary infrastructure projects to directing capital into endeavors that do little to make the economy more efficient.

One way Washington directed capital to fruitless ends came in the form of a financial reform bill called Dodd-Frank, which became law in 2010. This new law was advertised as necessary to prevent the kind of financial collapse that happened in 2008. Instead it has provided little additional protection against a future crash, made financial markets less flexible, and imposed new costs on the system (something many consumers saw in 2011 with new debit card fees). Combined with new health-care requirements, employment regulations, immigration rules, and constraints on innovation, it has led many of the country's largest companies to sit on substantial financial reserves even while the economy sputters. Uncertain about the future, they are saving their capital for the rainy days that seem to await them.

The way I've often described the problem we face is this: Rather than having the "war generals" (private entrepreneurs) lead our economy, we're being led by the "ordinance generals" in Washington. We need to replace the ordinance generals with war generals—those individuals who can actually create innovations that add value to society.

One way to do that would be to pull back the policies briefly mentioned above that are adding to uncertainty. But that's not enough. In a competitive global economy, we'll need to make advances in computing, information, and telecommunications technologies as well as other areas that will lead us to new ways of doing business. The goal is to increase our national output without increasing the resources we put into the economy. And to do that, we'll have to also build flexibility into our thinking.

What we know is that we must innovate before we build infrastructure. And here I am using a definition of the term *infrastructure* that includes much more than bridges and roads. I'm using a definition that includes government regulatory structures as well as private systems that range from rules to habits of business that surround our industries and often determine how our markets function.

Innovation must lead infrastructure for a simple, but compelling, reason: Innovation produces new types of products and markets, and it is virtually impossible to know how to run those markets efficiently before they are created. We can all be thankful that there wasn't a set of regulations in place that were so rigid that they would have made the iPhone impossible to create before Steve Jobs had rolled it out. If we seek to regulate future products and markets in advance, we'll impose rules that will almost certainly end up crushing innovation. R&D, creating new products, or developing new types of capital investments requires building infrastructure only after making gains in innovation.

We can't let infrastructure get too far behind innovation and creativity, of course. We need rules to run markets efficiently. But we can't let old infrastructure stifle new innovation, either. So we have to think about how to repeal old rules that stifle new ideas. We have to think about the rigidities that are already in place. Most of these rigidities exist in places where we don't allow individuals to use markets to compete or where we involve the government, which often won't allow old infrastructure to be upended in favor of new innovations and new types of rules.

If all of that seems a little abstract, consider a real-world example in the form of China. The Chinese economy has grown for the past thirty years and, notwithstanding those who believe otherwise, I think it will continue to grow for the next thirty years. The reason it will grow is that it has made great strides by pulling more of its population into industries that are more productive than agriculture. At the same time, China has achieved significant growth in tangible capital—it has built roads, bridges, and other physical assets. But there has not been corresponding progress of the same magnitude in homegrown technology and innovation. This is similar to the growth experienced in years past in South Korea, Taiwan, and even Japan.

China's growth has been hampered by overinvestment—by the habit of a centrally planned economy to invest not in things that make its economy as productive as it can be, but in hard assets that political leaders favor. These investments have been made with financial resources that come from a very high domestic savings rate. Essentially, China is funding its own overinvestment. So, in a sense, we can say that China both oversaves and overinvests. The net result is that its investments have produced some level of growth but have not made its economy nearly as efficient or as productive as it could be. In other words, its investments are paying off, but not nearly at the rate they should be.

One sign of that is this: About 30% of the labor force in China produces only 10% of the country's GDP, and there is also a supply of surplus labor that is mostly unskilled. China has a lot of people who could be vastly more productive.

Over time, as labor continues to move from farms to factories, China will experience real growth. And as the society becomes wealthier (a 1.3 billion person society, mind you) there will be a great increase in the demand for housing, transportation, education, and health care, things that wealthier individuals want to consume. In the years ahead we can expect China not only to react to its growing middle class by allowing new homes and new industries to be built, but to invest in education and in R&D as well. And both education and R&D will almost certainly be areas of significant and lasting growth for China.

But R&D could also be an area of significant growth for the United States. The United States has a huge advantage in R&D. China issues about 1,000 patents a year. South Korea and Taiwan issue about 8,000. And Japan issues maybe 10,000. The United States, on the other hand, issues something closer to 100,000. So R&D is one area that offers significant growth for the United States. All of these new patents offer the United States the chance to harness new innovation and new creativity and to take advantage of all of the cumulative know-how built up over the years and represented in all those previous patents. That knowledge is a tremendous edge in a global information economy.

Now, we've heard from some quarters that China has an edge of its own—that its economy is centrally directed and can therefore quickly marshal resources to productive ends. The argument is that China can be more nimble or more adept at directing investments in areas that will produce real economic growth than the United States. To the extent that this is true, it is because China is trailing the United States in innovation.

Think of it this way: When you are at the cutting edge of development, the only way to find new efficiencies is to conduct research. But when you are trailing behind someone who is conducting cutting-edge research, you can easily copy any critical breakthroughs that are made without doing much research on your own. You don't have to be too smart to figure out how to improve when others have already done the thinking for you. And in China's case, it can use the large trading firms of Japan and Hong Kong to import the ideas of financiers, intermediaries, managers of logistics, and so on to reduce innovation costs dramatically. If you reduce such costs, then obviously the deadweight costs of thinking and trying to address uncertainty are also reduced.

So we can expect China to close the gap with the United States relatively quickly, much the way Japan once closed the gap with the industrialized world. We've seen lots of growth in China in the coastal areas, and that growth will likely now extend into the center of the country. I think China will be self-sufficient and diversified but use a lot of imports and knowledge from the rest of the world. Some of those imports will come from the United States, which will work to access the sizable Chinese market for its goods and services.

Once China makes the relatively easy strides in its progress by borrowing our technology, the question will arise of whether it will be able to lead the pack with innovations of its own. If it can, it might be able to supplant the United States and claim to have the most productive workers in the world. But to do that, China will have to overcome the uncertainties and other challenges that the United States faces today. It will also have to compete head-on with the United States, something that will be a lot harder to do if we take the opportunity now to reduce uncertainty and rev up the engines of innovation in the United States.

So uncertainty really has a large effect on growth and innovation. The United States has been in the forefront of R&D and accumulative knowledge and can remain there and even grow dramatically if it concentrates on increasing the efficiency of its human and financial capital.

There are several ways to do that, and they start with developing new technologies and finding new ways to use existing technologies. The oil and gas industry is giving us one example of how we can profit by using existing technologies in new ways. Over the past several years it has started to adapt techniques first developed to extract gas from shale deposits to now extract oil. Similarly, we need to find new ways to apply technology in health care, retail, and education. And we need to rethink infrastructure and delivery systems to make them more efficient. Regulations can be streamlined, necessary roads can be built, advances in logistics can continue to allow retailers to free up capital previously committed to inventory, and better schools can help our students become more productive.

And we need to rethink our approach to success. We have to encourage success (and allow for failure), because that is how we grow. We also need to better understand what success actually requires. We tend to think that success is based on luck and not skill, and we tend to penalize success through excessive regulation and taxation. This approach has to end. We need to encourage long-term investing that leads to more R&D and a greater accumulation of valuable knowledge.

At the same time, we need to think about our human capital. The United States has been experiencing unusually high unemployment, so it has surplus labor. We need to get unemployed workers back to work in ways that actually increase value to society. Make-work infrastructure projects won't lead to long-term prosperity. But innovations that provide workers with jobs in new industries will.

To do all of these things, we need to remain flexible. I think in our global economy, uncertainty is ever increasing. So to accommodate for that, we need to build a dynamic economy and dynamic rules that can adapt to changing circumstances. In the coming decades, we're likely to see several surprising shifts as financial capital chases new opportunities and as human capital moves from one country to another or one region to another.

The world's population is expected to increase to nine billion people in the foreseeable future, with more than half living on less than two dollars a day. Aging of populations, movement of people from rural areas to cities, from south to north, and from country to country will create new challenges. We're going to have to worry about how vast movements of people affect scarce resources. And we are going to have to see all of these things as opportunities. If we position ourselves well, we'll benefit from shifts that await the world.

Likewise, advances in education and technologies will offer new opportunities to grow our economy. There are already innovations in the works that will make great strides in information technology, biology, nanotechnology, and neuroscience. We can nurture these innovations, in part, by allowing innovation to lead infrastructure. Too much infrastructure and entrenched infrastructure tend to stifle innovation. And stifling innovation on a grand scale can stifle the national economy. Rather than stifling our own success, we can unleash the creativity pent up in our economy. If we respond to our current situation by unleashing our war generals—our innovators—we'll put ourselves at the cusp of a new economic boom that will lead to benefits that will surprise even us.

Shocks create change. We had a shock recently. Let's not let a good shock go to waste.

Chapter 9

Entrepreneurs and Creative Destruction

By Peter G. Klein

Entrepreneurship research, teaching, and consulting activities have exploded in recent years. Academic organizations such as the American Economic Association and the Academy of Management now recognize entrepreneurship as a separate research field. Research and policy organizations such as the World Bank, the U.S. Federal Reserve System, the European Commission, the United Nations' Food and Agriculture Organization, the Organisation for Economic Co-operation and Development, and agencies involved in agricultural and rural development show a growing interest in studying and encouraging entrepreneurship. The Kauffman Foundation has substantially increased its funding for data collection, academic research, and education on entrepreneurship, and the Bush Institute has made entrepreneurship one of its core areas in research and policy activities aimed at increasing U.S. economic growth.

Entrepreneurship is also becoming one of the most popular subjects at colleges and universities. Entrepreneurship courses, programs, and activities are emerging not only in schools of business, but throughout the curriculum. Stories about entrepreneurs, about new companies, and about innovation are no longer confined to specialty magazines and trade publications, but appear in the major news outlets, the financial press, and countless blogs and Twitter streams. The death of Apple Computer cofounder and CEO Steve Jobs was one of the biggest news stories of 2011. Policy makers talk about entrepreneurship as a way of improving economic conditions in developing countries the way they used to talk about roads, dams, bridges, and other infrastructure projects. Even the Nobel Committee has recognized the potential impact of entrepreneurship, giving the 2008 Nobel Peace Prize to economist Muhammad Yunus, founder of Bangladesh's Grameen Bank, which specializes in microlending and the encouragement of small enterprise among the world's most desperately poor.

But what exactly is entrepreneurship? Is it simply self-employment or new-venture formation—a set of outcomes that can be measured, analyzed, and perhaps stimulated using the usual sorts of economic policy instruments—or a way of thinking or acting?

I see entrepreneurship not as a phenomenon, but as a behavior, what I call *judgmental decision making under uncertainty.* I have been developing the judgment-based approach to entrepreneurship and economic growth in a series of recent books and papers, and it is summarized in my book with Nicolai J. Foss, *Organizing Entrepreneurial Judgment: A New Approach to the Firm.*[1]

Unfortunately, economists have not, by and large, figured out how to incorporate entrepreneurial judgment into their models. Entrepreneurship was once central to theories of economic growth—one of the classic contributions, Joseph Schumpeter's 1911 *Theory of Economic Development,* makes the entrepreneur the central agent of economic change.[2] Ludwig von Mises, in his great work *Human Action,* published in 1949, called the entrepreneur "the driving force of the market."[3] But in the middle of the 20th century, economists turned increasingly to formal mathematical models of markets, and highly aggregate, Keynesian treatments of the economy, and they forgot about the entrepreneur. Economies grow through capital accumulation and through technological innovation, but these were treated either as exogenous, automatic trends or as variables controlled by government planners as they "fine-tuned" the economy.

However, entrepreneurship is not subject to government control. Nor is it limited to start-up companies. Instead, I want to suggest, following the classic contributions to the economic theory of entrepreneurship, that entrepreneurship is a fundamental aspect of human behavior, and the central part of a dynamic, vibrant, successful market economy. While new-firm formation and the growth of high-tech start-ups is critically important for economic growth, as Bob Litan argues in the next chapter, entrepreneurship is much larger, much broader, and more fundamental to economic performance.

THE ENTREPRENEURIAL FUNCTION

How should we think about entrepreneurship? The academic and practitioner literatures offer a bewildering array of definitions, perspectives, and units of analysis.[4] I find it useful to distinguish among "occupational," "structural," and "functional" perspectives. *Occupational* theories study entrepreneurship in the sense of self-employment and treat the individual as the unit of analysis. They focus on describing the characteristics of individuals (age, education, income, personality) who start their own businesses, and they focus on explaining the choice between employment and self-employment. *Structural* approaches treat the firm or industry as the unit of analysis, defining the "entrepreneurial firm" as a new or small firm. Research on industry dynamics, firm growth, clusters, and networks usually works with a structural concept of entrepreneurship. Indeed, the idea that one firm, industry, or economy can be more "entrepreneurial" than another suggests that entrepreneurship is associated with a particular market structure (that is, lots of small or young firms).

By contrast, the classic contributions to the economic theory of entrepreneurship from Schumpeter, Mises, Frank H. Knight, Israel M. Kirzner, and others model entrepreneurship as a *function*, activity, or process, not an employment category or market structure. This function has been characterized in various ways such as uncertainty-bearing, innovation, alertness to opportunities, coordination, and leadership. Importantly, these functions do not map neatly into occupational and structural categories. The entrepreneurial function can be manifested in large and small firms, in old and new firms, by individuals or teams, across a variety of occupational categories, and so on. By focusing too narrowly on self-employment and start-up companies, contemporary research and policy on entrepreneurship may be understating its role in the economy and in generating economic growth.

For Schumpeter, for example, the entrepreneur was a disruptive innovator, whose function is "creative destruction"—overturning the existing ways resources are configured by introducing new products, opening new markets, installing new production methods, or otherwise shaking up the existing ways of doing business. The result of such creative destruction is dramatic leaps forward in efficiency and growth. By Schumpeter's time, the automobile had virtually wiped out the horse-breeding and buggy-whip industries, to no one's regret but the former members of these obsolete industries. In our time, we've seen the personal computer dislodge the mainframe, and the rise of smartphones and "cloud computing" threatens to push the PC industry into oblivion. The AT&T Bell system employed four hundred thousand switchboard operators in 1970; today more than 99% of those jobs have disappeared, thanks to "disruptive" technologies.[5]

Kirzner takes a different approach, describing the entrepreneurial function as "alertness" to profit opportunities. His landmark 1973 book, *Competition and Entrepreneurship,* remains extremely influential in entrepreneurship research.[6] The simplest case of alertness is that of the arbitrageur, who discovers a discrepancy in present prices that can be exploited for financial gain. In a more typical case, the entrepreneur is alert to a new product or a superior production process and steps in to fill this market gap before others. Sergey Brin and Larry Page's creation of the Google search engine represents not only a technological improvement over previous search technology, but also the recognition and exploitation of an opportunity to raise funds by selling search-query-specific advertisements, an opportunity previous software engineers had missed.

My own work builds on the American economist Frank Knight and the Austrian economist Ludwig von Mises to conceive entrepreneurship as judgmental decision making under conditions of uncertainty. Judgment refers primarily to business decision making when the range of possible future outcomes, let alone the likelihood of individual outcomes, is generally unknown (what Knight, in his classic 1921 book, *Risk, Uncertainty, and Profit,* terms uncertainty, rather than probabilistic risk).[7] As former defense secretary Donald Rumsfeld famously put it, "The truth is, there are things we know, and we know we know them—the known knowns. There are things we know that we don't know—the known unknowns. And there are unknown unknowns;

the things we do not yet know that we do not know." In Knight's view, the entrepreneur's primary role in society is to deal with the unknown unknowns.

In the most general sense, then, all human behavior is entrepreneurial, as we are surrounded by Knightian uncertainty. For analyzing economic growth, however, it is useful to focus on a narrower conception of entrepreneurship, that of the businessperson who invests financial and physical resources in hopes of earning monetary profits and avoiding monetary losses. An entrepreneur has a vision, or imagination, of a business opportunity, but cannot encapsulate the details of this imagined opportunity in formulas, cash flow productions, reliable charts and figures, and other techniques for dealing with known unknowns. To exploit this imagined opportunity, the entrepreneur must acquire and invest productive resources—putting skin in the game. The set of possible resource combinations is huge, so this is no easy task. As Ludwig M. Lachmann put it: "We are living in a world of unexpected change; hence capital combinations . . . will be ever changing, will be dissolved and reformed. In this activity, we find the real function of the entrepreneur."[8]

JUDGMENT AND RESOURCE OWNERSHIP

The entrepreneur's critical function, in the judgment-based perspective, is *ownership*. To exercise the entrepreneurial function, the entrepreneur acquires and deploys resources. Entrepreneurs prosper as they, and the subordinates they employ, put these resources to their highest-valued uses. Private property and the profit-and-loss system give entrepreneurs incentives to make use of local knowledge, to experiment, and to learn from their mistakes as they seek to make the best use of resources, and to expand the capital under their control, in the face of an unknown future.

The entrepreneur's primary decision-making tool is what Mises called *economic calculation*, the use of present prices and anticipated future prices to compare present costs with expected future benefits.[9] In this way, the entrepreneur decides what goods and services should be produced, and what methods of production should be used to produce them. "The business of the entrepreneur is not merely to experiment with new technological methods, but to select from the multitude of technologically feasible methods those which are best fit to supply the public in the cheapest way with the things they are asking for most urgently."[10]

To make this selection, the entrepreneur must be able to weigh the costs and expected benefits of various courses of action—hence the importance of free markets for inputs and outputs.[11] Without private ownership of resources and a market-price system, there is no way for entrepreneurs to calculate the most effective ways of producing and innovating. This is the rationale for Mises's famous argument, in 1920, that Soviet-style central planners could not allocate resources rationally—an argument that was ridiculed at the time by socialist intellectuals (and many economists), and, of course, was proven right by the collapse of the centrally planned economies at the end of the Cold War.

Government actors, more generally, lack the incentives and resources available to private entrepreneurs. While government officials also command resources, at least nominally, and seek opportunities for gain (both public and private), they acquire some resources by coercion, not consent; they don't own the resources they control, and don't ultimately bear the gains and losses they create; their objectives are complex and hard to specify; and there is no mechanism for rewarding success and punishing failure akin to the market's competitive selection process among entrepreneurs.[12] Suffering from what Wilhelm Roepke called the "hubris of the intellectual," they try to replace entrepreneurial initiative with bureaucratic control.[13] But, in a world of Knightian uncertainty, such control can never be effective. It is only entrepreneurs, who bear the gains and losses from their own attempts to deal with an uncertain future, who can make an economy grow.

ENTREPRENEURIAL JUDGMENT, PUBLIC POLICY, AND ECONOMIC GROWTH

What, then, should government do to foster innovation, alertness, and judgment? Can entrepreneurship be stimulated, guided, or directed from above, or is it necessarily a bottom-up, market-driven phenomenon?

The answer, of course, is that entrepreneurship emerges from the initiative, creativity, and passion of individuals, not the guiding hand of the state. The best that government policy can do to encourage entrepreneurship is to allow an environment that encourages entrepreneurship to flourish—sound money, the rule of law, and free and open competition. Government cannot create entrepreneurs or tell entrepreneurs what to do. Government needs to get out of the way. Consider a few examples of what government should avoid:

Don't create and exacerbate business cycles. Government policy should not interfere with entrepreneurial planning, forecasting, and investing through bad monetary policy: creating asset bubbles by aggressive monetary expansion, trying to keep prices and wages artificially high through macroeconomic stimulus programs, and creating uncertainty that discourages investment through ever-changing monetary and fiscal policy. As described above, entrepreneurs rely on market prices to perform what Mises called "economic calculation"—forming judgments about what to produce, and how to produce it, based on today's prices for resources and beliefs about future product prices. Bubbles, for instance, hinder economic calculation—leading to over-investment in Internet companies in the 1990s and in real estate and mortgage-backed securities in the 2000s. Stimulus and forms of activist policy create "regime uncertainty"[14] that makes entrepreneurs favor short-term over long-term, growth-creating investments.

These arguments are central to the "Austrian" theory of business cycles, which has surged in popularity following the financial crisis and the obvious failure of the Obama administration's massive stimulus program. This theory, outlined by Mises and Hayek in the early 20th century, sees economic crises as the result of government policy errors.[15] Easy-money policies lower the interest rate below its "natural rate," leading to overinvestment in capital-intensive industries (what economists call "lengthening the period of production"). The result is an artificial boom, one that inevitably turns into a bust as market participants come to realize that there are not enough savings to complete all the new projects. Moreover, monetary expansion not only increases price levels, but also increases the variability of relative prices, making economic calculation particularly difficult.[16]

Even knowing that an artificial boom is under way, the entrepreneur must exercise judgment regarding its magnitude, duration, and effects on the entrepreneur's own markets, judgments that are particularly difficult to make under periods of rapid monetary expansion. Once a recession hits, programs to stimulate the economy, restructure industries, or allocate resources to politically favored firms and sectors make a bad situation worse, discouraging entrepreneurs from liquidating bad investments and directing resources to their proper, higher-valued uses.

Don't bail out failing enterprises. Schumpeter's creative destruction takes place as entrepreneurs experiment with different combinations of inputs and outputs, trying to find those that make the best use of the economy's scarce resources. For this, market feedback is essential. If a business cannot produce goods and services that consumers want to buy, it should be liquidated and its assets made available to other entrepreneurs to try again.

Indeed, a key function of competition—in product, factor, and capital markets—is to select not only for efficient combinations of different types of resources, but also for entrepreneurial skill. "What makes profit emerge," wrote Mises, "is the fact that the entrepreneur who judges the future prices of the products more correctly than other people do buys some or all of the factors of production at prices which, seen from the point of view of the future state of the market, are too low. . . . This difference is entrepreneurial profit."[17] Accumulation of profits and losses over time determines which individuals are best suited to own and control particular resource combinations. For this reason, bailouts, subsidies, and other forms of special privilege for particular entrepreneurs hinder the market process of directing productive resources to their highest-valued uses.[18]

Besides explicit bailouts, implicit subsidies from "too-big-to-fail" guarantees stymie the entrepreneurial selection process, not only by protecting unsuccessful entrepreneurs and entrepreneurial ventures, but also by rewarding lobbying and other forms of rent seeking, directing investment toward subsidized activities (at the expense of consumer preferences), and discouraging entry by nascent entrepreneurs who lack political connections.

Industrial planning, which attempts to substitute bureaucratic directives for market control of resources, further stymies entrepreneurial initiative. Consider, for example, the U.S. government's actions in rescuing General Motors from bankruptcy and engineering an alliance between Chrysler and Fiat.[19] The GM rescue proceeded under the assumption that the resources controlled by GM's current owners, and operated by its current management team, were more valuable in their current use than in alternative uses, owned and controlled by other entrepreneurs—an assumption clearly violated by the fact of bankruptcy. The Fiat-Chrysler merger was defended on the usual grounds of creating "synergies," despite a wealth of management research suggesting that such synergies rarely materialize. And if they would in this case, then it's likely market forces would have driven Fiat and Chrysler together without government help.

Focus on individuals, not aggregates. Recent discussion among academics and policy makers about the financial crisis has proceeded largely in Keynesian language, focusing on aggregates and downplaying the wide variety of firms, consumers, industries, and sectors of our economy. Despite the widely publicized failures of particular financial institutions, such as AIG, Lehman Brothers, Freddie Mac, and Fannie Mae, government officials spoke in terms of "the banking system," "the financial system," and the economy as a whole. The discussion of "frozen credit markets" concentrated on high-level indicators, with the focus on total lending, not the composition of lending among individuals, firms, and industries. But a decline in average home prices, reductions in total lending, and volatility in asset price indexes does not reveal much about the prices of particular homes, the cost of capital for specific borrowers, and the prices of individual assets.

In analyzing the credit crisis, the critical question is, which loans are not being made, to whom, and why? Focusing on total lending, total liquidity, average equity prices, and the like obscures the key questions about how resources are being allocated across sectors, firms, and individuals, whether bad investments are being liquidated, and so on. Such aggregate notions homogenize—and in doing so, suppress critical information about relative prices. The main function of capital markets, after all, is not to moderate the total amount of financial capital, but to allocate capital across activities or, more accurately, across entrepreneurs—to allocate capital in specific and individual cases.

Don't try to plan clusters of entrepreneurship and innovation. The remarkable success of America's information technology industry—centered in California's Silicon Valley, along with other technology clusters in places like Boston, San Diego, Austin, and St. Louis—has tempted policy makers to think they can engineer the next Silicon Valley through targeted subsidies, tax breaks, and other instruments. But technology clusters emerge from the bottom up, not the top down. Clusters often rely on powerful "anchor entities" such as universities, incumbent firms, research institutions, and the like, but these anchors cannot be planted for the specific purpose of creating a cluster. We don't know where the next cluster will emerge, what products it will produce, what new industries and markets will result—which is part of the beauty of capitalism.

As Mises pointed out, "The outcome of action is always uncertain. Action is always speculation."[20] Consequently, "the real entrepreneur is a speculator, a man eager to utilize his opinion about the future structure of the market for business operations promising profits. This specific anticipative understanding of the conditions of the uncertain future defies any rules and systematization"[21] This defiance of rules and systematization means that value-creating, growth-inducing entrepreneurship lies beyond the grasp of government planners, and can only come about through the dynamic interactions of free and responsible individuals.

INSTITUTIONS, POLICIES, AND ECONOMIC GROWTH

What government can do is support institutions—sound money, protection for private property, respect for the rule of law—that encourage capital formation, reward entrepreneurial initiative, and allow market competition to sort resources among actual and potential entrepreneurs. Tax policy is important. For example, the private-equity sector is subject to a 15% federal income tax rate. That's substantially less than the 35% that must be paid on "ordinary" income. And it's one reason why there is a healthy and growing private-equity sector in our economy. Private-equity firms put pressure on incumbent entrepreneurs to use their resources wisely and provide opportunities for newcomers to acquire and redeploy existing corporate assets.[22] More generally, there is a wealth of evidence that sound, market-encouraging institutions foster entrepreneurship and economic growth.[23]

To increase economic growth, we need not only high-tech start-ups, but also policies that encourage effective entrepreneurial judgment throughout all sectors and stages of the economy. We must allow profit-seeking individuals who command productive resources, and those who wish to command them, to create new goods and services, seek out new markets, find the best ways to produce existing products and serve existing markets, and exercise sound judgment about the best use of productive assets in an uncertain world. Figuring out how to best use our resources and grow our economy is not a job for Washington bureaucrats. In fact, it's a job bureaucrats cannot perform, precisely because they are insulated from the price signals and incentives of the marketplace. Rather, it is up to entrepreneurs at all stages, in all industries, in all places, to figure out how best to use our limited resources. If we allow the entrepreneurial function to flourish, we can be confident that the U.S economy will thrive and grow in ways we cannot today imagine.

Chapter 10

Baseball's Answer to Growth

By Robert Litan

Ask most economists how to create sustained 4% national economic growth and they are likely to outline policies designed to increase the nation's physical and human capital and accelerate its rate of innovation. They will recommend reducing or changing tax laws to encourage Americans to save and allow businesses to accumulate capital, invest in worker training, and fund research and development.

But there is a different way to approach the problem of economic growth and the challenge that the George W. Bush Institute has laid down—to achieve 4% annual economic growth over the long term. As readers will shortly learn, this other way of approaching the problem is not only well grounded in economics, but also has some analogues to the game of baseball, which is only fitting for a volume prepared by the Bush Institute, named for a man who more than any other president of the United States has a deep background in the nation's pastime.

But first to the economics: My approach draws on the simple insight that an economy's private-sector output in the aggregate is nothing more than the sum of the value added by its firms, or the entities that produce goods and services. Want to grow the economy at a faster clip? Then the economy needs to create new firms, especially rapidly growing ones, and to accelerate the growth of existing firms as well.

Over the past several years, a series of papers produced or funded by the Kauffman Foundation has made clear that new firms, or startups, are especially important to economic growth. For example, John Haltiwanger of the University of Maryland and two colleagues from the U.S. Census Bureau, Ron Jarmin and Javier Miranda, found that between 1980 and 2005, virtually all net increases in jobs were located in start-up firms, or firms that were less than five years old.[1] Firm age, not size, mattered for job growth. With my Kauffman colleague Dane Stangler, I was able to extend this analysis over a longer period, and found it to be true for the years 1980 through 2007.[2] And another Kauffman colleague, Tim Kane, found in an even more recent study that virtually all net job creation during roughly the three decades until the Great Recession was due to firms less than a year old, true start-ups.[3]

It is fair to ask whether jobs created by new firms last. But the answer is yes. In another study that I coauthored with former Kauffman researcher Michael Horrell, we found that fully 80% of the jobs generated by start-ups, in aggregate number, were still there five years later.[4] Kane's study was cited in the 2011 *Economic Report of the President* for a similar finding.[5]

This is not to say that the same firms were there, because we know that isn't the case. Indeed, one of the other surprising things unearthed by Kauffman research is the stability of firm survival rates: In good years and bad, after approximately five years just about half of all firms launched are still in business, and the other half are gone.[6] Of course, when looking over a longer period, failure rates go up considerably, as one would expect in any dynamic economy. Kauffman scholars Dane Stangler and Paul Kedrosky discovered that a company formed today has a 77% chance of disappearing over the next twenty-six years.[7] But the data also tell us that the jobs generated by the successful start-ups over their first five years offset almost all the job losses from the firms that fail, indicating that the jobs created by start-ups are not flashes in the pan.[8]

By implication, if start-ups are the source of net new jobs, then they must also be the source of a lot of output growth as well. Indeed, if it is true, as the evidence suggests, that start-ups were the source of all net new jobs from 1980 until 2007, then roughly one-third of all jobs and output currently produced in the economy have been generated by companies that did not exist before 1980.[9]

Start-ups also are vital to innovation and thus long-run economic growth. With no stake in the status quo, start-ups have disproportionately been responsible for many of the breakthrough or disruptive innovations that now characterize modern society. Examples include all types of computers and much of the software that operates them, many medical devices and an increasing number of pharmaceuticals, and air-conditioning, to name just a few. Large existing companies are important for partnering with start-up entrepreneurs or refining and mass-producing their innovations, but concentrate more on incremental innovations.[10] Since a considerably higher sustained national growth rate is likely to require continuous disruptive innovations, the U.S. economy thus will need a steady number of successful new high-growth start-ups launched each year.

4% GROWTH, HOME RUNS, AND OTHER HITS

Suppose the national base growth rate is 3%, which, judging from recent estimates by other economists and the government itself, may be a bit on the high side. How many new successful companies would it take to bump that growth rate up permanently by one full percentage point to reach the 4% target that is the objective of a research and policy initiative of the Bush Institute? That is a question I posed and tried to answer in late 2010—before I even knew there were others out there thinking equally ambitious thoughts.[11]

Given what I have observed about the importance of new firms to the economy, it may be tempting to answer the "How do we get 1% faster growth?" question by simply calculating how many more total firms need to be started each year. But this is too simplistic, because the real growth in output in jobs is generated largely by the most successful or the most rapidly growing new firms.

It is the truly innovative or inventive growing firms that bring to the market something new—a product, service, or process—that generates substantially more benefits for society as a whole than any single entrepreneur, inventor, or firm can capture for himself or itself. Economist William Nordhaus has estimated that inventors, whom I will assume to be reasonable proxies for innovative entrepreneurs, capture only 4%

of the total social gains from their innovations.[12] The lion's share of inventors' gains "leak out" to benefit many other firms and industries that use the inventions in some manner.

Think of the electric light, which opened up new horizons for all humanity. Or, more recently, consider breakthrough computer programs, such as the Microsoft or Linux operating systems, that establish a platform on which tens of thousands of other productivity-enhancing applications can run. The same is true of other platforms introduced by other firms, such as Apple's iOS or Google's Android, or new technologies, such as genetic sequencers or cloud computing, that facilitate innovation of many other complementary technologies.

To be sure, every innovation doesn't show up in measured GDP growth. Many health-care innovations—new pharmaceuticals, medical devices, and treatments—both lengthen and improve the quality of life for millions, if not billions, of people. In principle, firms that produce these types of innovations should also be included in our count of the innovative firms our economy needs in the future, even if not all of their benefits are captured in the traditional economic statistics.

If innovative firms are the drivers of growth in both output and jobs—largely because of the excess gains to society they generate over the private reward reaped by their founders, shareholders, and employees—then it stands to reason that the steady creation of more such firms will increase growth in the long run. How large or rapidly growing must these innovative firms be? There are no hard and fast rules, but for argument's sake, I suggest that a useful starting point is to consider inventive firms whose revenues eventually grow to an average of $1 billion or more. Using the baseball lexicon, I call these "home run" firms, because the benefits they deliver to the overall economy are themselves significant. So how many home run firms would we need to create each year to raise the national economic growth rate by one percentage point?

In a white paper I published in December 2010 for the Kauffman Foundation, I attempted to answer this question by drawing on Nordhaus's fundamental result that truly innovative firms capture just 4% of the gains they generate for society. Using some additional assumptions spelled out in that paper, I arrived at this answer: Depending on the assumptions, it probably would require the creation of 30 to 60 additional home run or billion-dollar firms every year beyond those currently being created to ratchet up economy-wide growth from 3% to 4%.[13]

How big is this number? Pretty big, it turns out. With the help of my Kauffman colleague Dane Stangler, we estimated from publicly available sources that since the mid-20th century, the average number of billion-dollar companies originating each year has been roughly 10–15—this, of course, being an average, smooths out the bad years and good years. Nonetheless, the baseline number itself might suggest that creating an additional 30–60 such companies each year in order to hit the 4% growth rate target looks deeply unrealistic.

Fortunately, the example of 30–60 home run companies is just one way to get to 4% growth. I looked at how many large firms we would have to create to make the work that's cut out for us easy to understand. I did it for effect, but it obviously is not how the economy really works. Many firms that are launched each year grow up to be less than home-run firms—instead they hit the economic equivalent of singles, doubles, and triples—but still deliver benefits to society. These firms still produce innovations, create jobs, and create great wealth. The more such sub-home-run companies are created each year, the fewer number of true home runs will be required to lift the growth rate by one percentage point.

Moreover, even if 4% growth requires only the estimated 30–60 home run companies, that range is equivalent to just .06–.12% of the roughly 500,000 businesses that are launched each year.[14] Expressed that way, adding another point to the growth rate only through home run companies looks far less daunting.

The challenge is to find ways to ensure that more of the firms that are launched grow quickly and produce more innovations than exist now. And here a hard look at the numbers reveals the task at hand. The number of new firms launched each year, as measured by the Kauffman Index of Entrepreneurial Activity (KIEA), has been relatively steady over the past fifteen years, even going up a bit since the recession began. That's the good news. The bad news is that the number of those firms that have hired employees, or employer-based firms, has been going down each year over this period (and most likely longer).[15]

This is worrisome and not easily explained. It is not necessarily inconsistent with the entrepreneurial energy in the U.S. economy, since employment growth among new firms is driven by a small fraction of the overall total of new firms. But still, when looking ahead to the steep challenge of trying to create more firms that create new jobs as a way of raising economy-wide growth, we find it disturbing to look back and discover that the overall numbers of those firms have been falling for some time.

So clearly, we have to do better. The question is how. By looking at current public policy, I have found three reforms that will cost the government virtually nothing, but that will nonetheless likely produce more innovation and job-creating companies in the United States.

TAKING IN MORE HIGH-SKILLED IMMIGRANTS

Let's begin with the low-hanging fruit, at least conceptually though admittedly not politically: letting more—lots more—skilled immigrants work and launch businesses in the United States.

This idea remains one of the very best ways to sustain higher economic growth. High-skilled immigrants, especially those who come here for an education, can benefit our society because human capital and one of its principal fruits, innovation, are the central keys to growth in any economy. This is especially true for economies at the technological frontier like ours, where faster growth can come only from the more rapid development and use of new products, services, and processes.

The past and continuing contributions of immigrants to our society and to our economy are well known. The emigration from Europe by scientists not only helped the United States win World War II, but also contributed to numerous scientific and technological breakthroughs with civilian applications. Immigrants also founded many of America's iconic companies, including DuPont, Procter & Gamble, Pfizer, and U.S. Steel. More recently, analysts have attributed 25% or more of successful high-tech companies to having at least one immigrant founder,[16] including Google, Yahoo!, and eBay. And it is not only immigrants who make important contributions to our society; their children do as well. Another recent study has found that almost three-quarters of the finalists in the 2011 Intel Math and Science competition for high schoolers were students from immigrant families.[17]

Allowing more highly skilled immigrants to live, work, and form new businesses here is thus a no-brainer as a matter of policy. Indeed, we already recognize this truth to some degree by accepting more than 100,000 immigrants per year into our universities for undergraduate or graduate study. We let in another 65,000 under the controversial, but very limited, H-1B visa program, which permits U.S. companies to bring in, for up to six years, immigrants with skills firms have difficulty finding among domestic workers.

But both of these entry points into our country are temporary. After getting their first-class educations in America, student and recently graduated immigrants must return to their home countries, even if they want to stay and work or start a business here. Likewise, when the six years of their H-1B visa runs out, these immigrants, too, must go home.

What a waste! It clearly would benefit the nation as well as the immigrants themselves if the United States had a far more sensible immigration policy, one that put much more emphasis on skills of immigrants. Given the human capital skilled immigrants bring to the workforce, there is also no need in principle to trade off their numbers against those in other categories. They're all a plus for our economy.

The most straightforward way to take in highly skilled immigrants is with those we already train in our universities but currently send home after they receive their degrees. Approximately 60,000 foreign students graduate each year with an undergraduate or graduate degree in science, technology, engineering, or mathematics (STEM), the fields most important for future technological innovation.[18] Why not, as an increasing number of analysts have suggested, just staple a green card to such diplomas to allow these individuals to work here permanently when they receive an undergraduate or graduate STEM degree?

The standard political answer to this sensible idea is that there isn't sufficient bipartisan political support for a narrower immigration bill that doesn't fix the ills associated with lower-skilled immigrants, especially from those countries south of our border. In addition, green cards for all STEM graduates may pit talented immigrants against their domestic counterparts in the labor market. This could conceivably drive down wages or cost some Americans their jobs (though raising overall national income in the process). Losers from any policy change speak more loudly in the political sphere than winners, especially if the latter are not already citizens. So, the idea of green cards for STEM graduates has some political risks.

There is a second-best way to bring in more skilled immigrants that has no political risks, however. And that is to permit immigrants to enter this country if they will start businesses and hire U.S. workers. Senators John Kerry and Richard Lugar offered a version of this start-up visa in 2010. It would have given a new visa to immigrant entrepreneurs who had raised at least $250,000 in outside capital. The capital requirement, no doubt, was added as a way to limit opposition to the proposal and also possibly to screen only for immigrants whose businesses could eventually scale.

The bill's capital threshold is considerably lower than the one in the existing "entrepreneur's visa" program, the EB-5, which carries a $1 million capital requirement (or $500,000 if the investment is in a business in an economically "distressed" area). But $250,000 is still a lot of money. It would clearly bar entry by many immigrants whose businesses do not require this amount of outside funding and yet are capable of launching businesses that hire Americans and later grow from self-financing or with outside capital once they've established a track record. Accordingly, the $250,000 capital requirement in the bill would have put a very tight limit on the numbers of potential immigrants who could benefit from it, and thus also limit the benefits to the nation.

To their credit, the two senators were responsive to the concerns about their initial bill, and in early 2011 introduced a revised version of their Start-up Visa Act. The new approach provides three different channels for immigrant entrepreneurs to come into the country, each channel having a significantly lower capital threshold than was the case in the previous proposal. Permanent green card status would be awarded only after the firms launched by the immigrants hire a minimum number of American residents. But the new version of the bill, like the earlier one, still caps the total number of start-up visas at 10,000 per year. Nonetheless, given the continuing controversy over broader immigration reform, it is not clear at this writing (November 2011) what the chances are that Congress will be able to pass even the narrower revised version of the Kerry-Lugar bill before the 2012 presidential elections.

At some point, however, if the economic recovery continues to be weak, the political case for passing reforms that bring in more immigrant entrepreneurs will grow stronger. Unlike the ideal solution of stapling green cards to STEM degrees, which could threaten the wages or possibilities of employment for some native-born Americans, start-up visas have only economic and political upsides. The visas would go to just job creators, so there aren't compelling reasons to oppose them. Indeed, this is the fundamental reason why *any cap* on immigrant entrepreneurs makes no economic sense. Politicians should easily be able to explain that these particular immigrants are different from all other immigrants because they will create more jobs for native-born Americans, and not "take" jobs from anyone.

If our political leaders need help explaining how this reform would work, they could point to Chile. That country recently passed "Start-up Chile," immigration reform that not only relaxes the entry requirements for entrepreneurs, but actually pays *$40,000* over a six-month period to three hundred highly promising would-be immigrant entrepreneurs each year. The program especially favors entrepreneurs who will use Chile as a global platform to build large-scale companies. Chile recognizes the obvious point that immigrant entrepreneurs create more jobs for domestic workers. I am told that the majority of the immigrants that Chile has let in under this new program are Americans.

Chile is both a warning sign and a challenge, because this kind of reform could easily spread to other countries, and thereby drain away even more talented Americans to build their companies abroad rather than here. Perhaps such policies are the kind of catalyst that will finally break the political logjam that so far has prevented narrower but highly important reform of U.S. immigration laws.

BREAK THE MONOPOLY UNIVERSITIES HAVE ON LICENSING INTELLECTUAL PROPERTY

Mention the need for the federal government to stimulate more innovation, and the response you are most likely to get is that Congress should spend more money on research and development. This impulse is well meaning, but it is also misplaced. First, spending money isn't the only way the federal government can encourage greater innovation. And second, given the budget shortfalls that face the nation in the years ahead, it is also an approach that is likely to end in failure (or at least come under continued pressure each year as Congress weighs spending).

But policy makers or citizens need not despair. By fixing the rules that govern the commercialization of faculty-developed innovations, the federal government can encourage more ideas and help bring them to market more quickly without having to spend any more money.

Typically, scientists sign a contract with their universities that includes two important elements. One part requires them to share any profits they may earn from the innovations they develop using the university's federal resources. The other key contract clause requires them to use their university's technology licensing office (TLO) to license all of their technologies. In other words, universities typically have a monopoly over the licensing rights of the intellectual capital their professors create.

We can now see that this monopoly stymies some innovation, or at least hampers the ability of scientists to bring their good ideas to the marketplace. But this monopoly actually grows out of an effort to create incentives for universities to support innovation and growth.

Back in 1980, Congress passed the Bayh-Dole Act, which gave universities the legal right to own the inventions discovered by their faculty when sponsored by federal research monies. This system has produced a steady stream of innovations that have raised living standards and expanded our economy.

We know, for example, that universities are increasingly becoming centers for innovation in America. One illustration of this fact is provided in an analysis of the top one hundred "most technologically significant new products" listed each year in *R&D* magazine. Fred Block and Matthew Keller report that universities and federal laboratories have become much more important sources of innovations over the last thirty-five years.[19] In 1975, for example, they note, private firms accounted for more than 70% of the R&D 100, while the academic institution share was just 15%. By 2006, just three decades later, these two shares were reversed: Academia contributed more than 70% of the top hundred innovations, while private firms accounted for about 25%. The Bayh-Dole Act seems to have given our universities a compelling reason to become far more active in commercially important research.

Academic entrepreneurship not only has been vital to U.S. economic growth in the past, but it could well be even more important in the future. As Jonathan Cole states in his impressive history of universities in the United States, "In the future, virtually every new industry will depend on research conducted at America's universities."[20] Given these facts, as we seek to spark significant economic growth in this country we must also confront the reality that no matter how successful the university innovation pipeline has been in the past, it must do better in the future.

One way to improve the flow of innovation would be to give faculty inventors ownership of their inventions or the intellectual property that results from their ideas. Doing so would give them an increased incentive to pursue ideas that have commercial applications. In a widely anticipated decision handed down in June 2011, the U.S. Supreme Court announced in *Stanford v. Roche* that Bayh-Dole does not automatically give universities the right to own their faculty inventors' intellectual property. Nonetheless, universities have a plausible counterargument that they deserve some of the gains from faculty-inspired successes because they pay their academics' salaries and give them a place to work.

It is virtually certain that universities will act on this strongly held view and find new contractual ways around the *Stanford v. Roche* decision (indeed, most university faculty contracts now require faculty to assign to their universities any IP rights in their inventions funded with government money).

Fortunately, there is one other straightforward way to better harness the genius of faculty inventors and give them broader incentives to commercialize their innovations, and at the same time benefit their home universities. Although university ownership of faculty discoveries has some rationale, there is no legitimate justification for universities to have a monopoly in deciding how to commercialize innovations. Universities don't act that way when it comes to faculty publications; why should they call all the shots on licensing of faculty ideas?

If faculty inventors had the freedom to make their own *licensing* decisions, they would no longer be at the mercy of TLO bureaucracies. A true market in licensing services would develop, just as it has for other inventors. Some universities might even specialize in licensing ideas from faculty across the country and thereby become particularly adept at bringing good ideas to market very quickly.

The agencies responsible for federal R&D funding could help development of such a market by simply requiring that universities that accept federal research grants also give their faculty freedom to license their ideas (if not initially, then perhaps after some short "right of first refusal period," such as ninety days). End this artificial monopoly on licensing and watch how the magic of the market can produce a win-win for all: benefiting universities with more licensing revenue and consumers with the more rapid availability of new products and services.

The only objections to this idea that I have heard have come from TLO officials themselves, who justify their positions (and salaries) by asserting that faculty inventors lack the knowledge and sophistication to license their technologies. If this were true—and I doubt it is—it would only be an argument for TLOs to provide information and training for faculty inventors who need or want it. This argument does not justify giving TLOs a monopoly on the decision of how and when to license or commercialize an inventor's ideas.

If so-called free agency for faculty inventors is deemed to be too radical, there is a fallback that government can easily pursue in the meantime. The University of North Carolina now has an "express license," which sets standard royalty rates (they are calculated as a percentage of sales and vary by industry). This allows faculty members to run with their ideas, rather than spending a lot of time working through their TLO to hammer out the fine points of a licensing agreement. The federal government could require universities to set up similar "express licenses" in order for them to receive federal research monies.

FINANCING SCALE COMPANIES

Home runs or less effective "hits" require financial muscle. Although a few privately owned firms can grow on internally generated funds, supplemented with some form of debt financing, truly scale companies at some point require publicly traded equity. Although such "initial public offerings" (IPOs) staged a modest comeback in 2011, especially with a new round of Web-based companies such as LinkedIn and Groupon, the annual numbers of IPOs since the bursting of the Internet bubble in 2000 have remained well below their prior peak, which in fact was reached in 1996, when more than 600 companies went public. During the decade spanning 2000 to 2010, the annual number of IPOs fell roughly in range of 50–150.[21]

Some falloff is natural because the numbers of IPOs were artificially inflated in the Internet bubble years, when, for a time, investors seemed more impressed with the eyeballs a company could claim on the Internet than with its cash flow. But there are other reasons as well for the dramatic decrease in IPOs.

One of them is a change in policy enacted in 2002. That was the year Congress passed the Sarbanes-Oxley Act (SOX), which significantly increased the cost of going public. SOX requires public companies to adopt many reforms related to financial reporting and corporate governance. And it was supposed to clean up corporate America after various accounting scandals (Enron and WorldCom topping the list) surfaced in the late 1990s and early 2000s. Among the more controversial, and ultimately most costly, of the new SOX requirements is that embodied in Section 404 of the act, which mandates that public companies certify the reliability of their "internal controls" and operating procedures.

Although members of Congress thought that the annual compliance costs associated with Section 404 would be no more than $100,000, actual expenses have proven to be much higher—by at least one estimate, $1.5 million, or an after-tax figure of about $1 million.[22]

This figure is a drop in the bucket for many large companies, but it is much more than an annoyance for rapidly growing companies that want to access the public capital markets. At a price-earnings ratio of 20, a not unreasonable figure for new-growth companies, a reduction in earnings of $1 million translates into a haircut in market value of $20 million. This is not an insignificant number for privately held companies with, say, market caps of around $100 million.

For several years after SOX was enacted, the Securities and Exchange Commission kept delaying the implementation of 404 for companies with market caps under $75 million, almost certainly for this reason. Eventually this exemption was made permanent as part of the Dodd-Frank financial reform legislation enacted in 2010.

The new permanent exemption is a step in the right direction, but Congress needs to do more. Although it is likely that SOX compliance costs have come down somewhat over time, as the SEC suggested in a report released in 2011,[23] Section 404 compliance costs still represent a significant reduction in market values for companies with market caps above the $75 million threshold. Many of these companies may not yet be in the black, so their after-tax compliance costs could still be in the $1 million range, which as the foregoing numerical example illustrates, represents a $20 million haircut off their market values. Even a somewhat smaller haircut, say $15 million, could act as a sizable deterrent to going public until sales and market value have reached higher levels. The catch-22 here is that going public is how many companies access the capital they need to scale. The problem with SOX is that it makes it too costly for companies to take the steps they need to take in order to vault themselves into faster-growing, larger, and perhaps more profitable companies.

Fortunately, there is a straightforward, sensible SOX reform that would remove its penalizing effects for would-be public companies: Simply give shareholders of companies below a threshold size (a market cap of $1 billion would be ideal) or during some initial period after going public (say, five years) the ability to decide whether to be covered by SOX. This would do a number of things, starting with only imposing costly SOX mandates on companies that can likely afford them or whose shareholders believe it is in their interest to have their companies subjected to all the SOX requirements. Giving shareholders the deciding voice on SOX compliance is a sensible reform. After all, SOX was enacted to protect shareholders. So shareholders should have the right to decide whether the reforms generate benefits for them in excess of their costs.[24]

There is also another policy reform, in addition to SOX, that could lead to a rise in IPOs in this country. A recent study that I conducted with my colleague Harold Bradley (chief investment officer at the Kauffman Foundation, and a longtime veteran of the equity markets)[25] suggested that exchange-traded funds (ETFs) give company officials compelling reasons not to go public.[26]

ETFs are financial instruments that bear a strong resemblance to mutual funds, but unlike those funds they can be traded throughout each day like stocks. The problem is not with all ETFs, but with just those funds that track small-company stocks, such as those making up the Russell 2000 index. And the issue is that ETFs that track small-company stocks typically have a trading volume that surpasses the trading volume of the stocks themselves. In these cases, trading in the ETFs can be far more important than trading in the underlying stocks. What's more, the values of the indices or other baskets the ETFs use to track small-cap stocks tend to lag behind the underlying value of the stocks themselves. For small-cap stocks, then, the ETFs become the proverbial tail that wags the dog.

Why should this matter? Because when investors are more interested in a basket of small-cap stocks than in the individual stocks within the basket, then information about the underlying stocks is not as relevant to investors as it is for larger-cap stocks. And more to the point, the whims of ETF investors thus become the dominant influence on the prices of the underlying stocks, rather than the underlying stocks influencing EFT investors. Knowing these facts, a private company that is trying to decide whether to go public could easily decide not to put its fate into the hands of rapid-fire traders of ETFs. Company executives understandably don't want to be the proverbial small boats on an ocean of capital, whose performance matters less to the market than the daily, and even hourly, shifts in attitudes of ETF traders.

Fortunately, there is an easy fix to this problem, too. Either prohibit ETFs from tracking small-cap companies with market caps below a certain threshold (such as $1 billion) or require ETF sponsors to gain the "opt in" consent of companies included in an index. This would likely mean that ETF sponsors would have to pay companies for the right to use their prices in an index, which could effectively halt the proliferation of small-cap ETFs.

Finally, and perhaps most important, entrepreneurs should be encouraged by public policy—tax policy in particular—to launch and grow scale companies, even before thinking of ever taking them public. Because of huge declines in computing and telecommunications costs, Web companies that have the potential to grow into the successful job-producing firms we need can be started without much—or any— outside financing. But more capital-intensive businesses in life sciences and clean energy, to take two prominent examples, generally do require outside investors, especially to cross over the "valley of death" in which many start-ups with good ideas fail for lack of adequate funding.

One powerful way to motivate investors to invest in such companies would be to exempt from any capital gains taxation any common or preferred equity investments in new enterprises if held for at least five years. Such a benefit would reward only patient capital and would be available to founders, limited (and general) partners of venture capital funds, and angel investors alike. Essentially this idea has been proposed by the Obama administration, but at this writing, congressional action on it is bound up with a larger debate over reform of the entire income tax code and what and how much spending to cut as part of a long-term deficit reduction package.

■   ■   ■

The U.S. economy faces its greatest challenge since the Great Depression, not just in recovering from a deep recession, but in finding ways to boost growth on a sustained basis. The launch and growth of new-scale firms will be central to meeting that challenge. Government must do its best to help and not hinder that process. And fortunately, there are significant things policy makers can do right now that do not carry with them large price tags or significant political risks. We know that start-ups produce the economic growth and jobs American workers depend on. By looking at the details of public policies and identifying where those policies put roadblocks in the way of the entrepreneurs, we can also determine which policies to change and how.

I've identified three ideas that involve bringing in more human capital, unleashing the creative innovators in our universities, and pulling out the obstacles that stop companies from going public and thereby gaining the resources they need to scale up to become the job-creating firms we need. Start-ups will likely power us toward greater economic growth. What we need to do is adopt policies that empower start-ups to get off the ground, quickly grow to scale, and become the leading firms of the future.

Chapter 11

The Role of Intangibles

By Nick Schulz

The United States is a rich country, the wealthiest large nation in the history of the world. But where does America's wealth come from? Part of it comes from our "amber waves of grain" and "fruited plains," as one of America's great national hymns puts it. And some of it comes from our industrial and manufacturing plants in the Northeast, the Great Lakes regions, and the Midwest. And still more of it comes from a hardworking labor force.

But while all these things are important to the American economy, they account for a small portion of our national wealth. The greatest source of American wealth is found elsewhere and is sometimes hard to see. That's because while the tangible sources of wealth noted above are important, it's America's *intangible* sources of wealth that have enabled it to become the richest nation of all time.

SOURCES OF WEALTH THAT ARE TANGIBLE AND INTANGIBLE

When looking for ways to kick-start economic growth, it's natural for human beings to focus on things they can see and touch. We think about fertile land producing food and agricultural goods for trading in global markets. Or we envision capital-intensive factories and heavy equipment churning out new products. Or we bring to mind a large labor pool providing services to satisfied customers.

And so what does a politician or policy maker do when he wants to communicate to the public that he cares about economic growth? He might go visit a factory near Detroit that builds tractors. Or he might visit a solar power array in the desert Southwest and talk up the importance of "green" jobs. Or he might visit a farm in the country's heartland and extol the virtues of farming and farm labor.

And make no mistake, this trio of traditional factors of production—land, labor, and capital—matters for economic growth. But it's not the only thing that matters. Indeed, it may not be the most important thing.

Over the past several decades, a new view of economics has started to emerge. This view focuses less on the tangible factors of production and more on invisible and intangible sources of wealth and growth. While these are things we cannot necessarily see or touch, they are nonetheless critical to economic success or failure. Indeed, over the long run, hardly anything else really matters.

So what is meant by these intangible factors of production? These include a nation's laws and rules; social norms and culture; entrepreneurship; attitudes about the future and about change; willingness to take risk; the ability to start new businesses easily; the receptivity of the market to new goods and services; and the overall quality of formal and informal institutions.

We know these intangible factors are important when we consider differences in economic performance over time. Tangible factors just don't fully account for the gaps.

Consider North Korea and South Korea. These two countries provide a dramatic but very useful example. There are no categorical differences between the two countries when it comes to land, labor, or capital inputs. But South Korea has experienced more than four decades of extraordinary economic growth, while North Korea's economy has performed miserably and in some ways has actually moved backward. If we want to understand the differences between the two, we need to focus on differences that are harder to see, such as their governance structure, the rule of law, and individual freedom.

Or consider the experience of Hong Kong. The city-state has always lacked such traditional factors of production as fecund agricultural land, a huge population, or large factories. And yet Hong Kong has long boasted economic growth rates and a high standard of living that are envied by the vast majority of mankind. Now, contrast Hong

Kong's experience with Argentina's. The South American giant has marvelous farmland and a big population. It has been able to attract and develop its own heavy capital stock. But it has experienced disappointing growth rates for much of the 20th and 21st centuries.

THE SOFTWARE LAYER

One way to think about the importance of intangible factors of production is to think about your computer. A computer is a tool for making you more productive. But from a productivity standpoint, what is most important about your computer? Is it the hardware in front of you—the screen, the keyboard, the battery, and so on? Or is it the software that you can't see or touch but that is running within the computer?

Two people can have identical hardware systems, but if they operate different software, they are likely to get very different productivity results. For example, imagine one computer is running software that consists of elegant code, with no bugs. The experience of the user is smooth and he is able to be as productive as possible. Now imagine another computer that looks the same because it has the same hardware. But that computer runs on flawed software, filled with bugs that jam the computer, force the user to restart multiple times, and lose important work. Which computer is more productive?

The economy is akin to a computer with hardware and software. Imagine two economies with the same "hardware" in that they have the same visible inputs of land, labor, and capital. But the economies differ in that they have different software operating systems. One country has honest government, the rule of law, and respect for property and contracts. It has a competent bureaucracy. And its cultural norms encourage saving, thrift, and hard work.

Now imagine another economy with corrupt governance and little respect for private property. Its civil servants are not interested in the long-run welfare of the country. Wealth can be confiscated by the authorities without warning or justification. It is not difficult to imagine which country's economy will perform better over time.

A simple example will help illustrate the point. One of the critical intangible factors of production for a country is its type of government—a democracy will have different rule sets that govern the nation's economic order than, say, a monarchy or a communist system or a kleptocracy.

The chart below divides the countries of the world into quartiles and ranks them depending on how democratic they are. It then looks at the living standards as determined by per capita income.

Democracy and Living Standards[1]

Quartile Ranking in Democracy	Average Income per Capita, 2002
Bottom 25%	$1,000
Second quartile	$1,600
Third quartile	$3,700
Top quartile	$12,000

As you can see, this table shows that more democratic governments tend to be more prosperous than less democratic governments.

Different governance structures and systems are like different software operating systems. And these differences in the software layer of the economy are dramatic. Residents of countries in the top quartile have an average income that is twelve times the income of residents in the bottom quartile. Intangible factors—a nation's software—account for much of the disparity we see in economic performance among countries over time.

HOW MUCH DO INTANGIBLES MATTER?

Economists, social scientists, and policy makers have only gradually come to appreciate the important role played by intangible factors in economic growth. Is it possible to get a firm handle on just how much these intangibles matter? In recent years, scholars have made progress in quantifying the relative importance of intangible factors of production.

For example, researchers at the World Bank have attempted to measure where the true wealth of nations really resides. Their findings are striking. The bank's researchers created an index that accounts for the natural, produced, and intangible capital in more than one hundred countries. Natural capital consists of resources such as oil, natural gas, and minerals; cropland; forests; pastures. Think of America's great farm belt in states like Nebraska and Iowa. Produced capital is all of a nation's machinery, equipment, and infrastructure. Think of America's chip fabricators in the Southwest and its steel mills in Pennsylvania and Ohio. Intangible capital is the difference between the total wealth of the nation and the combination of natural and produced capital.

"The most striking aspect of the wealth estimates," the researchers note, "is the high values for intangible capital. Nearly 85 percent of the countries in our sample have an intangible capital share of total wealth greater than 50 percent."

It is clear from the World Bank's findings that intangible capital matters greatly to economic success. Each resident of a low-income country has $4,434 worth of intangible capital available. Meanwhile, each citizen of a high-income country has an average of $353,339 worth of intangible capital at her disposal.

What's more, in high-income countries, intangible capital is a greater proportion of total wealth than in low-income countries. The natural capital that we see all around us, while still very important to poor countries, accounts for an insignificant amount of total wealth in rich countries. In poor countries, for example, natural capital—the minerals, oil, natural gas, forests, and so on—accounts for over one-quarter of total wealth. In rich countries it is a mere 2% of total wealth. Meanwhile, 80% of the wealth of nations in rich countries is to be found in intangible sources—capital neither natural nor produced.

In the chart below you'll find rankings of several countries based on their natural capital, produced capital, intangible capital, and their overall wealth per capita.

Intangible Wealth Around the World[2]

Income Group	Wealth per Capita	Natural Resources Share	Produced Capital Share	Intangible Capital Share
Low-income Countries	$7,532	26%	16%	59%
Middle-income Countries	$27,616	13%	19%	68%

Income Group	Wealth per Capita	Natural Resources Share	Produced Capital Share	Intangible Capital Share
High-income Countries	$439,063	2%	17%	80%
Switzerland	$648,241	1%	15%	84%
Denmark	$575,138	2%	14%	84%
Sweden	$513,424	2%	11%	87%
United States	$512,612	3%	16%	82%
Germany	$496,447	1%	14%	85%
Niger	$3,695	53%	8%	39%
Congo	$3,516	265%	180%	-346%
Burundi	$2,859	42%	7%	50%
Nigeria	$2,748	147%	24%	-71%
Ethiopia	$1,965	41%	9%	50%

It may not surprise you to see that countries such as the United States, Switzerland, and Denmark have very high levels of wealth and high levels of intangible capital. But some of the countries on the list have not only low levels of intangible capital, but they have *negative* levels. You might ask yourself, how is that possible?

The negative value of intangible wealth per person in countries like the Congo or Nigeria is the result of government and social institutions that are so dysfunctional that their adverse effect on the average worker's output more than offsets the positive boost to output that workers would otherwise enjoy from their country's natural resources and produced capital. Again, think of a computer that is so hampered by bugs and viruses that it actually makes anyone who tries to use it less productive. The person might be better off working without a computer altogether. That is how damaging the software layer in these countries has become.

The differences among nations when it comes to their intangible characteristics helps explain and contextualize such contemporary debates as immigration. Given the enormous differences in living standards depending on the intangible components of a given nation, who can blame men and women for risking life and treasure to leave a dysfunctional system so they can find a better life in a nation with a different operating system? By the same token, those who live in a nation with healthy and well-functioning institutions are keen to make sure nothing undermines the delicate order that has made their nation's economy strong, resilient, and wealthy. As a result, it is hardly surprising that immigration generates such intense debate.

Of course, intangible factors do not exist in a vacuum. Different intangible factors affect and influence one another. For example, the existence of political corruption can influence the broader national culture and how ordinary citizens view savings and investment. Virtuous intangible factors can have a positive, self-reinforcing effect. Harmful intangibles can trigger a negative feedback loop, much like when a computer gets infected with malware, with its performance steadily worsening over time.

The World Bank's estimates are a good first effort at trying to quantify just how important the software layer of the economy is to overall economic well-being. As more researchers work on the importance of intangible capital, we can expect further refinements in the results. But understanding the importance of intangible capital will become even more apparent as we think of the critical driver of growth-enhancing innovation and productivity in an economy—the entrepreneur.

THE ROLE OF THE ENTREPRENEUR

Entrepreneur is a great word. Its literal translation is "undertaker," as in one who undertakes risk. Of course, in contemporary English when we think of an undertaker we think of a person who prepares dead bodies for burial. And in a certain sense an entrepreneur in an economic context does exactly that—through his efforts, he attempts to bury old ways of doing things to replace them with something new.

Joseph Schumpeter was the 20th century's greatest theorist of entrepreneurship, and he captured the undertaker role well when in a discussion on the nature of dynamic capitalism he said, "[T]he problem usually being visualized is how capitalism administers existing structures, whereas the relevant problem is how it creates and destroys them." Entrepreneurs as "undertakers" bury existing structures; but they can only truly destroy them if they create something better.

When we think of entrepreneurs today we think of innovators such as Steve Jobs, who delivered many new products that helped bury established products and business methods. The iTunes store and the iPod completely buried the old way of distributing music (Tower Records, R.I.P.).

Part of what makes Jobs such a compelling figure, however, is not his myriad successes. It is instead his failures. What's often forgotten in media stories about Jobs is that he failed often and in spectacular fashion many times in his career. His Apple 1 computer was a commercial flop. The Lisa computer was an expensive failure. Jobs was forced out of Apple in the middle of his career and founded a company, NeXT, that had some interesting technical accomplishments but was also a commercial flop.

Successful entrepreneurship often goes hand in glove with failure. That's because successful entrepreneurs learn from trial-and-error experience. While successful entrepreneurs are often called "visionaries," it's more accurate to think of them as stumbling and fumbling in the dark, feeling their way toward often fuzzy and inchoate new economic and technological realities. Good entrepreneurs are undeterred by messiness and failure. Instead, they embrace the chaotic nature of economic dynamism as it propels them forward in fits and starts to upend the status quo.

Entrepreneurs are the critical actors operating within the software layer of the economy. They are the agents of change, pushing new products, techniques, and business models into the economy. Their primary talent is overcoming resistance to change. Established economies are characterized by entrenched market actors, firms, and business methods. Those entrenched interests have much invested in the status quo and thus much they are hoping to protect. It's the role of the entrepreneur to be the skunk at the garden party, the undertaker who is bent on burying the old way of doing things at a time when many people think those old ways of doing business have a lot of life left in them.

As a result, entrepreneurs are not necessarily the most welcome people in society. The extent to which they are enabled or encouraged to disrupt existing arrangements depends on the culture within which they find themselves.

Cultures that are more accepting of productive entrepreneurship will grow more rapidly over time, as their economies become more efficient and innovative and better able to satisfy the wants of their citizens. Cultures that are less hospitable to entrepreneurship will do less well.

But how can we know how welcome a culture is to entrepreneurship? It is difficult to measure culture directly. So it's useful to develop some proxies, some objective gauges that indicate how welcome entrepreneurs are in a given country. The chart below presents the cost of obtaining a business license. It looks at the time and cost of obtaining legal status to operate a firm in different countries. Time is measured in days, and cost is measured as a share of per capita GDP in that country. The chart gives a good sense of how different countries feel about *new* companies. New firms are important to entrepreneurial dynamism. They are by definition less invested in the status quo. And they are often the originators of new products, techniques, technologies, and business models. A country that makes it easy to start a new business is more hospitable to productive entrepreneurship than a country that puts up obstacles and roadblocks.

Cost of Obtaining a Business License[3]

Country	GDP per Capita, 1999	Time (days)	Cost (share of per capita GDP)
U.S.	$30,600	4	0.0049
Canada	19,320	2	0.0145
United Kingdom	22,640	4	0.0143
Germany	25,350	42	0.1569
France	23,480	53	0.1430
Russian Federation	2,270	57	0.1979
Japan	32,230	26	0.1161
India	450	77	0.5776

Country	GDP per Capita, 1999	Time (days)	Cost (share of per capita GDP)
Kenya	360	54	0.5070
Egypt	1,400	51	0.9659
Top quartile of GDP per capita	24,372	24.5	0.10
Second quartile of GDP per capita	5,847	49.3	0.33
Third quartile of GDP per capita	1,568	53.1	0.41
Bottom quartile of GDP per capita	349	63.8	1.08

As you can see, countries with a high cost of obtaining a business license have lower living standards than countries with a low cost of obtaining a business license. Of course, many other factors influence a nation's overall standard of living. But we should not be surprised to find that countries or economic zones where entrepreneurs are not discouraged by law are able to grow more rapidly than those where they are relatively discouraged.

The extent to which a country regulates new business entrants matters greatly to overall economic performance. Researchers have found that stifling entrepreneurs and new firms often leads to a greater level of corruption across an economy.

In the process these constraints on entrepreneurs also lead to the creation of a larger black market sector of the economy. This has serious negative ramifications for a nation's economic well-being. A country with a large informal economic sector has a harder time providing basic public goods and services such as education or roads or infrastructure. As a result, its economy is weaker relative to countries with a large formal sector and a small informal sector.

The chart below looks at the size of the informal sector, as measured by its estimated percentage of gross national product (GNP). A large percentage is a sign that a nation's institutions are weak or performing poorly. The larger this underground economy, the more likely it is that property rights are not secure and thus the black market becomes for some a preferred place for conducting economic activity.

The Underground Economy[4]

Region/Country (regional lowest and highest countries shown)	Informal Sector as a Percentage of GNP, 2000
Africa, average	42%
South Africa	28.4
Zimbabwe	59.4
Asia	26
Japan	11.3
Thailand	52.6
Latin America	41
Chile	19.8
Bolivia	67.1
Eastern Europe	38
Slovak Republic	18.9
Georgia	67.3
Western Europe	18
Switzerland	8.8
Greece	28.6
United States	8.8

So it is clear that the regions with large informal sectors are also relatively less wealthy and developed.

Every nation has entrepreneurs. But it's always an open question how those entrepreneurs will choose to exercise their talents. When avenues to legitimate businesses and enterprises are blocked or made difficult by bureaucratic hassles and corruption, the natural entrepreneurs in these countries can be pushed toward unproductive entrepreneurial activity in the black market sector. It is there they are unencumbered by rules and regulations thwarting their ambitions.

Everyone is made worse off by this kind of arrangement—the entrepreneur whose talents and energies would be more fully developed in the formal sector of the economy; the customers who are denied many of the fruits of the entrepreneurs' efforts; and the broader society, which can't reap benefits in the form of tax revenues from formal economic activity.

LESSONS FOR POLICY MAKERS

What has been described so far in this chapter is a conceptual shift. The old way of looking at the economy was to focus on the tangible economic inputs—land, labor, and capital. But it turns out there's more—a lot more—to an economy than just the tangible inputs. What matters most are intangible factors of production. These include a nation's system of governance, its laws, its culture, its respect for property, and other rules of the road that govern economic arrangements and incentives that drive GDP.

The implications of this shift in worldview are profound. When policy makers think about encouraging economic growth, they shouldn't think about helping established companies or industries. They also shouldn't think about funding or encouraging specific new industries.

Instead, they should be thinking about the economy's software layer—the intangible factors that determine long-run economic growth and prosperity. Some of these factors will be difficult to influence directly. For example, a nation's culture is the product of its people, history, traditions, and mores that have been passed down for generations. While culture is influenced by public policy, it typically changes slowly over time.

But policy makers can think constructively about the way policy influences key institutional arrangements and work toward making those institutions more conducive to long-run, entrepreneurial growth. Consider the following areas of public policy that are key elements of the software layer of the economy:

REGULATION

No one should oppose the prudent regulation of industry. For example, harmful externalities, such as pollution, that result from economic activity must be addressed by wise public policy. But it's also the case that regulations can benefit some economic actors at the expense of others. Of particular concern is the way in which regulatory hurdles and obligations make it difficult for entrepreneurs and new firms to get going. Policy makers looking to kick-start long-run economic growth should review regulations on the books and determine if they are making it more difficult for entrepreneurs to start new businesses.

The United States can draw on its history to find inspiration. In the 1970s, a bipartisan group of congressmen and policy makers came together to push deregulation of trucking, telecommunications, airlines, and other industries. This deregulation enabled entrepreneurs to enter these markets and transform how business was done. The efficiencies and new technologies forced into the marketplace proved a huge boon for consumers, who benefited from lower costs and improved quality over time.

TAXATION

Like regulation, taxation is an essential government function, but it is one that can be done well or poorly. There is widespread agreement across the political spectrum that the current tax system in the United States is too complex and distorts behavior too much and should therefore be reformed.

One example is the corporate income tax. Over the last several decades, other developed nations have learned that excessive corporate taxation is self-destructive. The revenues generated are not enough to make up for the distortions the tax introduces, like encouraging firms to locate plants and operations elsewhere to avoid taxes. So today the United States—thought by many to be a "low-tax" jurisdiction relative to other countries and regions—has one of the highest corporate tax rates in the world. This is an area ripe for reform.

It also surprises many people to learn that the United States has one of the most progressive tax codes in the developed world. That fact should influence policy makers as they seek to address the country's difficult fiscal challenges while also ensuring robust economic growth. One starting point is to ask just how much more progressive the American tax system can become while maintaining incentives to save, invest, form capital, and build wealth.

TRADE

International trade is another area where the intangible rules of the road matter as much as the tangible products that are themselves traded. And here is an area where the software layer has improved greatly over time. The liberalization of trade over the past two generations has proved enormously beneficial to consumers, who enjoy the world's bounty at lower cost.

Lawmakers can always do more to help the software that governs global trade. In 2011, the United States enacted free trade agreements with Colombia, Panama, and South Korea. But there are a lot of other free trade agreements that could be worked out. New agreements that continue liberalizing trade laws can be pursued over time.

NEW KNOWLEDGE

A significant source of intangible wealth is the stock of scientific and technical knowledge upon which innovators and entrepreneurs rely to develop new products and industrial platforms. This stock of knowledge is part of the overall stock of wealth available to people in the United States and around the world.

Policy makers can help expand that stock of knowledge by supporting basic research and development. Too often policy makers are tempted to support targeted research and development, pushing specific technologies or products. In this manner they end up picking winners and losers in the marketplace. This undermines the overall entrepreneurial landscape by encouraging a form of political entrepreneurship whereby entrepreneurs attempt to game the political system to their advantage instead of focusing on bringing new products and business practices to market that are demanded by consumers.

The private sector is best positioned to develop targeted R&D. The government can make a positive impact funding basic research, where the private marketplace has less incentive to invest.

■ ■ ■

Nobel Prize–winning economist Robert Lucas captured well the importance of thinking about intangible factors of economic growth when he said in 1988: "Is there some action a government of India could take that would lead the Indian economy to grow like Indonesia's or Egypt's? If so, *what*, exactly? If not, what is it about the 'nature of India' that makes it so? The consequences for human welfare involved in questions like these are simply staggering: Once one starts to think about them, it is hard to think about anything else."

It's hard to think about anything else because the beneficial humanitarian effects of sustained economic growth are so great: elevated living standards, greater social harmony, tolerance, peace, improved health, and education. It is difficult to think of a public policy goal that is more worthy than this.

Most important of all for policy makers is to grasp the importance of the intangible factors that yield robust economic growth. Policy makers must ask themselves what laws, rules, and regulations are inhibiting growth. They must ask what elements of a nation's culture are conducive to economic growth and make sure those elements are respected and bolstered. They must tolerate a certain messiness and unpredictability that are characteristic of dynamic, entrepreneurial economic growth. In this way, the goal of 4% growth for the United States can move from the realm of aspiration to reality.

Chapter 12

The Virtuous Cycle

By Maria Minniti

If **we were** to ask a sample of the population whether entrepreneurship matters for economic growth, the likely answer would be a unanimous yes. If we were to ask the same question to a group of policy makers, the answer would be definitely a resounding yes. In fact, it is difficult to find a recent political speech given about the state of the economy and ways to improve it in which the word *entrepreneurship* is not used repeatedly. Interestingly, we would get the same affirmative answer if we were to ask this question to a group of academics from various disciplines.

Indeed, recent years have seen an increased focus, both in policy and academic realms, on the entrepreneur as the driver of economic change and growth.[1] The importance of the entrepreneur in economic development has also been recognized by key international aid organizations. The World Bank, the U.S. Agency for International Development (USAID), and the International Monetary Fund (IMF) have all undertaken initiatives to understand and promote entrepreneurship in developing countries.[2]

Yet the role of the entrepreneur—why he is driven to innovate and how he, precisely, creates economic growth—is not well understood by policy makers or the general public. Thus, understanding the role entrepreneurship plays in the economy is critically important. As governments invest large volumes of capital in public policies, we need to understand whether those policies really will encourage entrepreneurs to create new jobs and increase economic growth.

■ ■ ■

Traditionally, analyses of the sources of wealth creation tended to focus on large corporations and neglected the role played by newer and smaller firms. Recent research, however, has shown that small and newer firms generate a significant amount of innovations, fill market niches, and increase competition, thereby promoting economic efficiency. Indeed, a realistic model of the economy involves the interplay of established, new, and small firms.

Understanding this interplay gives us a clearer understanding of why entrepreneurship is vital to the growth of the economy. In fact, the entrepreneur has a dual role engaging in productive activities. The first is to discover previously unexploited profit opportunities. This pushes the economy toward greater economic and technological efficiency. The second role takes place via innovation. In the role of innovator, the entrepreneur shifts the entire production possibility frontier outward. This shift represents the very nature of economic growth—an increase in real output due to increases in real productivity.

The purpose of this chapter is to explore the complex relationship between entrepreneurship and economic growth. Markets and competition are the two necessary conditions for economic growth. However, markets and competition work only because of risk-bearing and other important functions performed by entrepreneurs. This chapter will argue that there cannot be sustained economic growth without entrepreneurship.

WHAT DO RESEARCHERS KNOW ABOUT THE RELATIONSHIP BETWEEN ENTREPRENEURSHIP AND ECONOMIC GROWTH?

Although the relationship between entrepreneurial activity and economic growth is often taken for granted, the exact nature of such a relationship and the channels that allow entrepreneurial activity to influence growth are still largely unknown.

Economic growth has been of public and academic interest for a very long time, but it was not until the early 1950s that scholars began paying systematic attention to the need for sustainable growth. This was largely due to the fact that before World War II, researchers studying growth had focused primarily on wealthy economies and on the causes and effects of the industrial revolution. In other words, no scientific attention had been devoted to the reasons why some countries had grown rich and prosperous over time while others, with otherwise similar characteristics, had remained trapped in stagnant poverty.

Influenced by the experience of the industrial revolution and by the success of the Marshall Plan in postwar Western Europe, the wisdom of the time was that investment and savings, and their ability to mobilize a surplus of capacity in the labor market, were the key to achieving economic growth. It was thought that the accumulation of capital (which could then be invested) was the cornerstone of growth. It was on the basis of this analysis that large international organizations such as the World Bank spearheaded massive transfers of capital from wealthy to poorer countries—in the belief that such transfers would fill the gap in savings and put those countries on the same growth trajectory that North America, Western Europe, and even the Soviet Union had followed.

It was in this intellectual climate that, in 1956, Nobel laureate Robert Solow published his famous model of economic growth. According to Solow, the production of goods and services resulted from the interaction of capital and labor, and increases in production were possible thanks to technological advancements.[3] Going beyond the limited wisdom of his time, Solow's argument postulated that investment alone could not sustain growth and that technological change was necessary to increase the productivity that the interaction between capital and labor could produce.

He was right. But unfortunately, his model failed to explain how technological change comes about, and it failed to include the entrepreneur.

A shift in our understanding of economic growth occurred only significantly later, in the 1980s and '90s. Economist Paul Romer developed Solow's idea by incorporating technological change into his model. Romer's theory of economic growth included mechanisms that linked human capital to the creation of new technologies. In his view, technological progress was determined by the characteristics and capabilities of the people and firms in the economy.[4] The intuition behind Romer's theory is that research and development (R&D) expenditure produces knowledge, which in turn leads to technological change and growth. The knowledge generated by technological changes, however, spills over to other individuals, thereby increasing their ability to produce additional inventions. Thus a positive externality is set in motion that allows sustainable and possibly increasing technological change over time.[5] Research on "endogenous" growth, or growth developing within the economy, represents the state of the art on the causes and structure of economic growth, and it helps us understand the spreading and emergence of technological change and its relationship to growth.

Unfortunately, however, although the focus of economic thinking moved from investment in physical capital to investment in human capital, endogenous growth models continued to neglect the role of entrepreneurship in generating sustainable growth and economic development. Only in the late 1990s did it become evident that these models could not account easily for countries where growth has been remarkable in recent years even in the absence of significant expenditure in R&D, or for countries where plenty of expenditure in R&D has generated little if any growth.[6]

Over the past ten years, economists have worked to better understand what the distinctive characteristics of entrepreneurs are[7] and to incorporate explicitly what their role is in the process of economic growth.[8] Among studies that consider the role of the entrepreneur, economist Claudio Michelacci[9] has proposed a model of endogenous growth in which technological change requires both researchers (who produce inventions) and entrepreneurs (who transform those inventions into economically viable ventures). Michelacci's work shows that entrepreneurs are a key element to growth; without them R&D investments yield very little return. We need entrepreneurs in order to convert new, innovative ideas into tangible gains for the economy.

One of the important contributions of endogenous growth theory is the idea that investments in human capital create economic growth through the spillover of knowledge. In other words, as new ideas are developed, those ideas spark creativity and imitation among others. Zoltan Acs, David Audretsch, and a few other economists have argued that the link that connects economic growth to entrepreneurial activity is the mechanism that converts knowledge into "economically relevant" knowledge. They focus on entrepreneurship as the critical element that converts knowledge into commercializable knowledge (products and services that consumers will buy).

As in the works discussed above, the recent growth literature that does include entrepreneurs focuses on their role as agents who bring research-based technological discoveries to the market. Nevertheless, the characterization of technological change or innovation (the two words are used synonymously) is not sufficiently refined. As a result, there isn't enough attention paid to the fact that innovation and technological change may result from a variety of activities and that only some of those activities require R&D expenditure, but all of them require the presence of entrepreneurs. Moren Lévesque and I collaborated on research published in 2010[10] that looked at the gap between R&D and entrepreneurial activities that lead to growth. In our research we realized that the characterizing features of entrepreneurs are their alertness to opportunities[11] and their willingness to incur up-front costs, not their involvement with original technological discoveries that, instead, only differentiate their types. Building on existing scholarship,[12] Lévesque and I showed that higher economic growth is found when the number of research-based or imitative entrepreneurs, or both, is increased. Specifically, we argued that entrepreneurs are the lubricant for the engine of economic growth.

Whether imitating an existing product or technology or transforming a new invention into a marketable technological change, entrepreneurs are the economic actors who make growth possible. And they do that by risking their own capital in exchange for an expected profit. Which type of entrepreneur is more important for economic growth depends on the type of country or specific economic circumstance.[13]

For example, in a relatively rich country, growth is generated by increases in productivity. To remain competitive, such a country will need more original technological discoveries than poorer countries do. On the other hand, a country characterized by a large quantity of unused resources may increase its wealth simply by mobilizing those resources. This country may specialize in imitating technology developed elsewhere and, depending on the level of development of the country and the cost of technological change, imitative entrepreneurs may be more important than research-based entrepreneurs. So determining which type of entrepreneur is more important for growth is country-specific, and answering the question requires careful empirical analysis.

WHAT DOES THE DATA SAY ABOUT THE RELATIONSHIP BETWEEN ENTREPRENEURSHIP AND ECONOMIC GROWTH?

Clearly, entrepreneurship is a complex phenomenon and can be found in a variety of settings and situations. Thus no single measurement, no matter how precise, can capture the entrepreneurial landscape of a country. This is why the empirical literature addressing the relationship between entrepreneurship and economic growth is broader than the theoretical one, spanning a large variety of methods (ethnologic approaches, case studies, interviews, surveys, and countrywide indicators) and countries. In most macroeconomic studies that are relevant to our current discussion, entrepreneurship is measured through self-employment, the prevalence of start-up initiatives, or the existence of new or small businesses. Although these measures can all be criticized on various grounds, each of them provides important insights. For example, recent studies have shown the existence of a systematic relationship among the per capita GDP of a country, its economic growth, and its level and type of start-up activity.

Countries with similar per capita GDP tend to exhibit a similarity in both the prevalence and type of new firm formation, while significant differences exist across countries with different levels of GDP per capita. At low levels of per capita income, start-ups provide job opportunities and scope for the creation of new markets. As per capita income increases, the emergence of new technologies and economies of scale allows larger and established firms to satisfy the increasing demand of growing markets and to increase their relative role in the economy.

This increase in the role of large firms is usually accompanied by a reduction in the number of new firms, since a growing number of people find stable employment in large industrial plants. As further increases in per capita GDP are experienced, however, the role played by the entrepreneurial sector increases again, as more individuals have the resources to go into business for themselves in an economic environment that allows the exploitation of opportunities. In high-income economies, through lower costs and accelerated technology development, entrepreneurial firms enjoy a newfound competitive advantage.[14]

As a result of the analysis just described, some agreement has begun to emerge among scholars that the empirical relationship between entrepreneurship (using as a proxy the number of start-ups) and economic growth (proxied by per capita GDP) can be illustrated by a shallow inverted U function as shown in Figure 1 below.[15]

Figure 1

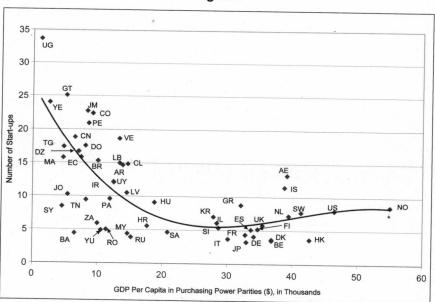

Economists Sander Wennekers and Roy Thurik,[16] for example, have suggested the existence of a U-shaped relationship between the number of self-employed individuals and the stages of economic development. Similarly, economists André van Stel, Roy Thurik, and Martin Carree[17] have found that entrepreneurial activity by early stage entrepreneurs affects economic growth, but that this effect depends on the level of per capita income. This suggests that entrepreneurship plays a different role in countries in different stages of economic development. Entrepreneurship researcher Leo Dana,[18] for example, has shown that the business environment in Uruguay does not lend itself to the reproduction of entrepreneurial policies that have been successful in Argentina even though the two countries have much in common. Along similar lines, entrepreneurship researcher G. A. Giamartino[19] has argued that when one considers many developing economies around the world, it is not unreasonable to conclude that the status of internal and external components varies widely across countries and within regions of countries and that these differences may lead to different experiences in how entrepreneurship influences economic development.

If we accept the definition of an entrepreneur as someone who is alert to opportunities and willing to incur up-front costs, Figure 1 shows that entrepreneurial activity will tend to be higher in countries with lower levels of GDP than entrepreneurial activity in high-income countries, but that after bottoming out, the rate of entrepreneurship increases again as a country become wealthier.

Although this may seem counterintuitive, we need to remember that innovation is context-specific. Entrepreneurship can take many forms. We also need to remember that the poorer a country is, the more unexploited opportunities there are, and many of those opportunities might consist of very simple subsistence activities.

It is also important to point out that, although the idea of a U-shaped relationship illustrates an association between entrepreneurship and economic growth, in fact the linkage between entrepreneurship and macroeconomic activity is complex. Different levels of development determine the environment in which entrepreneurial decisions are made and, as a result, determine the type, quality, and quantity of entrepreneurship in a country. In turn, the type, quality, and quantity of entrepreneurship contribute to the growth and development of that country. Thus it may be said that a "virtuous cycle" characterizes the relationship between entrepreneurship and aggregate economic activity. Entrepreneurship can create economic growth, which in turn creates new conditions that lead to different types of entrepreneurship. Such a virtuous cycle therefore can not only lead to new entrepreneurship, but can also influence the type of entrepreneurship a country experiences.

However, it is also important to know what motivates individuals to start businesses, since motivation influences what type of businesses will be created and for what purposes. For example, researchers have shown that it is important to distinguish between business owners who start their ventures out of necessity and those who do so out of opportunity.

Back in 1943, economist Alfred Oxenfeldt[20] argued that individuals confronted with unemployment and low prospects for formal employment will turn to self-employment as a viable alternative. Thus high unemployment should be associated with increasing start-up activity because the opportunity cost of starting a firm is lower.[21] Additional empirical evidence from poorer and developing countries confirms this hypothesis and shows that this is particularly true for the uneducated and for women. Facing the reality that there are few employment opportunities available to them, individuals in poorer countries will start new business ventures.

On the other hand, new ventures hire workers, enter markets with new products or production processes, and increase efficiency by increasing competition.[22] In addition, people who have a job are more likely to start a business because they are more likely to have sufficient resources to do so and a financial cushion to fall back on if the venture does not succeed. These contradicting effects are reflected in the fact that while some studies hypothesized and found evidence of a positive link between unemployment and entrepreneurship, others have found evidence supporting a negative link.[23] As a result, the relationship between labor market conditions and entrepreneurship (described as start-up activity) cannot be univocally determined.

To make things more complex, economist David Blanchflower, writing in *Labour Economics* in 2000,[24] found no positive impact of self-employment rates on GDP growth. Other economists, however—such as Carree, van Stel, Thurik, and Wennekers[25]—have suggested that countries with relatively low self-employment rates benefit from increased self-employment in terms of GDP growth, but that countries with relatively high self-employment rates do not. In other words, the state of the labor market seems to play an important role in the relationship between entrepreneurial activity and economic growth. The state of the labor market also seems to determine the type of entrepreneurship a country experiences, which in turn also influences growth. How this relationship works exactly, however, is not easy to determine.

Dutch economist Roy Thurik, referenced above, and his coauthors[26] tested empirically self-employment and unemployment using a rich data set of OECD countries. They found that increases in unemployment have a positive impact on subsequent rates of self-employment while, at the same time, increases in self-employment rates have a negative impact on subsequent unemployment rates. Because these are dynamic intertemporal relationships, previous studies estimating contemporaneous relationships had confounded what are, in fact, two relationships each working in opposite directions and with different time lags. What Thurik and his colleagues have proven is that the net impact of entrepreneurial activity on macroeconomic performance increases with per capita income. Their robust empirical results confirm that entrepreneurship has a positive (albeit slow) effect on economic growth.

So why do countries with comparable levels of per capita GDP exhibit different levels of entrepreneurial activity? The reason is that, ultimately, *people* start businesses, and *people* do not act in a vacuum. But what drives people to start businesses? What conditions create entrepreneurs or spur entrepreneurship? To answer that, let's take a look at the incentives involved in entrepreneurship.

ENTREPRENEURIAL DECISIONS AND INSTITUTIONAL INCENTIVES

Nobel laureate Douglass North demonstrated why institutional change matters in terms of creating incentives. His work essentially allows us to understand the dynamics involved—why certain incentives spark entrepreneurial activity in one setting, but don't spark such activity in a different setting.

According to North,[27] formal and informal institutions influence the behavior of individuals of all cultures and traditions, and, regardless of cultural background, the same individuals will tend to act very differently under different sets of institutional circumstances. Entrepreneurship is universal (the desire to innovate, take risks, and so on exists everywhere). Thus when applied to entrepreneurship, North's theory of institution suggests that certain types of incentives are more conducive to entrepreneurship and that basic rights such as freedom, certainty of the law, and personal safety are necessary, albeit not sufficient, conditions for productive entrepreneurship to take place anywhere in the world.

This has major implications for the way we understand economic change and progress (or lack thereof). Alertness to unexploited opportunities and willingness to bear risk are universal human characteristics that can be found everywhere, and regardless of level of development. Thus the question we need to ask is no longer how to create more entrepreneurial individuals, but how to motivate individuals to behave entrepreneurially and to channel their entrepreneurship toward beneficial activities.

In 1990, economist William Baumol developed what has since become a key component of our understanding of why specific levels of entrepreneurship emerge in different countries. Baumol argues that the institutional environment of a society determines the relative payoffs attached to various opportunities. He goes on to argue that these payoffs direct the entrepreneurial efforts of individuals toward activities where the returns are relatively higher. In other words, entrepreneurs will gravitate toward the activities that will earn them higher profits.

Thus, in order to experience a virtuous cycle between entrepreneurs and economic growth, what we need is the right institutions—such as, say, a body of law that protects property rights. If individuals can earn a profit by taking advantage of an opportunity (such as by starting a new business venture), we can expect them to do so. The exploitation of such opportunities will be beneficial for the community and country where these individuals live and work, and economic growth will follow. On the other hand, if the profits attached to this type of activity are low compared to, say, those provided by opportunities that have negative social implications (for example, by engaging in an illicit business), then individuals will undertake the latter. Some people will become richer, but the country as a whole will not grow.

Overall, we observe different outcomes from entrepreneurial behaviors because the type of opportunities yielding the highest returns varies across societies.[28] Economic growth and progress requires that higher payoffs be attached to productive entrepreneurial activities. Of course, the big question then becomes how to establish institutions that encourage entrepreneurial behavior toward productive activities.

Some recent research in economics provides interesting insights on the role that governments may play in fostering or hindering entrepreneurial behavior.[29] The number of studies in this area is quite significant, which reflects the increasing attention paid to entrepreneurship by governments at all levels around the world. Some researchers argue that entrepreneurship policies were developed as a measure to absorb workers displaced by corporate downsizing and privatization waves in the 1980s.[30] Others argue that entrepreneurship policies are emerging as one of the most essential instruments for economic growth and that, just as monetary and fiscal policy were the mainstays for creating employment and growth in the postwar economy, entrepreneurship policy is likely to emerge as the most important policy instrument for a global and knowledge-based economy.[31] Still others argue that even the success or failure of a transition economy can be traced in large part to the performance of its entrepreneurs, since much of the task of devising new ways of doing business in transition economies has been taken on by entrepreneurs who end up acting as reformers.[32]

Overall, the issue of what institutional environment is more conducive to growth is an open one. What we do know is that when it comes to entrepreneurship policy, one size does not fit all, and different types of entrepreneurship and different types of policy may be desirable depending on the level of per capita GDP in a country. As mentioned earlier, the exploration of opportunities that in some countries may be considered the source of mere subsistence activities may in fact make a significant difference in other contexts. There is not yet a general agreement among economists about the role of innovation, and whether it will necessarily lead to an increase in entrepreneurship. The two may be connected, but if so it is not a simple connection. Entrepreneurs need something more than a new idea to jump into the fray. They need institutions that can ensure they will profit from adding their creative energies to the innovations that are available.

Along similar lines, economists David Audretsch and Max Keilbach[33] have suggested that entrepreneurship is crucial in driving the process of selecting innovations, and hence in creating diversity of knowledge, which in turn serves as a mechanism facilitating the spillover of such knowledge across individuals. Their results support the hypothesis that the innovation efforts of firms lead to an increase in regional technical knowledge, which in turn improves local economic performance. In addition, regional innovation efforts are shown to increase entrepreneurship capital, which in turn also increases regional economic performance, albeit indirectly. Within this context, Paul Geroski[34] has pointed out that entrepreneurship plays a critical role in the behavior of large, established firms when they are faced with competitive pressure generated by new technologies. Indeed, a primary feature of entrepreneurship is its ability to generate experimentation. This means that the role of the entrepreneur is critical outside the specific contributions of each entrepreneur—without entrepreneurship sufficient experimentation will not occur. To understand how the entrepreneur contributes to growth, we must not only understand the virtuous cycle of entrepreneurship, but also consider the limitations that established firms may encounter in the absence of entrepreneurial strategies. Faced with new, emerging competition, established firms will start to experiment themselves with new ways of doing business and new technologies. This additional form of experimentation is vital to economic growth.

Finally, in recent years, a particularly important aspect of the entrepreneurial landscape has become countries' attitude toward external market openness, usually referred to as globalization. Globalization is an important element of entrepreneurship because the economic gains from international trade can enhance entrepreneurial incentives. In an economy open to international competition, entrepreneurs can seek out new market opportunities while, at the same time, they will have to meet the highest global standards. That pushes them to be increasingly efficient and to continue innovating in order to compete. This competitive element of globalization is perhaps the single most important push toward economic growth. Thus an institutional context aimed at promoting entrepreneurship must support the progressive liberalization of global markets.

■ ■ ■

To sum up, the entrepreneurial market process consists of the daily decision making of many independently acting entrepreneurs, each striving to establish and develop a business. The aggregate level of entrepreneurial activity and its relative distribution across alternative forms of entrepreneurship emerge as the unintended consequence of the actions taken by all independent entrepreneurs while attempting to exploit profit opportunities. Clearly, the process is decentralized and therefore unplanned, even though each individual entrepreneur makes his or her own plans. Thus, as Roger Koppl[35] has pointed out, "the entrepreneurial market process does not know where it is going until it gets there, nor does it need to. A government wishing to control the outcome of the entrepreneurial market process, however, must do what the market does not do: plan the overall result of the process in advance."

Koppl's argument is important because it shows that when entrepreneurship policy requires policy makers to predict the outcomes of the market process, it sets them up to execute a task that is truly impossible. Policies ensuring institutional transparency, stable monetary values, predictable taxation, and secure property rights do not require policy makers to compute specific outcomes in order to achieve their intended goal of promoting entrepreneurial ventures. Such policies are desirable and necessary to create the proper incentive system. In other words, these things are necessary to create the "rules of the game" by which individuals, and entrepreneurs, operate. Policy makers cannot predict which entrepreneurs will be winners and which ones will be losers. They can, however, put in place policies that protect the dynamics of the market and enable it to produce favorable outcomes. In other words, by creating the proper underlying conditions, policy makers can influence the institutional conditions that will allocate efforts toward productive rather than unproductive or destructive activities.

Policies that attempt to control outcomes, on the other hand, are not likely to succeed. By definition, entrepreneurs are individuals who deviate from the norm and who have superior knowledge and experience about a particular market and process. That is what gives them a competitive advantage and makes them perceive opportunities that others do not see. To control outcomes, policy makers would have to substitute their own decisions for those of entrepreneurs and be able to guess which start-ups should be more likely, let's say, to contribute the most new jobs to the economy. This is equivalent to saying that policy makers who wish to control or greatly influence the results of the entrepreneurial market process should be able to pick winners and predict the future. Policy makers would not only have to get the policies right, they would also have to guess which businesses to create and which ones will succeed. In a world where most start-ups fail within their first three years, that seems an arduous task, even for the most enlightened of policy makers.

Markets, on the other hand, have a crucial advantage over such overambitious policy makers in that they do not need to predict outcomes in advance. The process of alertness to unexploited opportunities, innovation, and competition generates the market discipline necessary to take the economy where it needs to go in the most efficient way.[36] Sometimes the process may take a long time, and sometimes it may involve economically painful side effects. Nonetheless, it is still the best way we have available for a country to grow. Growth needs entrepreneurs, not bureaucrats, no matter how well-meaning. Providing conditions conducive to productive entrepreneurship is challenging enough.

Entrepreneurs are a crucial element in the growth process. There is no growth without entrepreneurship. Governments wishing to promote productive entrepreneurship need to provide the proper institutional frameworks. This calls for justice, peace, certainty of the law, and fiscal transparency, among other important elements of the macro economy of a country. Within such a context, entrepreneurs then make their decisions and, through the trials and errors of innovation and the dynamics of competition, the virtuous cycle of entrepreneurship produces sustainable economic growth.

Chapter 13

Growth Needs Trade

By Carlos Gutierrez

I**t's not often** that a congressman tells you that he is about to vote against what he believes to be good for the country. So I was a little taken aback in 2005, when I was pressing for the passage of the Central American Free Trade Agreement (CAFTA) and found tepid support among some members who had backed trade measures in the past. One by one, they told me essentially this: They agreed that passing CAFTA would be in the best interests of the United States, but they were going to vote against it anyway.

It was disappointing to watch. For decades—really since the end of World War II—there has been strong bipartisan support for trade in this country. Presidents in both parties from Harry Truman to John F. Kennedy to George W. Bush had pushed for opening up trade. And in recent years other nations have heeded our call and have adopted the tenets of free trade. So at a point when we are finding new allies abroad willing to lower trade barriers, Congress is flirting with protectionism.

The reasons seemed clear enough. Some pressure groups, including labor unions, had come out against CAFTA, and the House Democratic leader, Representative Nancy Pelosi, called on all of her members to vote against the bill. Some members of Congress who might have otherwise supported the trade agreement worried that voting for CAFTA could cost them reelection and were therefore wavering.

In the end, CAFTA (which included trade provisions for Central American countries and the Dominican Republic) passed the Republican-controlled House by just two votes (217–215). It did so in large part because fifteen Democrats defied their leadership and voted for the bill. Afterward, I would often hail the "CAFTA 15" as courageous members who were willing to put immediate political demands aside and support legislation that in the long run would create jobs in America. But the episode was a warning sign. Bipartisan support for trade was starting to crack.

In the years that followed, I saw additional warning signs that the United States might turn away from trade. The United States had negotiated free trade agreements (FTAs) with Colombia, Panama, and South Korea before the end of the Bush administration. Each of these agreements seemed like an easy thing to support. Why? Because the United States typically has lower trade barriers than other nations, so these FTAs lowered barriers to selling our goods abroad. Yet each one of these agreements bogged down in Washington politics for years. They passed only in 2011, when high unemployment and an unsteady economy compelled lawmakers to act.

My concern has been that governments have a habit of making the same mistakes over and over again. The last time the United States went deep on protectionist policies was at the start of the Great Depression, with the passage of the Smoot-Hawley tariff.[1] What began as a misguided attempt to protect American jobs by imposing tariffs on goods made outside the country turned into a trade war that saw retaliatory tariffs imposed on our goods across the world. That trade war fed into the Great Depression, helped prolong high unemployment, and left America economically weaker than it should have been.

Trade is something that is often misunderstood and therefore too quickly maligned. In fact, free trade gives exporters access to new markets, and competition from imports forces firms to become more productive. Consumers in particular benefit from lower prices and more choice, which raises their standard of living. Almost all countries seem to recognize the benefits of trade, regardless of political leanings. Brazil, Chile, China, Vietnam, and Mexico have been active participants in trade. Chile, for example, has fifty-seven bilateral or regional trade agreements, the most of any country.[2] The development success stories of the last half of the 20th century are a clear testament to open economies.

Of course, trade also leads to change. And change is not only disruptive; it can be painful for workers in industries that shift jobs overseas. To help affected workers and communities, the federal government has traditionally provided Trade Adjustment Assistance (TAA) to those who lose their jobs due to increased imports. The program, which was first created in 1962 under the Trade Expansion Act and was later revised under the Trade Act of 1974, provides displaced workers with job training, income support, and relocation assistance.

However, TAA can only be a temporary help. The reality is that economies change. Imposing tariffs on imported goods to protect domestic industries is self-defeating for two reasons. First, as we saw with Smoot-Hawley in 1930, tariffs can lead to destructive trade wars that hurt everyone. And second, tariffs aren't able to hold back the economic tides. If jobs shift overseas because it is cheaper to produce a given product there, imposing a tariff will force Americans to pay more for goods than they should. That takes money out of the pockets of consumers while doing little to encourage American workers to shift to jobs or industries where they can be the global leader. In other words, high tariffs can make us a poorer and weaker country.

As in so many instances, overcoming the negative impact of trade so we can all reap the benefits of it comes down to leadership. As commerce secretary I visited communities in North and South Carolina. Some communities had seen the future years before and had planned ahead. It was clear that low-wage foreign competition would one day hurt the textile sector, so some community leaders realized they needed to get away from competing with poor countries on wages. Instead, these communities turned toward producing higher-end goods that required skilled workers. To do that, they attracted technology investments that supported higher-paying jobs.

Meanwhile, other communities featured leaders who chose the road of demagoguery; they insisted that the loss of textile jobs was the fault of free trade and railed against the economic tides washing over them. These would-be successors to Huey Long promised their communities that the textile mills would stay open forever. They were wrong, and as a consequence, their communities suffered. They failed to recognize the lessons of history.

Textile manufacturing began in Manchester, England, in the 18th century. Eventually the industry shifted out of England in favor of Massachusetts and other states in the Northeast. Those states later saw textile mills move again, this time to cheaper labor markets in the American South. In recent years, the textile mills have been on the move again. Now the trend favors Bangladesh, China, Honduras, Vietnam, and other countries. The lesson is that no one can stop an industry from moving to where it can run more profitably. Instead, the future of U.S. jobs will be in innovative high-value-added, differentiated products that are difficult to replicate. Sometimes these products will be manufactured goods (such as microchips) and other times they will be intellectual or service-oriented goods (such as financial products, computer software, and consulting services).

It seems to me that the leader who years ago confronted his constituents with the bad news did a greater service to his community than the politician promising outcomes that would be beyond his control to achieve. It can take months or years for workers to acquire new job skills, so it pays to have a head start on the process. It pays to have strong leadership.

■ ■ ■

The current trading system is a product of committed leadership over decades. It started with the creation of the General Agreement on Tariffs and Trade (GATT), which was signed in 1947. Although the GATT was only a provisional agreement, eight rounds of trade liberalization were signed during its existence from 1948 to 1994. The first few rounds focused on tariff reductions. Then in the 1960s and '70s the Kennedy Round and the Tokyo Round began to address nontariff barriers as well.

In 1994 the Uruguay Round expanded trade talks to new areas such as services and intellectual property, and established the World Trade Organization. The WTO was a significant step because it formalized how we resolve trade issues, including negotiating and implementing trade agreements and settling disputes. Both of these things—negotiating new pacts and resolving lingering disputes—have become increasingly important as countries sign new trade agreements and specific regions start acting as new unified trading blocs.

Europe has led the world in regional integration. In 1957 the Treaty of Rome created the European Economic Community, which led in 1993 to the creation of the European Single Market. Today, the European Union has twenty-seven members, seventeen of which use the euro as a common currency. One result is that trade within the EU is the largest for any unified bloc in the world—approximately $3.36 trillion worth of merchandise was traded inside the EU in 2010. In addition to integrating internally, the EU has been active in negotiating FTAs with others. In 2011 the EU struck a trade deal with South Korea and as this book went to press was negotiating agreements with the Association of Southeast Asian Nations (ASEAN),[3] Canada, India, Malaysia, Mercosur (a bloc that comprises Argentina, Brazil, Chile, Uruguay, and Paraguay), and Singapore.

The North American Free Trade Agreement (NAFTA) began a process of regionalization in the Western Hemisphere that has yet to be completed. In 1988 the United States signed an FTA with Canada and then expanded it to include Mexico in 1994 by passing NAFTA. The United States has also signed FTAs with Australia, Bahrain, Chile, Jordan, Morocco, Oman, Peru, Singapore, Israel, South Korea, Colombia, Panama, and five Central American countries (Costa Rica, El Salvador, Guatemala, Honduras, and Nicaragua), plus the Dominican Republic (CAFTA-DR). While the United States has more FTAs in the Western Hemisphere than in any other region, most of these trade pacts are agreements with individual countries. The U.S. trade agreements in the region are not linked together; this makes doing business more costly. With a unified trade agreement, where any two countries that have an FTA with the United States also have an FTA with each other, companies could establish more efficient supply chains that take advantage of individual country strengths. If we had this system, a lot of the textile trade, which the United States has lost to Asia, could have remained in the hemisphere with U.S. participation.

Perhaps the most significant example of the new drive toward regionalization—and one that should get our attention because it could prevent us from gaining easy access to a very large market—is China's goal of creating an integrated Asia through something called ASEAN + 3 (the ten Southeast Asian countries plus South Korea, Japan, and

China). If China succeeds at hammering together this trade agreement, it will create the largest trading bloc in the world, surpassing the EU as number one in a few years after implementation. An integrated Asia will not include the United States and will most likely establish the renminbi as the currency of settlement. In the United States, we wonder when China will make its currency fully convertible and increase its value; the change must happen well ahead of a regional agreement.

China joined the WTO in 2001 and has FTAs with ASEAN, Pakistan, Chile, New Zealand, Singapore, Peru, and Costa Rica. But it started to open its markets to international trade decades ago. Today, China's import-to-GDP ratio—a measure of openness—is about 25%, up from 7.5% in 1978. Even before joining the WTO, China was the fastest-growing market for our exports, and today it is our number-three export market and the number-one source of imports.[4]

In surveying this data, you will spot the trend. The world is moving toward bilateral and regional agreements, and those agreements don't always involve the United States. In fact, usually they do not. So as time goes on, the United States could find itself facing tariffs and other barriers to selling its goods in markets across the world. And each time we find ourselves on the outside looking in on other nations' FTAs, we'll be at a disadvantage. If we turn protectionist now, we could be outcompeted in part because we aren't a party to FTAs being negotiated around the world.

U.S. exporters are already at a disadvantage. The United States has FTAs with only seventeen countries. There are more than 260 FTAs in existence worldwide. The United States is involved in only one of the more than one hundred bilateral and regional trade agreements that were under negotiation as this book went to press. And in 2008 our best shot at a worldwide free trade agreement evaporated when the WTO's Doha Development Round collapsed. The goal of those negotiations was to iron out a comprehensive trade agreement that would cover all 140 countries in the WTO. Its collapse only increases the need for us to strike regional and bilateral agreements across the world. Unless the United States negotiates more FTAs, we will lose out to countries, such as China, that have a more active trade agenda than we do.[5]

■ ■ ■

Fortunately, if we do act there is plenty of reason to expect that expanding trade will help fuel a new economic boom in America. One constant bright spot in our economy, for example, has been our trade in services. For years we've run a trade surplus in telecommunication, financial, technical, and other professional services. In 2010, for example, we had a $146 billion trade surplus in services (compared to a $646 billion trade deficit in goods). The United States has a comparative advantage in services (our college system is one reason why), so in our trade negotiations we should be especially focused on opening up new markets to our service industries.

What's more, the statistics indicate that trade creates jobs and allows Americans to earn more money than they would otherwise. According to the Department of Commerce, exports support more than 10 million jobs in the United States. Between 2003 and 2008 the number of export-related jobs increased by about three million.[6] Furthermore, jobs in export industries tend to pay more. The Commerce Department's International Trade Administration estimates that "exports contribute an additional 18% to workers' earnings on average in the U.S. manufacturing sector."[7] Another study shows that in U.S. export-intensive service industries, workers earn 15–20% more than their counterparts in other service industries.[8]

In 2008, 19% of jobs in the U.S. agricultural sector were supported by exports[9] and 19% of U.S. agricultural commodity output was exported.[10] That means we produce about one-fifth more than what we consume and therefore our farms can sell our surplus to other nations. The USDA notes that "anywhere from 26–30 percent of farm cash receipts in any one year comes from exports," and that "every dollar of exports creates another $1.40 in supporting activities." Agricultural exports support about one million jobs in the United States.[11]

Manufacturing numbers are even more impressive: 27% of all U.S. manufacturing jobs are supported by exports; that accounts for 3.7 million jobs.[12]

Free trade agreements play an important role in U.S. trade overall. In 2009, U.S. trade with its FTA partners made up 31% of its imports and 38% of its exports. And U.S. exports to FTA partners generally grew much faster after an FTA was implemented compared to the three years before; furthermore, export growth to FTA partners has significantly outpaced growth to non-FTA partners. In other words, trade with FTA partners has been particularly important for expanding exports, as Table 1 from the U.S. Chamber of Commerce shows.[13]

Table 1
Average Annual Growth of U.S. Merchandise Exports to FTA Partner Countries

	Three Years Prior to FTA	Implementation of FTA through 2008
Australia	9.9%	11.7%
Bahrain	-6.6	30.3
Canada	6.7	5.0
Chile	-8.0	36.3
Dominican Republic	7.9	11.9
El Salvador	3.5	10.0
Guatemala	10.5	19.1
Honduras	7.7	14.3
Israel	-5.1	7.1
Jordan	0.4	15.4
Mexico	9.5	6.1
Morocco	-1.8	44.6
Nicaragua	11.8	20.5
Singapore	-2.3	11.6
Total of 14 FTAs	3.2	17.4
Non-FTA Countries, 1998–2008	6.0	

Source: Bureau of the Census

FTAs have had significant benefits for the U.S. economy. A 2010 study by the U.S. Chamber of Commerce shows that U.S. FTAs led to an increase in exports of $462.7 billion in 2008 and supported 5.4 million jobs.[14] Dan Griswold of the CATO Institute notes that both U.S. exports and imports with our fourteen most recent FTA partners[15] have grown more quickly than overall U.S. trade since the enactment of each agreement. Thus FTAs both expand export opportunities for U.S. producers and lower prices for U.S. consumers. But contrary to fears that recent FTAs would undermine U.S. jobs and competitiveness, manufacturing exports have actually grown faster than imports with those fourteen FTA countries. The U.S. manufacturing trade surplus with these countries improved from under $7 billion ten years ago to $36 billion in 2010. Why the increase? Before signing a trade agreement, U.S. FTA partners tended to have higher barriers against U.S. exports than we imposed on their goods.[16]

The United States does more two-way trade in goods with the six CAFTA-DR countries ($48 billion in 2010) than it does with either Russia ($31.7 billion) or Indonesia ($23.4 billion), and about the same as with India ($48.8 billion).[17] In spite of that, CAFTA-DR was particularly controversial. But as Griswold notes, U.S. manufacturing exports to the six countries covered by this agreement increased by 34%, while manufacturing imports increased 25% between 2005 and 2010. The most telling statistic: The manufacturing trade balance was a deficit of $5.2 billion from 2001 to 2005, compared to a surplus of $13 billion from 2006 to 2010.[18]

Similarly, the controversy over NAFTA, which entered into force in 1994, demonstrates how the costs of trade are often exaggerated. During the 1992 presidential campaign, Ross Perot warned of a "giant sucking sound" of jobs going from the United States to Mexico if NAFTA were to pass. A quick look at macroeconomic statistics before and after the agreement shows these fears were unwarranted. Perot failed to recognize that there isn't one example of a country that has improved living standards or created broad prosperity without engaging in international trade.

Take, for example, India, which for a long time pursued an economic policy of *swadeshi* (self-sufficiency, or autarky). After this strategy unraveled and economic reforms were introduced in the early 1990s, India's economy performed well (averaging 6.8% growth since 1992). In fascist Spain under the caudillo Francisco Franco, the policy of autarky actually caused famine among the Spanish population. Many of today's fast-growing countries at one time had protectionist policies, only to change course in order to ignite a period of economic growth.

■ ■ ■

The United States needs to spark an immediate and sustained economic expansion. Trade is not only a vital component of economic growth; it is one area where policy changes can lead to almost immediate benefits to the American economy. It doesn't take an entrepreneur long to figure out how to profit from falling tariffs and other trade barriers. In surveying our policies, there are six areas where policy makers can give a boost to our economy by expanding trade.

Let's start with China. Trade with China has become extremely controversial in the United States. The complaints include the following: Our trade deficit with China was $273 billion (in 2010); intellectual property right protections are weak; and their currency, the renminbi, has been kept low, making Chinese exports to the United States artificially inexpensive.

Policy makers have at their disposal three ways of addressing trade issues with China. They can use existing trade mechanisms, such as the Strategic and Economic Dialogue and the Joint Commission on Commerce and Trade, to promote dialogue; they can use WTO rules and arbitration mechanisms if dialogue fails; and they can enforce trade law through the use of antidumping and countervailing duties.

Dialogue should always be the first choice, but we need to be firm with China. Our policies should pressure China to do more to open its markets, to intensify its efforts to clamp down on intellectual property violations, and to make its laws and regulations both more transparent and apply equally to Chinese and American companies. We must also ensure that China isn't using the value of its currency to give Chinese companies an artificial edge over American companies. The U.S. Treasury has the authority to label China a currency manipulator, which carries a corresponding tariff to offset the undervaluation of the renminbi. At some point this authority may have to be used.

Second, we need to diversify our trade in Asia. Only 25% of our exports are destined for Asia, although 60% of the world's population lives in Asian countries. Why? One reason is that at the moment we only have two FTAs in Asia (Singapore and South Korea). Some people may want to count Australia as one of our FTAs in Asia because of its proximity, but in any case the list is not an impressive showing for the world's one-time champion of free trade and open markets.

The biggest FTA prize in Asia is Japan. It's a sizable modern economy that already conducts a lot of trade with the United States. In the past, such an agreement would be unthinkable for political reasons. But the South Korean agreement could prove to be a catalyst for change. Preliminary discussions with Japan should begin immediately. This would be the boldest move in trade since NAFTA.

During the Bush administration, discussions were begun with Thailand and Malaysia. Those talks stalled, but should now be restarted. Without more trading partners in Asia, we will be overly reliant on China. Ironically, those who criticize free trade agreements cite a litany of complaints against China as proof that FTAs don't work. What these uninformed critics of trade need to know is this: The United States doesn't have an FTA with China.

If the ASEAN + 3 trade agreement is implemented by 2016 (as some are pushing for) then our government needs to move decisively to avoid putting U.S. exporters at a critical disadvantage. Fortunately, we have some leverage. Many Asian countries see the United States as a counterweight to China and therefore have an interest in helping us expand trade and other connections in Asia.

Third, as discussed briefly earlier, we need to better integrate the Western Hemisphere. We can do that with a Free Trade Agreement for the Americas with like-minded partners. An FTAA has already been discussed. The idea was brought up at a meeting with thirty-four nations in Argentina in 2005. Unfortunately, five nations opposed the idea, so talks never started in earnest. However, we can build on the success of CAFTA-DR and the support of the other twenty-nine countries in the region that are open to the idea of establishing a unified trading bloc. We will always have opponents in the region—Cuba and Venezuela come to mind—but we can still accomplish a tremendous amount with countries that are open to free trade. An FTAA team should be established in the office of the U.S. trade representative to begin work immediately.

And, it is worth noting, an FTAA would not only expand our economy by making it easier to set up efficient supply chains; it would also serve national security interests. It is in the interests of the United States to have prosperous Americas—from Canada to Argentina. Economic success to our south would help stem the flow of illegal immigrants and illegal drugs. It would also bolster Latin American efforts to counter the spread of anti-American ideologies, like the ones we see today in Cuba, Bolivia, Ecuador, Nicaragua, and Venezuela.

Fourth, we need to invest in commercial infrastructure. It has become fashionable to call for "infrastructure" projects as a way of stimulating the economy. Talk of fixing roads, building bullet trains, painting schools, and building new bridges abounds. But resources are limited. The challenge for policy makers is to allocate capital to where it generates the most return. Policy makers must set priorities based on a project's ability to help our competitiveness and create jobs on a sustained basis.

For this reason, commercial infrastructure projects should be given the highest priority; a failure to invest in commercial infrastructure will weaken our ability to compete globally. A recent report on the state of U.S. infrastructure notes that "freight bottlenecks and other forms of congestion cost about $200 billion, or 1.6% of the U.S. Gross Domestic Product (GDP), a year." Unfortunately, this will get even worse unless we act—the volume that ports handle is expected to double by 2020, and freight tonnage could increase by 88% by 2035.[19]

The Panama Canal expansion, which will be completed by 2014, represents an immediate challenge. The expanded canal will use larger, deeper ships, known as "post-Panamax." Ports in the United States will have to be dredged so these ships can use them. According to Dave Sanford of the American Association of Port Authorities, only one port on the East Coast, Norfolk, Virginia, meets the required channel depths.[20] Ports along the Gulf of Mexico are in particular danger of not being ready. If we fail to accommodate these new ships, U.S. exporters and consumers will be hurt, jobs will be lost, and we will demonstrate to the world that we aren't giving trade the importance it deserves.

Fifth, we need to invest in our Foreign Commercial Service. The Commerce Department has more than 1,400 employees in some seventy-five countries. These officials are effectively America's sales force. They help exporters navigate the maze of bureaucracy in countries around the world; they advocate on behalf of U.S. business; they bring potential partners together; and, most inspiring, they do it with a great sense of service to their country. While federal government expenses need to be reduced nearly across the board, the Foreign Commercial Service has a direct impact on our economy. By greasing the wheels of trade, the service helps American businesses employ Americans.

And finally, one of the most effective things Congress could do would be to grant every president Trade Promotion Authority (TPA). TPA was created by the 1974 Trade Act. It allows an administration to negotiate all the details of a trade agreement and then requires that Congress vote it up or down without tinkering with any of its provisions. TPA is essential to trade negotiations because each FTA is a carefully constructed agreement that balances opening trade against specific concerns by one country or another. Changing even seemingly small details can blow apart a trade deal that took months or years to hammer together.

TPA lapsed in 1994 but was restored by the Trade Act of 2002. The original version of the 2002 Trade Act passed the House by just one vote (215–214), in what one observer called "the most partisan congressional vote on such a bill since the 1930s."[21] This authority again expired on July 1, 2007—though, thankfully, TPA extended to the Colombia, Panama, and South Korean trade bills because they were negotiated prior to the authority's expiration.

President Barack Obama has not requested a renewal of TPA, a tactic that itself sends a very negative signal. His administration is calling for a doubling in exports in the next five years. If successful, the president's Export Initiative could create some two million new jobs. But without TPA, the president's negotiating authority will lack credibility. We will not be able to make significant progress on trade until TPA is renewed.

■ ■ ■

The United States benefits a great deal from trade. Approximately 95% of the world's consumers live outside the United States, and trade will only become more important in the future as developing countries become wealthier and better able to afford our goods. The International Monetary Fund estimates that over the next five years, 83% of global growth will occur outside the United States.[22] Given the superiority of jobs in the export industry, the importance of exports to manufacturing and agriculture, and the competitive advantage in services, the United States should be aggressively advocating for its exporters' interests, rather than voluntarily standing back while other countries pursue FTAs. The United States must become an export powerhouse if the economy is to grow substantially in the coming years.

Winning support for expanding international trade will require extraordinary leadership. Our CEOs and other business leaders need to start letting their employees know the benefits of trade and explain that many of their coworkers' jobs exist because they are supported by exports. Members of Congress should also get a crash course on the Smoot-Hawley tariffs and the consequences of protectionism. Those who don't know this history may be doomed to repeat the mistakes of the Great Depression.

The Bush Institute has set an ambitious goal of 4% growth annually over a sustained period of time. If this level of growth is going to be possible, we will need to increase our productivity, find new customers for our goods and services, and put a relentless emphasis on creating jobs that allow Americans to take advantage of the technologies of the future. Trade will clearly have to be a central component of that effort. But no matter at what rate we aim to grow, we are facing an increasingly competitive world. China, the European Union, and others aren't waiting for us. They are working out trade agreements of their own and doing what is best for their own economies. We can thrive in this competitive world and even prosper from the trends now under way.

After all, Americans are among the most innovative and industrious people the world has ever known. It is up to us to take the necessary steps to continue being the most competitive and prosperous.

Acknowledgments

Carlos Gutierrez would like to thank Peter Tillman for the time, energy, and research that much informed this chapter.

Chapter 14

Market-Friendly Energy

By Steven F. Hayward and Kenneth P. Green

In a striking report released in late 2010, the Congressional Research Service captured the essence of our energy problem. The report didn't wade into current debates over alternative fuels or even mention energy independence. Instead, it touched on something more fundamental. The report looked at coal, natural gas, and oil supplies around the world and gave us this simple fact: Today, the United States has within its borders more fossil fuel reserves than any other country in the world.

In other words, the United States has more sources of domestic fossil fuel energy than Saudi Arabia, Iran, Russia, Venezuela, or any other country we depend on for oil. The United States is an energy-rich country. It just doesn't tap its reserves as extensively as it might.

The implication of the report is not that the United States can shut its borders to foreign oil and still have a thriving economy. Most of our fossil fuel deposits are coal—which is great for producing electricity, but not capable of fueling the average American's car or truck. What's more, energy is a global commodity. If we isolate ourselves from the global market, we'll pay more for energy than we should and deny ourselves the benefits of new discoveries being made around the world.

Rather, the implication of the report is this: The United States has enough resources to unleash a new economic boom driven by cheap and abundant sources of energy.

To see how, let's first drill down into the CRS report. To give us a fair comparison of various forms of energy, the report converts gas and coal reserves into a common standard of measure: "barrel of oil equivalent."

Using these calculations, we can see that the United States has approximately 900 billion BOE of coal, or about a third more coal than Russia. In total, the United States has 972.6 billion BOE in all types of fossil fuels. That exceeds reserves in Russia (954.9 billion BOE), China (474.8 billion BOE), and Saudi Arabia (309.1 billion BOE).

But what's really interesting is that the CRS report looked at "undiscovered" but technically recoverable oil and gas supplies. These are reserves we have strong reason to believe are buried in the ground, but are not now being exploited. If we add this supply to proven reserves of all fossil fuels, we find that the United States still leads the world in overall energy supplies with 1,324.1 billion BOE. Russia (1,248.6 billion BOE), Saudi Arabia (540.4 billion BOE), China (503.2 billion BOE), and Iran (442.4 billion BOE) all have less than the United States.

In other words, the energy problem facing the United States isn't a lack of domestic energy. It's not even necessarily a lack of the right kind of energy. The numbers listed above—particularly the potential oil and gas reserves locked up in the country's ground—indicate that there are abundant sources of all kinds of energy yet to be tapped in this country. The United States has a lot of energy economic potential.

And if we survey our economic history, we will see that energy has always been the lifeblood of America's growth. In many ways, the story of America has been the story of the increasing development of energy resources, and the technologies powered by that energy. From John D. Rockefeller to Henry Ford, the rise of oil and the rise of the internal combustion engine transformed the American economy. Through coal- and diesel-fired power plants (and hydro as well as nuclear power), we can also see an electric grid being rolled out across the country. These new energy sources have made heating one's home, traveling across the country, or running a business cheaper and easier.

Of course, it's not just Americans who have thrived with cheaper sources of energy. As recently as 1850, the physical exertions of humans and animals accounted for 94% of the world's total energy use; only 6% of the world's energy came from concentrated energy sources such as oil or coal. Today those figures are exactly reversed. The energy revolution of the 19th and 20th centuries—predominantly fossil fuels—has made it possible for the average citizen throughout the world, increasingly even in poor nations, to use the energy that just two centuries ago required thousands of human beings. For example, a jet airplane uses the equivalent of the manual labor energy of seven hundred thousand human beings, and does so at an affordable price because of the abundance of modern, concentrated energy sources.

In his sweeping history of economic growth, *The Wealth and Poverty of Nations: Why Some Are So Rich and Some So Poor*, economic historian David Landes sums up the power of energy: "All economic revolutions have at their core an enhancement in the supply of energy, because this feeds and changes all aspects of human activity." His point is that by making energy cheaper, we also reduce the cost of producing nearly every other economic good; when we make advances in energy, we produce wealth across the broader economy.

■ ■ ■

The energy problem the United States faces today—and the problem that stands in the way of using energy to unleash a new era of economic growth—comes in three parts. First, several trends that have lowered energy costs over the past few decades appear to have run their course; unless we enact reforms soon, we may face a future of rising energy prices. Second, the United States has specifically put vast tracts of territory off-limits to energy exploration either by outright prohibition or by slow-walking a permitting process and thereby discouraging energy development. And third, over the past several decades we have seen the rise of an environmental movement that is capable of demonizing energy exploration regardless of the facts involved. These problems are compounded by the reality that the United States doesn't have a coherent energy policy, so we aren't setting benchmarks that will allow us to know whether we are making progress toward unleashing a new energy revolution.

Let's take each one of these issues in turn, starting with the trends in energy over the past several decades.

Throughout the late 1800s and early 1900s, America's energy economy was largely a free-enterprise story. In the transitions from wood to coal, oil, and natural gas, the vast majority of the energy that

Americans used was secured by private investors using private capital, seeking private profit. Sort through the archives and you'll find photos and stories of wildcatters taking risks and building derricks that brought oil to the surface. Discoveries of oil in California, Texas, and other states transformed the local and national economies.

However, the government didn't take a hands-off approach for too terribly long. The federal government came to impose price controls on oil and natural gas that lasted for decades and created burdensome regulations that energy markets had to live by. Part of the story of the New Deal often left untold is that it crushed energy innovation and turned instead to large government-backed energy projects aimed at bringing electricity to every corner of this nation. Think of the Tennessee Valley Authority, which is still in operation today. Rather than opening the door for entrepreneurial companies to bring electricity to a large swath of the country, TVA essentially grabbed the market on energy production for its area. At the time, electricity production, which often required large tracts of land and posed civil engineering challenges, was thought to be a "natural monopoly" requiring close government regulation if not outright government control.

Fortunately, some reforms and energy advances have lowered prices. The Reagan administration repealed price controls on oil and natural gas. This gave energy markets greater flexibility and thereby led ultimately to lower prices. There has also been a great deregulation of public utilities, which has opened the door to competition among energy providers. In Texas today, for example, residents can decide from whom to buy electricity and can choose among companies competing not only on price but on support for environmental causes as well. That kind of competition seems simple today, but before deregulation it was thought impossible.

We have also seen tremendous advances in the efficiency with which we use energy. Anyone who thinks Americans are wasteful of oil has missed one of the greatest stories in energy over the past three decades. American oil consumption has remained virtually flat over the past thirty years, because Americans have become very efficient in their use of energy. Today we use only slightly more oil than we did in 1978, even though the economy has more than doubled in real terms. Since 1975, energy consumption per dollar of economic output has fallen 50%. These are stunning achievements and are testimony to the steady improvement in energy efficiency we've made over the last generation, including even—yes—our cars and trucks.

Perhaps the most significant trend recently has been advances that have opened up new sources of energy. The shale gas revolution that is under way not only is transforming Pennsylvania and other states where gas reserves are suddenly becoming economically viable; it is also transforming energy markets across the country and the world. A decade ago the United States was looking to build liquefied natural gas terminals to import vast quantities of the fuel. Today the emphasis is shifting toward using LNG terminals to export the stuff.

The trend here is that we're increasingly able to use a technique called hydraulic fracturing, also known as "fracking," to extract gas (and more recently, oil) from deeply buried shale deposits. Fracking is bringing energy to the surface in places where it was scarce before and where, in many cases, it is close to a potentially lucrative customer base. Pennsylvania's gas fields, for example, are not all that far from the populous East Coast. Thanks to fracking and other new methods for extracting oil and gas, domestic oil production in the United States has actually increased over the past three years, reversing a twenty-five-year decline. (This is particularly significant given the fact that we haven't opened up sizable new areas to energy development.)

The result of these and other trends is that the overall cost of energy (measured as a proportion of household income) has been falling for decades. In the 1930s, households spent, on average, about 5.5% of their income, on energy. By the late 1990s, according to numbers compiled by the Bureau of Economic Analysis, the cost of energy had fallen to about an average of 2.3% of household income. It was not a straight-line decline; price shocks from global events and inflation periodically sent energy costs soaring. But the trend clearly pointed down.

However, over the past decade this long-term trend has reversed. Since 2002 the cost of energy as a proportion of personal consumption has risen to near 4% today. This rise preceded the onset of the recession in 2008 and chiefly reflects the higher recent global prices for oil, which have risen from a band between $20 and $60 a barrel a decade ago to recent spikes of as high as $150 a barrel.

Some of this price volatility reflects political uncertainty in the Middle East in the post-9/11 era. But some of it reflects the fact that other countries—such as China and India—are now consuming much more oil than they once did. We've also seen new controls imposed on carbon-based energy that are raising the cost of gasoline and electricity. The United Kingdom and Germany, for example, have put in place new curbs on carbon for environmental reasons. California and other states have similarly imposed new environmental mandates on utility companies, which drive up the price of electricity.

The end result is that we may be reaching a point where we will need to develop new sources of cheap, clean energy if we are to provide the power for a new economic boom. The shale gas (and oil) revolution may have come along just in time—at a point when we've squeezed all the efficiency we can reasonably expect to get out of the energy economy and at a point when we need new sources of energy in order to replace the fuel we are losing to the Chinese and Indian economies.

Unfortunately, the second component of our energy problem is that we've made vast tracts of territory off-limits to oil exploration. In fact, much of America's energy potential is locked away by state and federal fiat. As the Energy Information Administration observes, "Today, natural gas and oil drilling is prohibited in all offshore regions along the North Atlantic coast, most of the Pacific coast, parts of the Alaska coast, and most of the eastern Gulf of Mexico." These prohibitions prevent us from tapping into sizable deposits. As the Congressional Research Service report sketches out, the United States has a staggering amount of conventional fossil fuel resources that, with new technological advances, are now becoming recoverable.[1] What we need now in order to tap into those reserves is corresponding political advances.

A decade ago, we had a heated debate about opening a small portion of the Arctic National Wildlife Refuge (ANWR) to drilling. Proponents of drilling won elections and pushed for changes, yet ANWR remains off-limits. Similarly, a few years ago, we had a raucous debate over opening up parts of the Outer Continental Shelf (OCS) and other areas for oil exploration and eventual oil production. Laws were changed and politicians supporting the drilling were elected. Yet the rigs were never set up to drill or fulfill the promise of a significant amount of new domestically produced oil. We've seen similar things occur in Alaska, where Shell Oil and others have spent years and large sums of money battling for the right to drill in the Chukchi Sea.

While U.S. proven oil reserves are usually estimated at around 19 billion barrels, CRS estimates that the actual figure is closer to 145 billion barrels (this figure includes oil shale deposits not currently under development). Most of the barriers to producing this oil are political rather than technical.

Oil from these sources would not lower gasoline prices immediately, and perhaps not much at all, depending on global market conditions. But over time, by decreasing U.S. imports, tapping these resources could provide us with supplies that buffer us against fluctuations in world oil prices. Most important, however, drilling in American waters would create jobs in the United States—importing oil creates jobs abroad; producing it domestically creates jobs at home.

Perhaps the prospect of new jobs is one reason why exploration and development of Outer Continental Shelf reserves was supported by 60% of the respondents to a poll taken by the Consumer Alliance for Energy Security, a coalition of industrial and institutional energy users. Americans seem to know intuitively that energy is a boon as a well as a boom. It's not a coincidence that the state with the lowest unemployment rate during the Great Recession is North Dakota. The unemployment rate in the state was about 3.4% as this book went to press, an achievement made possible by a boom in conventional energy production, most of it occurring on private or state land that is largely immune from the process that prevents or delays development of federal lands and coastal waters.

Advances in natural gas production technology have unlocked previously unimaginable amounts of shale gas and coal bed methane—perhaps more than a century of domestic supply. And the superabundance of coal has never been questioned. If we can get beyond the hurdle of carbon emissions, coal could even end up powering a large number of the cars and trucks on our roads, but first we have to transition to electric vehicles that recharge their batteries through an electric grid.

Rather than thinking about developing new energy ideas that can transition us to a more prosperous economy, we've allowed ourselves to get caught up in debates that effectively shut off access to new sources of energy. So before we can make sensible changes to our energy policies we need to address the third component of our energy problem: the rise of environmentalism.

It's perhaps fitting that the modern environmental movement traces its roots in part to a nearly two-decade-long fight over a proposed hydroelectric power plant on the Hudson River. After all, the Hudson is named for an explorer who sailed up it with great hopes of finding new riches by developing a trade route to the Far East, but instead discovered a vast uncharted wilderness.

The power plant was to be built just north of West Point by the Consolidated Edison Company, otherwise known as Con Ed, in the early 1960s. Because the plant involved pumping vast amounts of water from the river and carving out the side of a mountain, a collection of environmentalists waged a concerted campaign to block it with public demonstrations and protracted court fights. In the end, the legal strategy worked: The environmentalists won their fight, marking a watershed moment in environmental politics. The fight proved that the courts could be used to defeat a major corporation's plans to build a power plant, and energy debates have never been the same since.

Over the decades that followed, environmentalists have been able to use common concerns over air and water quality to build strength and momentum for their movement. Today litigation is common in energy fights, but in the early 1970s it was hard to predict where the battles were headed. Back then we were getting serious about reducing air and water pollution, so environmentalists had a receptive audience in calling out some of our biggest polluters and broadly blaming fossil fuels for a wide variety of environmental ills.

The result is that today large pieces of public lands and most of America's coastal waters have been placed off-limits to energy exploration, with the notable exception of one-half of the Gulf of Mexico. And still environmentalists are pushing for a new set of regulations. This time they want to regulate carbon as a backdoor way of imposing a broad set of new mandates on the energy industry.

So far efforts to place caps on carbon emissions have failed on the national level. But over the past several years environmentalists have made headway on the state level. Many states now require their utilities to derive a significant portion of their electricity from alternative or renewable fuels, such as wind, solar, or biomass. Several European countries now aim to produce 20% of their electricity from alternative or renewable sources by 2020. Several American states are following along. One of them is California. Only, in the case of the Golden State, the mandate is to produce 33% of the state's electricity from renewable resources by 2020. The stated goal here is to reduce carbon emissions, but in practice these targets will drive up the price of electricity.

From the early moments of the modern energy fights the debate has broken down along the familiar fault line of whether to emphasize production (more supply) or conservation (less use), with a large amount of "alternative" or "renewable" energy romanticism thrown in. The typical dynamics of legislative compromise have tended to produce an "all-of-the-above" mix of policies that lack consistent objectives.

Generally, the hodgepodge of policies we have enacted have not used markets to solve problems or ensure that we maintain a steady source of affordable energy. Instead we have manipulated energy markets with mandates and regulations. Vehicle performance standards were put in place, and the country's gasoline market has been fragmented into many smaller, less resilient markets. Mandates to use ethanol were also instituted, creating a voracious appetite for corn to convert into ethanol—a fuel that creates its own environmental concerns and has driven up the price of food here and abroad.

Other mandates took aim at specific problems, such as cleaning up after an oil spill. Two major spills in particular drew significant policy reactions. One was off California's coast, the Santa Barbara spill of 1969. It led to new restrictions on drilling off the coast of California. The other was the 1989 *Exxon Valdez* spill in Alaskan waters. What followed was the Oil Pollution Control Act of 1990, which prescribed protocols for responding to oil spills and required oil companies to keep expensive equipment and trained workers on hand in the event of a spill.

Fortunately, the trend over time is that there are fewer and fewer oil spills. This reflects changes in shipping (especially double-hulled tankers after the *Exxon Valdez* spill) and offshore-drilling technology. There are about 3,500 offshore rigs active in the Gulf of Mexico and more than 6,500 worldwide. As the National Academy of Sciences (NAS) brief for the 2003 book *Oil in the Sea III* notes, "Spillage from vessels in North American waters from 1990 to 1999 was less than one-third of the spillage during the prior decade, and, despite increased production, reductions in releases during oil and gas production have been dramatic as well."

And the spills we do have typically don't come from oil wells or pipelines. Over the past sixty years, there have been ten offshore-drilling accidents that released more than five thousand tons of oil into ocean waters. During this same period, there have been seventy-two oil spills from tanker accidents that released five thousand tons of oil or more. In other words, for every offshore-drilling accident, there are seven major tanker spills and numerous tanker accidents of smaller size. Most tanker spills also tend to be larger in magnitude than offshore-drilling accidents. In aggregate, tanker spills have released into ocean or coastal waters more than four times the amount of oil as offshore-drilling accidents have.

So it's unfortunate that British Petroleum's 2010 spill from a blown-out well in the Gulf of Mexico has hardened some policy makers against offshore drilling. The United States produces over one million barrels per day from offshore platforms in the Gulf of Mexico—nearly one-quarter of total domestic oil production. If this production is restricted, the United States will lose a significant portion of its domestic supplies. These supplies would have to be replaced by expanding onshore production in areas such as the Bakken field in North Dakota or in the currently closed ANWR; by developing oil shale deposits found in western states (for this oil to be economically viable, market prices for oil would need to be consistently higher than they have been over the past few years); or by importing more oil from overseas.

None of these options would likely reduce the risks of a spill in the Gulf of Mexico. As we've seen, tanker spills are more common than offshore drilling spills, and imports would bring more foreign tankers to our shores. Furthermore, other countries are unlikely to curtail their offshore exploration in the Gulf. Cuba is already drilling for oil one hundred miles off the Florida coast. Mexico is also drilling in the Gulf, and both Venezuela and Brazil are expanding their offshore exploration and production in deep water and are likely to expand to the Gulf of Mexico if the United States scales back. So if we curtail drilling in the Gulf, we'll lose energy production yet do little to reduce the risk of oil spills.

■ ■ ■

As we face the prospect of higher energy prices in the long run, it is time for the United States to overcome all three components of its energy problem and develop a pro-growth energy policy. To do that we need to develop a coherent strategy that answers this basic question: How do we provide energy to a broad cross section of Americans that is relatively cheap, safe, and clean? Answering this question will help us cut through all three components of our energy problem, while also developing the new sources of energy that will fuel a new economic expansion. To do that, we suggest taking the following steps.

First, open up more of North America to energy exploration. This can be done in a way that is safe and that doesn't raise environmental risks. We've already mentioned the possibility of new drilling in Outer Continental Shelf regions of the country, Gulf of Mexico, Chukchi Sea, and ANWR. Drilling can be conducted safely in all these places and with the appropriate level of safety review. However, they are far from the only places that are essentially off-limits now yet nonetheless hold significant energy deposits.

We now have the technology to tap into oil and gas in vast shale deposits. These advances in technology have led to discoveries in places we didn't expect to be drilling—including large shale deposits in Texas and Louisiana, as well as a large deposit that runs beneath parts of New York, Pennsylvania, West Virginia, and Virginia. We also have shale deposits in Colorado and other western states. Some of these deposits run under federally controlled land. We need an extensive review of federal lands and a new process that will allow us, where appropriate, to tap into energy deposits that will otherwise be off-limits.

· If we are to be successful at opening up new land to energy development, we need also to streamline the permitting process for major projects. That process has become so protracted that its deadweight cost now far exceeds the protections it is supposed to provide. The case of the Keystone XL pipeline to bring crude oil from Canada down to U.S. refineries near the Gulf coast is a prominent example. The eventual approval of the pipeline has never really been in doubt. It is just too good an idea to stop; in addition to bringing in new oil, estimates of the number of new jobs the pipeline would create approach two hundred thousand. But the process has dragged on for several years as environmentalists have found creative new ways to block it.

The multiple agency reviews, repeated layers of public hearings, and the numerous jurisdictions available for obstructionist litigation for these types of projects should be reduced. Energy-related permitting should be centralized in the Department of Energy, with the Environmental Protection Agency and the Department of the Interior participating in a streamlined hearing process on par with other interested parties. Also, specific regulatory regimes such as the Clean Air Act should be amended to require that proposed regulations and standards pass a cost-benefit test. The aim in all these reforms is to inject economic growth into the equation as we strike a balance between the need to regulate the energy industry with the imperative that we reignite the economy and create the jobs Americans need and the wealth that ultimately leads us to a cleaner environment.

The second step to move toward a more coherent energy policy that promotes economic growth is to eliminate subsidies.

Only in the government does it make sense to fix one bad idea—the subsidizing of fossil fuel energy—by giving even larger subsidies to less efficient forms of energy such as ethanol, wind, and solar power. The best policy regarding energy subsidies is to eliminate them entirely.

Subsidies subvert the efficient functioning of the market, which is our only effective mechanism for matching supply with demand. They also create a fertile garden for rent seekers, who conspire to get a share of the pie. Rent seeking happens when people who cannot sell a good in a free market tap the coercive and redistributionist force of government to lever their uncompetitive good into the market at the public's expense. Rather than contribute to overall social welfare by giving consumers the best goods at the lowest cost, rent seekers undermine social welfare by foisting inferior or overpriced goods onto the market while taking money that could be used to actually grow the economy. In other words, they make all of us poorer.

Subsidies are also often inequitable. High gasoline taxes create an incentive for new fuel-efficient cars—in a sense creating a subsidy for vehicles that get a lot of miles to the gallon. But only people in higher economic brackets can afford the new cars; poorer people are left to drive less efficient vehicles and spend more on gas taxes. When the California government wanted to subsidize electric vehicles, it offered more than $8,000 to people who leased General Motors' EV1. The only people who could do so were households that earned more than $100,000 annually and had a regular gasoline-powered car as their primary mode of transportation.

Finally, subsidies pave the way for adverse consequences that inevitably result when legislators decide that their few hundred heads are wiser than the nearly infinite number of nuanced economic decisions made by their millions of constituents.

Government efforts to protect the environment are rife with unintended consequences. Mandating fuel-efficient vehicles led people to drive more, not less (known to energy economists as the "rebound effect"), delivering much lower fuel savings than forecast. Manufacturers receive subsidies for selling flexible-fuel vehicles that most people run on gasoline. That allows the companies to sell SUVs with their ruinous miles to the gallon and still maintain proper "average" fuel economy.

Both the Democrats and Republicans are pushing energy subsidy plans that, by further distorting markets and degrading price signals with hidden subsidies for fuels such as ethanol, are likely to weaken our energy-intensive economy further. By adding more mandates to fuel production and use, these plans also make our energy production and distribution system more fragile and subject to disruption.

The right thing to do is to strike all energy subsidies, tax the environmental harms that energy demonstrably creates, and let the market sort it out.

And the third step we need to take to a more coherent energy policy is to invest in a few target areas of research that will likely lead to new innovations.

Today's federal research investments, whether for solar and wind or ethanol and nuclear, are structured around scale and quantity, not innovation. Most of these current technologies are not cost-competitive with fossil fuels, and probably retard progress toward making commercially scalable breakthroughs in energy technology. There is a limited role for the federal government to be a customer for some experimental technologies in specific, well-defined cases (such as developing portable energy sources for the military), but the government should move away from promoting the general deployment of alternative energy technologies that cannot compete without subsidy.

A $35 billion loan guarantee program brought us the Solyndra scandal, which involved the Energy Department giving a well-connected solar company a $500 million loan. The program's other projects, while less scandalous, are likely to be no less dubious in their practical results.

A better approach is offered by the ARPA-E (Advanced Research Projects Agency–Energy, modeled after the Pentagon's legendary Defense Advanced Research Projects Agency) unit of the Department of Energy. ARPA-E is intended to conduct research into ways of overcoming the formidable technical barriers necessary to make alternative energy sources from batteries to biofuels scalable at a reasonable price.

Like DARPA (the research agency that has developed a long string of cutting-edge technologies for the military), ARPA-E is exempt from the usual civil service bureaucracy and costly union-driven mandates, so it can be much more nimble than other government agencies. ARPA-E was set up by legislation passed in 2007 but wasn't funded until 2009. Its total budget was a paltry $400 million in its first year—less than the Solyndra loan. But the thing to note is that research efforts like ARPA-E aren't about creating jobs, green or otherwise, which is why it has been of little interest to Congress or the White House. It is meant to expand our base of technical knowledge, leading to new and better options in the future.

Above all, the energy future is open-ended and unpredictable. While the role of energy in economic growth is important, American energy policy ought to be about generating the amount of energy we need and the kinds of energy we want, rather than being treated primarily as a jobs program. Moving toward a more market-friendly energy policy will make possible faster economic growth that will boost employment in all sectors.

Chapter 15

Social Security Reform and Economic Growth

By Charles Blahous and Jason J. Fichtner

Regardless of whether we aim for 4% growth, a lower figure, or a higher one, reforms to federal entitlement programs are essential. To engender a pro-growth economic environment, entitlement reform must not only rein in the rising costs of these federal programs, but also remove the barriers to labor force participation and existing disincentives to personal saving that arise from them. Entitlement spending growth is the primary driver of unsustainable federal spending growth; without effective entitlement reform our future economic growth potential will be buried under a mountain of federal taxation and indebtedness.

Any discussion involving entitlement reform must first overcome the misconception that it is possible to close these programs' funding shortfalls mainly by raising taxes. The primary alternative to containing spending growth from a budgetary perspective, raising taxes isn't a credible long-term solution to the entitlement policy problem. Even taking the perspective of those who might prefer to raise taxes substantially rather than to cut significantly into entitlement cost growth, we see clearly that relying on tax increases alone would represent an ineffective and economically crippling approach to this policy challenge. The Congressional Budget Office (CBO) estimates that federal tax rates would have to more than double to address currently projected spending increases.[1] Such high tax rates would have devastating economic effects.

Robert Barro and Charles Redlick of Harvard estimate that for each $1 in new tax revenue, the economy tends to decline by about $1.10.[2]

Economists Christina Romer and David Romer also recently examined more than sixty years of U.S. tax data. After controlling for other factors, they found that "a tax increase of 1 percent of GDP lowers real GDP by about 3 percent."[3] Many other economists agree—beyond just taking money directly out of the wallets of individuals, such tax increases would also reduce the size of the economy at large.

Moreover, there is little reason to suppose that a revenue increase alone would solve the fiscal problems caused by entitlement spending. Harvard economists Alberto Alesina and Silvia Ardagna examined numerous instances of fiscal adjustments throughout the world. They found that attempts to close deficits that relied on spending reductions were far more successful than those that relied on tax increases. Spending reductions were also less likely to lead to recessions.[4]

Similarly, relying on a policy of borrowing to fund entitlement programs would be shortsighted and would severely damage the economy. Most economists agree that high levels of debt pose a significant problem for economic growth. Carmen Reinhart and Kenneth Rogoff recently examined debt levels in forty-four countries over a period of up to two hundred years. They found that if national debt expands from 30% of GDP to 90% or more, economic growth rates fall in half,[5] and that this phenomenon occurs in developing countries and in more advanced economies alike. Economists at the Bank for International Settlements found similar results. Their research showed that when government debt in Organisation for Economic Co-operation and Development (OECD) countries exceeds a threshold of about 85% of GDP, economic growth slows.[6] While there remains some question as to the applicability of international comparisons to the United States, there is little reason to believe that the United States occupies a sufficiently unique position to allow it to accumulate escalating levels of debt without consequence.

While some debt-financed spending can stimulate short-term economic growth, long-term economic growth is undermined when a nation's debt becomes so large that servicing that debt redirects substantial resources away from productive activity. Like most nations, the United States finances its sovereign debt[7] by issuing securities. As the government borrows to finance its spending, it competes with private entities that also borrow to finance their own activities. Thus every dollar the government borrows is one less dollar that can be used by private business. Moreover, excessive government borrowing drives up interest rates, which makes borrowing more expensive for everyone else.[8]

Because businesses need capital in order to survive and grow, the dynamic that raises interest rates increases the cost of doing business. Projects are less profitable than they would otherwise be. At the margin, some producers may decide not to produce at all.[9] For the nation as a whole, this leads to a decrease in the level of capital accumulated[10] as well as a decrease in the level of goods and services produced.[11] These adverse outcomes are virtually assured in the absence of meaningful entitlement reform since, as we noted, federal taxes cannot practicably be raised to the level necessary to pay for currently projected spending. A failure to reform our national entitlement programs would thus almost certainly lead to enormous further increases in the U.S. national debt, and to all of their ancillary adverse effects.

A failure to address these issues would also undermine our nation's real and perceived macroeconomic stability.[12] Put simply, until we clarify how we intend to pay for currently projected entitlement spending, businesses (and individuals) will have to operate under the assumption that taxes will eventually be raised to pay the government's bills. The uncertainty of those tax hikes—when they are coming and how large they will be—serves as a drag on the economy.

A brief review of federal finances makes clear the central role of entitlement spending in driving these fiscal strains. In fiscal year (FY) 2011, for example, the federal government spent approximately $3.6 trillion, or almost 24% of GDP, while collecting $2.3 trillion in revenue. The result was a $1.3 trillion deficit.[13] While debt held by the public exceeded $10 trillion by the end of FY2011, or roughly 67% of GDP, the national gross debt, which includes bonds such as those held in the Social Security trust fund, now stands at nearly $15 trillion and is estimated to climb to more than 100% of GDP in FY2012.[14] Spending on the three largest federal entitlement programs (Social Security, Medicare, and Medicaid) accounted for more than $1.5 trillion in FY2011, or roughly 43% of the federal budget.[15] Over the next couple of decades, both federal spending in general and the proportion attributable to entitlement spending are projected to rise dramatically.

The magnitude of the spending problem becomes even more obvious when one examines current policy projections. The CBO's "Alternative Fiscal Scenario" is considered by many to be the most credible projection of current federal fiscal policy.[16] Under these estimates, revenues, which have fallen considerably due to the recession, are expected to return to their historical share of GDP (approximately 18%) within the next decade. Under this alternative fiscal scenario, by 2035 total federal outlays will have further increased by 10 percentage points to roughly 34% of GDP.[17] Also in 2035, the net ratio of debt held by the public to GDP will be an enormous 187%.[18]

Again, the primary driver of this projected fiscal crisis is federal entitlement spending. By 2035, Social Security, Medicare, and Medicaid alone are projected to encompass roughly two-thirds of all noninterest federal spending, or nearly one-sixth of the nation's total economic output. As shown on the following chart, the consequence of a failure to constrain these entitlement spending costs would be an explosion of the government's fiscal imbalance.

The sheer size of our federal entitlement spending commitments is thus by itself a grave threat to future U.S. economic growth. But even considered separately from their magnitudes, the designs of federal

Figure 1: Federal Long-Term Spending Is Unsustainable

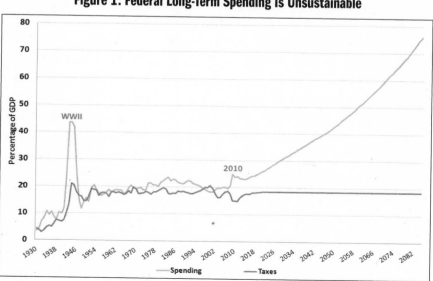

entitlement programs are problematic because they undermine economic growth in at least three ways: They encourage us to save less, have fewer children (the productive taxpayers of the future), and stop working earlier.

The pressing need for further reforms to Medicare, Medicaid, and other federal health entitlements has been widely documented. This chapter, however, will focus directly on the more easily understood Social Security program, where changes to encourage labor force participation, improve incentives for saving, and other pro-growth reforms can be presented free of the complexities of problems unique to our health-care system. We will now turn to specific ways in which Social Security might be reformed to contribute to a brighter outlook for national economic growth.

SOCIAL SECURITY REFORM AND NATIONAL SAVING

Faster long-term economic growth is positively correlated with higher national saving. Furthermore, such saving is inversely correlated with government expenditures, government debt, and public health expenditures. In other words, as government spending and debt decline (or grow less rapidly), saving generally increases—and vice versa.

Data from the World Bank's World Development Indicators data catalog demonstrate this correlation. Specifically, a simple regression model using data from the 31 high-income countries of the Organisation for Economic Co-operation and Development spanning the years 1971–2009 exhibit a clear correlation between saving and growth rates.

A robust literature suggests that Social Security negatively impacts personal saving.[19] The reasons are rooted primarily in Social Security's design as a traditional pay-as-you-go (PAYGO) financed system, in which contributions paid by current younger workers are used to finance current benefits for older retirees. Another factor contributing negatively to personal saving behavior is the design of Social Security's benefit formula.

The essence of a PAYGO system is that it does not attempt to amass savings so as to finance future benefit obligations. Instead a PAYGO system operates as a pure income transfer process without adding to the national stock of capital available to finance retirement benefits. A PAYGO system by its very nature requires maintaining a sufficient number of workers per retiree to support benefit payments. If the ratio of workers to retirees falls, higher taxes or borrowing is necessary— both of which further retard economic growth.

In some respects, the current design of Social Security creates the worst of both worlds from the standpoint of facilitating retirement saving. This is largely because the accumulation of a large Social Security trust fund creates the *illusion* of savings already put aside to finance future benefits, thereby deterring some personal saving that might otherwise take place. But while the Treasury bonds in the program's trust fund represent assets of the Social Security program and increase its authority to make benefit payments, most academic studies have concluded that the bonds' presence has stimulated additional federal consumption rather than adding to national savings.[20] The existence of the trust fund thus causes many workers to believe that more retirement saving is being put aside on their behalf than is actually the case.

Facing financing challenges to PAYGO social retirement systems, some countries in Latin America, Eastern Europe, and Asia have transitioned away from such systems toward those based on private accounts or on a hybrid of PAYGO and advance-funding.

Though personal account systems introduce a number of important policy challenges and contentious value judgments, research generally shows them to have positive effects on private saving. For example, in 1998, Carlos Sales-Sarrapy and other researchers estimated an increase in private saving of 2.18% of GDP in the first year Mexico introduced private accounts.[21] Chile also moved its social retirement system away from a PAYGO-financed system toward private accounts, and the positive results on personal saving were dramatic:

> According to economist Klaus Schmidt-Hebbel, the rate of growth of the Chilean economy went from an average of 3.7 percent per year, in the period from 1961 through 1974, to 7.1 percent per year in the period from 1990 through 1997, and of that extra growth of 3.4 percentage points per year, the pension reform would have

contributed .9 percentage points per year, that is, more than a quarter of the total. Of the total increase of 12.2 percentage points in the rate of savings during those two periods, the pension reform contributed 3.8 percentage points, that is, 31 percent of the total increase.[22]

Beyond the question of whether a national pension system should be financed on a PAYGO or advance-funded basis, the growth of national pension benefits themselves bears directly on individual savings incentives. For many lower-income, liquidity-constrained individuals, it is simply not rational for them to engage in additional long-term saving if they believe that most Social Security benefit promises will be honored. Research by Andrew Biggs and Glenn Springstead[23] shows that retired beneficiaries in the second income quintile receive Social Security benefits that exceed 80% of their final previous earnings, and that those in the bottom income quintile routinely receive benefits that far exceed 100% of previous earnings. For millions of low-income individuals, progressive and wage-indexed Social Security benefits render it irrational to put aside further retirement saving.

Millions of Americans have independently reached this conclusion, with 64% of all aged beneficiary units[24] relying on Social Security for 50% or more of their income, and 34% relying on Social Security for 90% or more of their income.[25] This would not be the case if Social Security had left these individuals with both the incentive and the discretionary income to put aside substantial additional savings during their working years.

As a result, analyses of proposals either to constrain the growth of scheduled Social Security benefits, or to incorporate a savings component into the program, show higher projected savings and growth rates than proposals that do not. For example, CBO published separate analyses of two different Social Security reform proposals in 2004. One proposal by Peter Diamond and Peter Orszag[26] relied primarily on raising taxes, while the other proposal by President George W. Bush's bipartisan 2001 commission would have both reduced the growth of PAYGO benefits and created private accounts. When considering the impact on saving, the CBO stated that under President

Bush's commission plan, "national wealth (the sum of private wealth and cumulative budget surpluses) would be 10 percent to 12 percent higher in 2080 than it would be under the baseline scenario."[27] By contrast, CBO found that the Diamond-Orszag proposal would reduce projected GNP relative to the baseline.

In sum, adequate personal and national saving is a requirement for robust economic growth. So as not to inhibit the realization of this objective, Social Security and other federal entitlements should be reformed to constrain the growth of unfunded PAYGO liabilities and to remove disincentives for personal saving.

SOCIAL SECURITY AND LABOR FORCE PARTICIPATION

Labor force participation bears a straightforward relationship to economic growth: Aggregate growth is equal to the growth in productivity per worker times the growth in the number of workers. To realize our potential for future growth, the reforms we must inevitably make to repair the finances of federal entitlement programs should also involve close attention to influences upon work participation, particularly at the margins when those in late middle age are weighing whether to continue their working careers or to begin their transition into retirement.

Most analysis of Social Security has concluded that its current design discourages work in paid employment, especially for younger seniors and for secondary earners. Research by Gayle Reznik, David Weaver, and Andrew Biggs has found that Social Security's return on payroll tax contributions by those aged 62–65 is -49.5%,[28] meaning that the program offers literally just pennies of return for each additional dollar contributed.

Social Security also aggressively redistributes income from two-earner married couples to one-earner married couples, thus penalizing a household decision to have both spouses of a couple work and contribute payroll taxes. For example, a medium-wage two-earner couple, both born in 1955, expects to receive back only 80 cents from Social Security on each dollar contributed (in present value), whereas a one-earner couple would expect to receive $1.39.[29]

Despite the complexities of determining one's net effective tax rate on Social Security–covered work, there is evidence that individuals do respond rationally to these incentives. As Jeffrey B. Liebman, Erzo F. P. Luttmer, and David G. Seif determined in a 2008 paper, "Our estimates conclusively reject the notion that labor supply is completely unresponsive to the incentives generated by the Social Security benefit rules. We find reasonably robust and statistically significant evidence that individuals are more likely to retire when the effective marginal Social Security tax is high."[30]

Because of its origins during the Great Depression, Social Security was designed with scant attention to providing reasonable returns for those seniors who remained in the workforce.[31] The focus then was instead on providing for their departure and on clearing employment opportunities for the young. The Social Security Act well succeeded in its aim of nudging older Americans out of the ranks of those seeking employment. Civilian labor force participation rates for those 65 and older dropped from 26.7% in 1950 to 12.5% in 1980.[32] The decline was particularly sharp for males over 65, some 45.8% of whom were in the workforce in 1950 but only 19.0% in 1980, despite national gains

Figure 2: Civilian Labor Force Participation Rates, U.S. Males 65 and Older

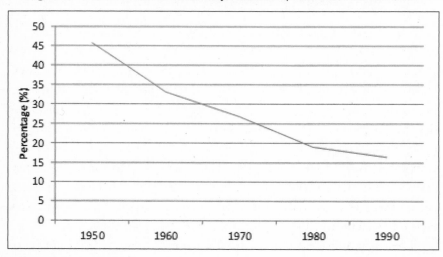

Source: Bureau of Labor Statistics

in longevity and health during the intervening time period. The Bureau of Labor Statistics (BLS) attributes this decline to Social Security: "In the 1950s, a sharp drop occurred in labor force participation for men 65 and older, as Social Security retirements affected labor force participation rates."[33]

Notably, labor participation did *not* immediately decline for those younger than 65 (and thus ineligible for Social Security benefits)—that is, until Social Security's Early Eligibility Age (EEA) of 62 was established.[34] After the creation of EEA, labor participation by middle-aged males aged 55–64 also began to trend downward, from 87.3% in 1960 to 67.7% by 1990. As BLS notes, "Labor force participation decreases started in the 1960s for those 55 to 64. Since this time, some of the 20-percentage point decrease for men in this age group has to be attributed to the availability of Social Security benefits to men 62 years of age."[35] Though this sustained trend toward early retirement has since bottomed out and begun to reverse somewhat in recent years, Social Security on balance clearly remains a substantial barrier to labor participation by Americans in their late middle age. For example, seniors who continue to work after claiming Social Security benefits at 62 (but before Normal Retirement Age, or NRA) are subject to an earnings limitation under which they are required temporarily to give up as much as $1 in benefits for every $2 earned above a $14,160 threshold.[36] This is but one of the program's facets that nudge individuals into early retirement.

Social Security's EEA of 62 is the most common age of benefit claiming.[37] More than 70% of beneficiaries take advantage of the opportunity to claim Social Security retirement benefits prior to NRA, despite receiving lower monthly benefits when doing so.[38] For years, early retirement was often encouraged by Social Security Administration (SSA) field offices under the mistaken belief that it leaves beneficiaries better off. Fortunately, SSA has more recently adopted policies recognizing that individual circumstances must be carefully considered when determining one's optimal age for claiming benefits.[39]

The basic Social Security benefit formula is designed to impose net incremental income losses on those who extend their working careers.

Previous writings of Charles Blahous,[40] of Gopi Shah Goda, John B. Shoven, and Sita Slavov,[41] and of others have explained how returns on contributions generally diminish the longer one works.

A primary reason for this effect is that the current Social Security benefit formula attempts to perform two functions simultaneously. On one hand, the formula reduces one's lifetime wage history to a single number: the *average* earning of one's top 35 earning years. On the other hand, the formula is progressive, redistributing income from high-wage to low-wage workers.

When an individual first begins his working career, his "earnings history" consists of 35 zero-earning years. Each year that he works, he replaces one of those zeroes with a positive earnings year. Each time he does so, his career "average earnings" rises. But because the benefit formula is progressive, it delivers lower and lower returns as this average rises. In other words, the longer he works, the worse his financial return under the current Social Security benefit formula.[42] This worsened treatment becomes particularly pronounced after he reaches the limit of 35 years of earnings,[43] at precisely the time that a retirement decision is likely to be made.

Social Security's nonworking-spouse benefit also discourages work. An individual without any history of paid employment can be entitled to receive a benefit equal to 50% of his or her spouse's earned benefit. Consequently, an individual who is married to a high-wage earner may receive a benefit well exceeding what another individual might earn based on an entire working career of payroll tax contributions.

These various features of Social Security—from benefit eligibility at age 62, to the earnings limitation, to the nonworking-spouse benefit, to the technical details of its benefit formula, to others—all act as a drag on labor force participation and thus interfere with the goal of maximizing future economic growth.

It is only barely an exaggeration to state that the financial unsustainability of current federal entitlement programs is entirely attributable to insufficient projected growth in the U.S. labor force. This conclusion can be substantiated by some simple math. Social Security's initial benefit formula increases along with growth in the national Average

Wage Index. Because program payroll tax revenues also automatically grow with national wages, this benefit formula would be financially sustainable within a stable tax rate if the worker-to-beneficiary ratio never declined.[44]

This is not, however, what is taking place. Worker-beneficiary ratios are projected to become much more unfavorable going forward, as shown.

Figure 3: Social Security Worker-Beneficiary Ratios, 1960–2030 (past and projected)

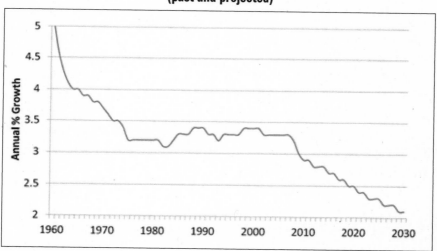

Source: Social Security Trustees' Report

The previous decline in Social Security's worker-beneficiary ratios during the 1960s reflected the gradual implementation of various program expansions. Worsening future ratios, however, reflect one phenomenon more than any other: the withdrawal of the baby boom generation from the labor force. Whereas from 1963 through 1990, annual labor force growth rates never once dropped below 1.2% despite the existence of periodic recessions, from 2019 onward our future labor force growth rates are projected never to exceed even half that rate (0.6%). See Figure 4, next page.

Trends in labor force growth rates can readily be seen to correlate

Figure 4: Labor Force Growth Rates, 1960–2030 (past and projected)

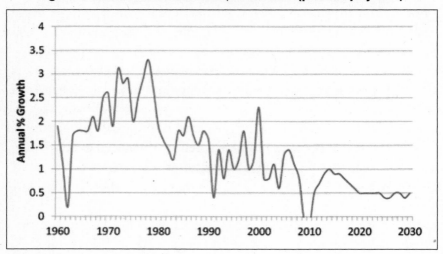

Source: Social Security Trustees Report

closely with rates of real GDP growth. Though a graph of past and projected real GDP growth exhibits more noise than labor force growth, the general correlation with labor force growth is nevertheless clearly visible:

Figure 5: Real GDP Growth Rates, 1960–2030 (past and projected)

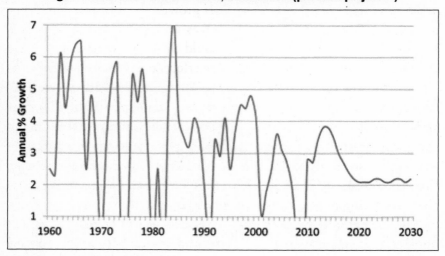

Source: Social Security Trustees Report

The economic benefits of increasing labor force participation through longer work careers would likely well exceed what is shown in federal scorekeepers' analyses of program finances. Repeal of the Social Security earnings limitation, for example, is scored under current Social Security Administration methodology as actuarially neutral although it would almost certainly incentivize longer working careers, both generating additional government tax revenue and benefiting the economy as a whole. This is similarly true of proposals to raise Social Security's EEA of 62, which is not scored by the Social Security actuaries as producing direct financial gains for the program, though the change would clearly incentivize taxpaying work by those in their early sixties.

A recent CBO analysis of raising the EEA acknowledges this effect conceptually but does not attempt to quantify it: "[T]his option also would probably lead workers to remain employed longer, which would increase the size of the workforce and boost federal revenues from income and payroll taxes." But: "The 10-year estimates for this option do not include those . . . effects."[45]

Other CBO analyses, however, quantify some potential advantages of Social Security reforms in promoting economic growth by constraining the growth of PAYGO benefits and stimulating additional work. The aforementioned 2004 CBO study found that President Bush's 2001 commission proposal to cut cost growth "could cause some people to work longer or harder"[46] whereas under the Diamond-Orszag proposal to raise taxes "households would choose more leisure."[47] Thus the two plans would produce opposite effects on economic growth.

Extended workforce participation would pay dividends for individual seniors as well as for the economy as a whole. As Barbara Butrica and colleagues noted in 2004, "[P]eople could increase their annual consumption at older ages by more than 25 percent simply by retiring at age 67 instead of age 62. The increased tax revenues generated by this work could be used to support a wide range of government services, including public support for the aged."[48]

For these and many other reasons, Social Security reform as well as broader entitlement reform should be undertaken with an eye toward rewarding those in late middle age who make the decision to extend their working careers. Some of these changes would produce net direct savings for the program, whereas others would benefit individual participants at some expense to program finances.

The often-discussed proposals to raise Social Security eligibility ages would likely have a positive effect on worker output and economic growth. Age 62 now being the most popular age of benefit claim, raising the EEA would necessarily delay many claims and likely be correlated with continued work.[49] Andrew Biggs has estimated that raising EEA to 65 would increase long-run GDP by 3–4%.[50]

Though raising eligibility ages is politically controversial, certain key points should be borne in mind about this option. One is that an EEA increase of even three years would merely bring the age of earliest claim again to what it was at the program's inception, without beginning to adjust for substantial health and longevity gains since then. Life expectancy at birth, meanwhile, has grown by more than fourteen years since 1940, while life expectancy at 65 has grown by more than six years.[51] A second critical point to remember is that raising EEA to bring it closer to the NRA would likely reduce poverty among seniors, as they would be subject to less of an early retirement penalty.

Another positive work incentive could be created by increasing the program's actuarial penalty for early retirement as well as increasing its delayed retirement credit (DRC). The current actuarial penalty for early retirement is a 25% reduction in annual benefits for those who retire at 62, four years before the current NRA of 66, or about a 6% reduction for each year; the delayed retirement credit is an 8% increase in annual benefits for each year (up to age 70) that claims are delayed beyond NRA.[52] Increasing these adjustments may better reflect the value of additional payroll taxes contributed by working seniors.

The various reforms mentioned above would likely be useful if enacted separately but would work best in tandem. Steepening the actuarial penalty for early benefit claims could, despite its other policy benefits, potentially worsen some early claimants' subsequent risk of poverty if enacted as a stand-alone measure—but would not do so if accompanied by an increase in the EEA.

Only a minority of beneficiaries take advantage of the DRC as currently structured.[53] An option potentially more attractive to workers would be to allow an individual to receive the entire DRC as a lump sum when claimed (while also receiving the basic monthly benefit as it would have been calculated at NRA). This could potentially allow claimants to receive a lump sum of tens of thousands of dollars on the date of their delayed claim—an additional incentive for continued work but with no financial cost to the system.

Another potentially important work incentive reform would be to redesign the basic benefit formula so that it operates on each separate year of work rather than on one's career average earnings. Such an alternative would apply the current formula, divided for example by 38 or 40, to *each* of one's earnings years separately, so that one continues to accrue benefits at the same rate no matter how long one works.[54]

For example, consider a person who has worked a full career with wage-adjusted average earnings of $60,000. The worker is considering a part-time "transition job" on the way to full retirement that would pay $30,000 annually. Applying the 12.4% Social Security payroll tax to these earnings, the worker would contribute an additional $3,720 in Social Security taxes. Now assume for illustration that the $30,000 transition job displaces the "35th highest earnings year" in that worker's wage history, in which he earned $19,500 (wage-adjusted). Under the current system, this substitution would only slightly increase his career average earnings, from $60,000 to $60,300. Applying the benefit formula's 15% "bend point factor" to the additional $300 in average earnings generates only $45 more in annual Social Security benefits. To recover the nominal value of the extra payroll taxes paid over this working year, this worker would have to collect retirement benefits for over 80 years—and for centuries to recover their interest-compounded value. For this reasonably typical worker, Social Security offers little incentive for continued work.

Changing the benefit formula as we have suggested might somewhat lower this worker's benefits (depending on his personal wage history) relative to current law if he *stopped* working after 35 years. The reforms would, however, offer much greater rewards for this worker to *remain* in the workforce. Depending on the number of years included in the benefit formula calculation, his extra year of work would result in an additional $373–$393 in annual Social Security benefits—a rate of return on his continued work more than eight times higher than under current law.

Another work incentive reform would be to gradually restrain the growth over inflation of nonworking-spouse benefits associated with higher earners. The nonworking-spouse benefit does play a useful role within Social Security, recognizing the value of stay-at-home work and of raising the next generation of wage earners. It is, however, inefficiently designed in that it is both regressive and a significant disincentive to paid employment.[55] It is not necessary to eliminate the nonworking-spouse benefit to address its worst inequities. One option is simply to constrain its growth. For example, a low-wage worker retiring today might receive a Social Security benefit of $11,000 as a result of contributing to the program his or her entire working life. The benefits of the nonworking spouses of the highest wage earners could be limited to that amount. No future nonworking spouse would receive a benefit exceeding the inflation-adjusted value of the benefits that today's low-wage workers receive based on a full career of payroll tax contributions.

Payroll tax relief could also be offered to seniors who extend their working lives, as has been proposed by Mark Warshawsky[56] and by John Shoven.[57] The basic idea would be to establish a status of being "paid up" under Social Security after a given number of years of contributions (forty-five in the Warshawsky formulation), after which no further payroll taxes would be collected. Notably, this would offer a work incentive to individuals on the way to paid-up status, and not only upon reaching a given age.

One policy challenge associated with improving Social Security's work incentives is that doing so will likely shift the distribution of Social Security income somewhat from women (who are more likely to have work interruptions to bear and raise children) to men (who are more likely to have longer working careers). This concern is readily addressed, however, by making the basic benefit formula incrementally more progressive at the same time that work incentive improvements are enacted.[58]

Evidence from Jeffrey B. Liebman and colleagues suggests there would indeed be a positive labor supply effect to such incentive improvements, and thus a positive effect on federal revenues, retirement income security, and broader economic growth.[59] At a time when America desperately needs the labor productivity of our skilled, healthiest younger seniors, we would do well to have a Social Security system that sides with those who provide us with the benefits of their continued work.

SOCIAL SECURITY AND FERTILITY

The relationship between fertility levels and broader economic growth is an issue one must approach with delicacy. Few of life's decisions are more personal than those pertaining to whether to bear and care for a child. Americans have historically, and rightly, taken a dim view of governments that attempt to control, manage, or even influence these family decisions too closely. As an analytical matter, however, the issue cannot be entirely avoided for the simple reason that future economic growth depends greatly on the growth in the working-age population, which in turn depends enormously on fertility rates.

In various inexact and somewhat haphazard ways, U.S. economic policy recognizes and implicitly places value on caring for a dependent child. The U.S. income tax code contains various exemptions and credits that reflect burdens assumed with child-rearing.[60] Proposals for new "family-friendly" policies proliferate from time to time; for example, suggestions in recent years for a new "KidSave" entitlement, in which the federal government would provide start-up funds for savings accounts for newborn children.[61] Whenever such policies are enacted, government officials are effectively choosing to redistribute income from the childless toward those who are assuming the burden of raising children.

Although the broader benefits of child-raising elude quantification, there is at least one area of federal policy where they are comparatively easy to calculate: Social Security financing. Social Security's pay-as-you-go structure, in which benefits for previous generations are paid from the taxes of subsequent generations, depends directly on the growth of the working-age population, and thus to a great extent on fertility. This raises the policy question of whether the benefits of child-rearing would be more sensibly recognized in Social Security law than through the general income tax code.

Social Security's long-run finances are more sensitive to fertility projections than to any other demographic or economic variable.[62] Under current projections, the gap in 2085 between annual program costs and income is estimated at 4.24% of the payroll tax base—that is, 4.24% of all wages workers would earn that are subject to the Social Security payroll tax. This assumes a long-term fertility rate of 2.0 children per woman. If instead the fertility rate decreased to 1.7, the long-term gap would swell by more than 50%—to 6.50% of the payroll tax base. If by contrast the fertility rate increased to 2.3, the long-term shortfall would be cut by more than 40%, to 2.43% of the payroll tax base. For further perspective, consider this: If American birthrates were to return immediately and permanently to peak baby boom levels, under current law there would not be any long-term Social Security shortfall as now projected.

It has long been understood anecdotally that nations with expansive social welfare systems tend to have lower birthrates. There is a vicious cycle connecting low birthrates and rising tax burdens. On the one hand, lower fertility rates lead intrinsically to higher tax burdens, because whenever there are fewer workers each must bear an individually higher tax burden to finance a given level of aggregate government benefits. But it is beginning to be better understood that the effects flow the other way as well: Rising social insurance costs lead in turn to lower birthrates. This self-contradiction at the heart of existing European social insurance programs has influenced those nations' population growth to wither at precisely the historical moment when the productivity of younger workers is most needed to support the benefit promises made to older citizens.

Michele Boldrin, Mariacristina De Nardi, and Larry E. Jones found that "an increase in government old-age pensions is strongly correlated with a reduction in fertility."[63] Isaac Ehrlich and Jinyoung Kim (2007)[64] also suggest that 48% of the reduction in fertility rates in OECD countries between 1965 and 1989 may be due to the rise in tax rates caused by growing pay-as-you-go Social Security benefits. This suggests that if U.S. Social Security taxes are increased as a means of alleviating its financing shortfall, American fertility might decline and further exacerbate the demographic shifts already negatively impacting program finances.

We explore here how the Social Security payroll tax structure might theoretically be redesigned to more equitably treat those shouldering the responsibility of raising the payroll taxpayers of the future. We take as a fundamental philosophical starting point that the objective is not to replicate the vagaries of other federal economic policies in compensating for child-bearing via arbitrarily negotiated subsidies. In sum, we explore whether Social Security's tax revenue stream could be adjusted in a simple way to become more "fertility-neutral" (while still falling somewhat short of being truly "family-friendly").

We focus on the tax side rather than the benefit side of Social Security for a number of reasons, but mainly owing to considerations of potential complexity. The benefit side of Social Security already attempts to recognize some of the value of parenting, both through its nonworking-spouse benefit and through specific benefits for dependent children, among other features. None of these, however, attempts to recognize the ultimate financing contributions made and current burdens borne by parents during the time of their parenting.

Social Security's payroll tax structure, by contrast, provides an obvious and simple way to pursue more equitable treatment of those who nurture Social Security's future supporters. Under current Social Security law, benefits are directly tied to the total amount of wages subject to the payroll tax. The payroll tax rate can thus be readily altered without unintended spillover effects upon program outlays.

This in turn suggests that the most straightforward method of creating a "fertility-neutral" payroll tax would be to increase the basic payroll tax rate while creating exemptions or deductions for each dependent child. This, of course, is already done in the federal income tax. But whereas in the federal income tax structure the current exemptions reflect the results of a political negotiation, it is at least theoretically possible to base adjustments to create a fertility-neutral payroll tax structure solely on what is actuarially fair.

In approaching this policy problem, we will observe the following principles:

1) Revenue-neutrality.
2) Treat all children equally, even though the actual relationship between birthrates and Social Security's actuarial balance is nonlinear.
3) Establish per-child deductions as a percentage of wages rather than a dollar amount, to ensure that all families of the same sizes pay the same payroll tax rates.

Incorporating these factors, conducting the relevant actuarial calculations, and simplifying somewhat produces a modified payroll tax structure of:

- A basic payroll tax rate of 14.4% for workers with no children, with
- A deduction of 2.5% for each dependent child.

In this simplified system, therefore, a worker with two children would pay a 14.4% payroll tax rate in years with no dependent children in the household, 11.9% during years that there is one at home, and 9.4% when both are present. This would lead us back to an average rate roughly equal to the current-law 12.4% tax rate for parents of two children.

Under this formulation, if U.S. fertility rates remained consistent with current projections of 2.0, then the average payroll tax rate would remain roughly 12.4% and program finances would be mostly unaffected. If instead fertility rates rose to 3.0, then the average payroll tax rate would decline to roughly 11.4%. This would result in a small net improvement in Social Security's long-term finances.

This illustrative policy would also protect Social Security finances from downside risk. Under current law, a decline in fertility rates from 2.0 to 1.5 would be truly disastrous for program finances. Under this alternative policy, such a demographic change would be automatically accompanied by an effective increase in average payroll tax rates from roughly 12.4% to 12.9%, somewhat cushioning the financing blow of lower fertility. This feature would thus serve as a partial automatic stabilizer, which various experts have proposed be incorporated into Social Security.[65]

Clearly, enacting such a policy as a stand-alone measure would shift Social Security financing burdens from those workers with children to those without. In all likelihood, this change could only be enacted if compensating changes were made in other areas of federal policy, such as, for example, the federal income tax. An example of a compensating change would be to reduce or eliminate the personal income tax exemption for dependent children, using the savings to lower marginal income rates for all income taxpayers.

To change our broader tax system's recognition of the benefits of parenting in such a way would of course be a fundamental change from historical practices. There are reasons, however, that such a policy may make greater sense than current law. It would somewhat broaden the base of federal income taxpayers while at the same time help the poorest working parents through payroll tax relief. And it would more directly tie the benefits of (and incentives for) parenting to what such parenting explicitly does for Social Security finances, in contrast with the more nebulous justifications for various "pro-family" exemptions and deductions in current federal income tax law.

■ ■ ■

Social Security reform, as well as broader entitlement reforms that encompass Medicare and Medicaid, should be undertaken with a focus on reining in program costs, encouraging personal saving and investment, and rewarding those in middle and early retirement age who make the decision to extend their working careers. Only by approaching reform in this manner can we ensure that the operation of federal entitlement programs is compatible with facilitating the levels of economic growth that we hope for America throughout the 21st century and beyond.

Acknowledgments

The authors wish to thank Jakina Debnam and Brandon Pizzola for their invaluable assistance with researching, editing, and developing substantive content for this chapter.

Chapter 16

Education Quality and Economic Growth

By Eric A. Hanushek

Since the recession of 2008, the United States has been debating how to restore and enhance the health of its economy. But what has been lost in this short-run focus on stimulus spending and federal deficits is the need to reform the nation's public schools, the engine behind any long-run growth.

An economy's ability to grow over time—its ability to innovate and raise both productivity and real incomes—is strongly tied to the quality of education provided to the vast majority of workers. Skills and intellectual capital are increasingly important in a modern economy, and schools play a central role in the development of valuable skills. We've seen this to be true in the United States as, over the past century, it expanded its economy in large part through expanding the number of people in society who receive a strong, basic education. The economy of the United States today leads the world, in significant part because the vast majority of Americans received an education that gave them an ability to innovate and to adapt to new technologies.

Unfortunately, there is now increasing evidence that the United States is reaching a point where, to achieve rapid growth of its economy, it will need to increase the quality of education it provides to its students. There is little evidence that today the K–12 education system in the United States is in fact competitive internationally or that it can be counted on to fuel future U.S. economic growth. Indeed, as far back as 1983 the United States was given a warning, with a government report, *A Nation at Risk*,[1] that its schools needed reform. Had we undertaken policies after *A Nation at Risk* was published that truly reformed our schools, we could today be enjoying substantially higher national income. We did not rise to the challenge then, and now it is much more critical that we do so.

Fortunately, the challenge before us is not insurmountable. If we raise education to levels experienced today in, say, Canada, Germany, or Finland, we would dramatically improve our economy and the well-being of our society. To see how, let's first consider the importance of what economists call "human capital," or the stock of valuable knowledge, abilities, and other things possessed by an individual.

HUMAN CAPITAL AND ECONOMIC GROWTH

Economists have devoted considerable attention to understanding how human capital affects a variety of economic outcomes. The underlying notion is that individuals invest in themselves by attending school or otherwise acquiring skills and intellectual abilities. The valuable skills accumulated by these investments over time represent the human capital of an individual. Much like a business investing in machinery (physical capital), an individual can reap economic rewards from making investments in human capital. Acquiring valuable skills allows a worker to become more productive than he would be otherwise and therefore earn higher pay. In the case of public education, parents and public officials essentially act as trustees—they determine many aspects of the initial investment a student makes in his or her human capital (although factors outside school also affect human capital).

Much of the early empirical work on human capital by economists concentrated on the quantity of schooling—the number of years of education students attained. This focus was natural. Through the 20th century the United States adopted a policy of universal education and was rewarded for its investment with high productivity growth. Moreover, quantity of schooling is easily measured, and data on years attained, both over time and across individuals, are readily available and formed the basis for studying the impacts of greater human capital. And the typical study reports that quantity of schooling is highly related both to individual earnings and to economic growth rates. Individuals with more schooling typically earn more than those with less, and the longer a nation's students stay in school, the more likely it is that its economy will grow.

The early study of human capital, developed during the 1960s and '70s, focused almost entirely on its importance for individuals and their wages in the labor market. Strangely, over much of the period after World War II, economists did not pay as much attention to economic growth as they did to macroeconomic fluctuations. Subsequently, with the revival of the study of economic growth in the 1990s, the role of human capital in determining economic growth became an important issue for macroeconomists. Even as there has been a variety of models and ideas developed to explain differences in growth rates across countries, these models and ideas invariably include (but are not limited to) the importance of human capital.[2]

But quantity of education attained is a very crude measure for the quality of skills students possess, particularly when comparing the human capital of different nations. Few people would be willing to assume that the amount learned during the sixth grade in a rural village in Peru equals that learned in an American sixth grade. Yet that is what is implicitly assumed when empirical analyses focus exclusively on differences in average years of schooling across countries. What's more, in the United States over the past quarter century, high school and college completion rates have been roughly constant. To continue to make gains in skills, and to reap the commensurate economic rewards, the United States will need to focus on what students know as they progress through school and what skills they have upon graduation.

These attributes—what students know, and what knowledge and skills they have that are applicable to the labor market—are the ones that matter in discussions of economic growth. A more educated society can be expected to lead to higher rates of invention; to make everybody more productive (when workers have more skills, companies can more easily introduce better production methods); and to lead to more rapid introduction of new technologies.

The better measurement of human capital for application to economic growth was made possible in the fortuitous development of international cognitive tests by a group of psychometricians. In 1963 and 1964, the International Association for the Evaluation of Education

Achievement (IEA) administered the first of a series of mathematics tests in a voluntary group of countries. These assessments were subject to a variety of problems, including issues of developing an equivalent test across countries with different school structures, curricula, and language; issues of selectivity of the tested populations; and issues of selectivity of the nations that participated. The first tests did not document or even address these issues in any depth. The tests did, however, prove the feasibility of such testing and set in motion a process to expand and improve on the undertaking.

Subsequent testing, sponsored largely by the IEA and the Organisation for Economic Co-operation and Development (OECD), has included both math and science and has expanded on the group of countries that have been tested.[3] In each, the general model has been to develop a common assessment instrument for different age groups of students and to work at obtaining a representative group of students taking the tests. The United States is the only country to participate in all the testing, although relatively little attention has ever been given in the United States to the results.

The world ranking of the United States in terms of student achievement is now easily seen. With the development of the common testing within the OECD through the Programme of International Student Assessment (PISA), it becomes obvious that the United States is lagging badly in terms of student outcomes. Figure 1 shows the U.S. position in mathematics in 2009.

American mathematic achievement is below the OECD average, trailing the highest-achieving countries of the world by a substantial margin. Note, for example, how far the United States trails Canada. Some people have suggested that performance on these assessments has no real impact. But they are very wrong.

Beginning with recent work by Dennis Kimko and me,[4] a variety of analyses goes beyond simple school attainment and delves into quality of schooling.[5] This early work incorporates the information about international differences in mathematics and science knowledge that has been developed through testing over the past five decades. And it finds that school quality has a remarkable impact on differences in economic growth.

Figure 1. PISA Mathematics Achievement, 2009

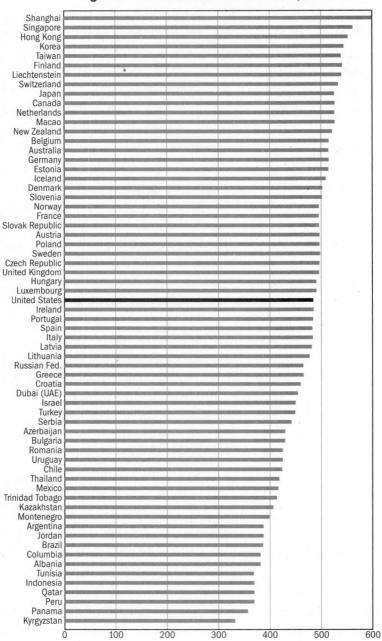

The analysis of economic growth is quite straightforward. The available test scores are combined into a single composite measure of quality, referred to alternately as the quality of human capital or simply as cognitive skills. The simplest growth analysis considers statistical models that explain differences in growth rates across nations. The basic statistical models, which include the initial level of income of a country, the quantity of schooling, and quality of human capital measured by math and science tests, explain the vast majority of the variation in economic growth across countries.

Most important, the cognitive skills of the labor force as measured by math and science scores are extremely important in an economic sense. One standard deviation difference on test performance (100 points on the PISA assessment) is related to a 2 percentage point difference in annual growth rates of gross domestic product per capita. Moreover, adding other factors potentially related to growth, including aspects of fundamental economic institutions, international trade, private and public investment, and political instability, leaves the effects of cognitive skills unchanged.

The relationship between math and science test scores and growth is extraordinarily important. If the United States could rise to the level of Germany (approximately one-quarter standard deviation on PISA), past history suggests that the U.S. long-term growth rate would increase by 0.5 percentage points. Rising to the level of Canada would imply an annual long-term growth rate that is approximately 0.8 percentage points higher. The impact of such changes is hard to overstate.

The implications of such a difference in growth rates can be seen by tracing out what happens to U.S. gross domestic product (GDP). In an article for *Economic Policy* in July 2011, Ludger Woessmann and I provide some indication of what would happen to GDP if it were possible to boost the achievement of the population. In particular, we calculate the time path of the annual growth rate engendered by education reform designed to move students from their current performance to a given new level. This pattern of economic outcomes represents the confluence of three separate dynamic processes: 1) changes in schools lead to the progressive improvement in student achievement until students fully reach the new steady-state level of achievement; 2) students with better skills move into the labor force and the average skills of workers increase as new, higher-achieving workers replace retiring workers; and 3) the economy responds to the progressive improvement of the average skill level of the workforce. Based on the historical pattern of growth rates, we project the future development of GDP with and without the education reform. Finally, we determine the total present value of the reform by calculating the discounted values of increases in GDP after reform.

These projections of the growth relationship vividly show the importance of achievement. We simulate the impact on the U.S. economy (and other OECD economies) of a series of scenarios representing different school improvement programs: 1) moving to the level of Germany or Australia (a gain of 25 points, or one-fourth standard deviation on the PISA tests); 2) movement up to the level of Finland, the world leader on PISA; and 3) movement of all U.S. students to a level of basic skills (400 points on PISA, generally Level 1). In each, for the sake of illustration, it is assumed that the United States takes twenty years to reach new achievement levels, and the labor force quality reflects the average achievement of those in the labor force at each point in time. The simulations presume that the cognitive skills-growth relationship observed across the past half century hold into the future, and this permits estimating how much higher GDP would be with added achievement compared to the current levels.

The implications for the economy with these differences are truly astounding. Economic growth is projected over an eighty-year period (the expected life of somebody born today), and then the present value of the gains is calculated (where the future gains are discounted at 3% per year).[6]

A 25-point improvement (something obtained within the past decade by a number of other countries in the world) would have a present value of $44 trillion for the United States (and $123 trillion for the entire OECD). Reaching the performance levels of Finland would add $112 trillion in present value to the U.S. economy. Just bringing everybody up to basic skills (400 points on PISA)—something akin to achieving the goals of No Child Left Behind—would yield a striking $86 trillion.

To put these gains into perspective, the current U.S. economy has a GDP of $16 trillion. The recession of 2008 cost the United States something on the order of $3 trillion in lost output, and the amount of stimulus applied to move out of recession was $1 trillion. In other words, the prospective gains from improving our schools dwarf the economic issues currently occupying all of the policy attention. This is not, of course, an argument for ignoring the current economic slowdown. But it is an argument for heeding the importance of education as a long-run growth issue.

Another way to get a perspective on these increases is to consider the added GDP relative to the accumulated GDP over the same period but without improvements in cognitive skills. Moving to the level of Finland would yield 16% higher GDP over the eighty-year period of the projections. Achieving proficiency as under NCLB would yield a 12% higher value of output over the period.

From a policy point of view, these calculations underscore the need for aggressive (and successful) policies aimed at improving achievement and skills. From a research point of view, the ability to uncover such fundamental relationships highlights the enormous value of the underlying large-scale international surveys.

WHY HAS U.S. GROWTH BEEN SO STRONG?

The United States has been at best mediocre in mathematics and science ability. Some people find this anomalous. How could math and science ability be important in light of the strong U.S. growth over a long period of time? The answer is that a variety of factors clearly work to overcome any deficits in quality. It is important to highlight some issues that are central to thinking about future policies.

Almost certainly the most important factor sustaining the growth of the U.S. economy is the openness and fluidity of its markets. The United States maintains generally freer labor and product markets than most countries in the world, along with clear and enforceable property rights. The government generally has less regulation on firms (both in terms of labor regulations and in terms of overall production), and trade unions are less extensive than those in many other countries.

Even broader, the United States has less intrusion of government in the operation of the economy—not only less regulation but also lower tax rates and minimal government production through nationalized industries. These factors encourage investment, permit the rapid development of new products and activities by firms, and allow U.S. workers to adjust to new opportunities. While identifying the precise importance of these factors is difficult, a variety of analyses suggest that such market differences could be very important explanations for differences in growth rates.[7]

Additionally, over the 20th century, the expansion of the education system in the United States outpaced that of other countries around the world.[8] The United States pushed to open secondary schools to all citizens. With this came a move to expand higher education with the development of land grant universities, the GI Bill, and direct grants and loans to students. In comparison with other nations of the world, the U.S. labor force has been better educated, even after allowing for the lesser achievement of its graduates. In other words, more schooling with less learning each year has yielded more human capital than found in other nations that have less schooling but learn more in each of those years.

The analysis of growth rates across countries considered the quality of elementary and secondary schools in the United States. It did not include any measures of the quality of U.S. colleges. However, by most evaluations, U.S. colleges and universities rank at the very top in the world. The quality of U.S. colleges and universities has undoubtedly helped foster high growth through an expanded science and engineering base.

The high quality of U.S. colleges and universities has contributed in an additional way. By attracting an ever-increasing number of foreign students, the United States has implicitly taken advantage of the high-quality elementary and secondary education provided abroad. A significant proportion of these foreign students have stayed in the United States after finishing college and thereby contributed to the growth of the U.S. economy. (Other highly trained immigrants have also come to the United States and contribute to the American economy.)

While the United States has benefited from these factors in the past, its advantages in terms of attracting highly skilled immigrants and college students are evaporating. As other countries have improved their economic institutions, the United States is losing out in the competition for highly productive workers. Perhaps no place is this as evident as China, which has removed a variety of very bad economic policies to unleash spectacular growth over two decades. But similar improvements are found around the world.

Other nations, both developed and developing, have also rapidly expanded their schooling systems, and many now surpass the United States. Currently, the United States falls just slightly below the OECD average secondary school completion rate. And overall students in the United States are not completing more schooling than students in many other countries, even when college attendance is taken into account. As economic conditions elsewhere in the world improve, highly skilled workers no longer uniformly seek to emigrate to the United States. Instead they find productive opportunities in their home countries and in other nations around the globe.

Thus it appears unlikely that the United States will continue to dominate other countries in innovation and in human capital unless it can improve the quality of the education it offers students. The raw material for U.S. colleges is the graduates of our elementary and secondary schools. And as has been frequently noted, many American students arrive at college unprepared for the coursework ahead of them and therefore have to take remedial classes. This lack of preparedness makes American colleges and universities less effective at producing highly skilled workers than they would be otherwise, while also making it more likely that foreign-born students will make up a greater proportion of our science and engineering graduates.

IMPROVING QUALITY: THE ROLE OF TEACHERS

A Nation at Risk issued a call in 1983 for improved schooling, but this call went unheeded.[9] Of course, over the past three decades American schools have introduced new programs, pursued different visions of improvement, and spent considerably more on education.[10] But student performance has remained essentially flat. One simple lesson we've learned over the past three decades is that *how* money is spent is much more important than how *much* money is spent.[11]

It is now widely recognized that teacher quality is the most important aspect of schools. A variety of studies have shown the impact of teacher quality. These studies, relying on observed differences in student achievement, provide consistent estimates of the impact of effective and ineffective teachers (Hanushek and Rivkin, 2010).

There has often been some confusion about the effects of specific teacher characteristics with the overall contribution of teachers. The consistent finding over four decades of research—frequently called education production function research in economics—has been that the most commonly used indicators of quality differences are not closely related to achievement gain, leading some to question whether teacher quality really matters.[12] The two most commonly used indicators of teacher quality are experience and graduate education. These two measures have little or no relationship with the effectiveness of teachers. (The one exception to this general statement is that teachers typically become more effective over the first couple of years of experience, even though subsequent experience does little to change teacher effectiveness.)

These findings about teacher experience and teacher degrees are particularly important because these factors are the primary determinants of teacher salaries. As a result, teacher salaries are essentially unrelated to effectiveness in the classroom. The research also demonstrates that just raising teacher salaries will not solve the teacher quality problem, because such increases in salaries go to both effective and ineffective teachers—thus encouraging ineffective as well as effective teachers to stay in teaching.

Recent research has not relied on the measurement of specific teacher characteristics. Instead it has focused on the estimation of the value added by a teacher. Effectively, this research attempts to uncover the independent impact of the teacher (as opposed to families, peers, neighborhoods, and the like) on student achievement. Heuristically, it looks at whether the average growth in achievement of one teacher's students is greater than that for other teachers. In other words, value-added estimates for teachers are a performance-based measure to describe which teacher has been effective and which has not. Using administrative databases, some covering all the teachers in a state, such research provides strong support for the existence of substantial differences in teacher effectiveness.

Although this approach circumvents the need to identify specific teacher characteristics related to quality, it has introduced additional complications and has sparked an active research debate on the measurement and subsequent policy use of estimated teacher value added. For the purposes of this discussion, however, we are not so much interested in identifying and measuring effectiveness of individual teachers—the source of much of the current policy controversy. We simply want to build on the implications of having a wide variation in teacher effectiveness, something that is less subject to controversy. Moreover, the analysis indicates that much of the variation in teacher effectiveness is found within schools, and does not simply reflect "good" and "bad" schools or disadvantaged schools or inner-city schools.[13]

Starting with the estimates of the difference in effectiveness of teachers, it is possible to project the long-term economic impact of policies that would focus attention on the lowest-quality teachers from U.S. classrooms. Consider what would happen if the very lowest-performing teachers could be replaced by "average teachers." Based on the estimates of variations in teacher quality identified in the research and calculating the impact through a cycle of K–12 instruction, we can see that modifying the stock of teachers could dramatically change U.S. achievement.[14] While there is some uncertainty about the precise variation in teacher effectiveness, Figure 2 provides an indication of what the overall impact could be (based on the range of available estimates of the importance of teacher quality).

From this figure, replacing the least effective 5–8% of all teachers with an average teacher would bring the United States to a level of student achievement equivalent to that in Canada. Replacing teachers performing in the bottom 7–12% of teachers would bring the United States to the level of the highest-performing countries in the world, such as Finland.

The previous estimates of economic impacts of achievement then

Figure 2. Alternative Estimates of How Removing Ineffective Teachers Affects Student Achievement

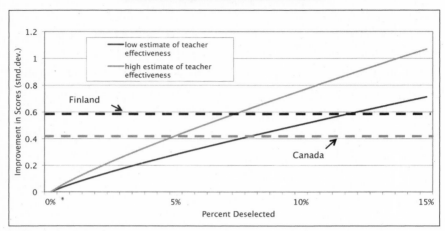

Source: Hanushek (2011)

underscore the economic ramifications of altering the quality of teachers. Approaching Finland's achievement would, by the historical pattern of economic growth, yield a gain in present value of more than $100 trillion over eighty years.

The appropriate policies to achieve these changes in teacher quality are beyond this discussion. Suffice it to say that the rewards for improvement are enormous. The economic benefits of reforming America's public schools far exceed the potential gains of a short-term focus on flattening out business cycles and from recovering from recession.

■ ■ ■

In February 1990, in an unprecedented meeting of the nation's governors with President George H. W. Bush, an ambitious set of goals was established for America's schools. One of those goals was that by 2000, "U.S. students will be first in the world in mathematics and science achievement." By 1997, as it was evident that this goal was not going to be met, President Clinton, in his State of the Union speech, returned to the old model of substituting quantity for quality: "We must make the thirteenth and fourteenth years of education—at least two years of college—just as universal in America by the twenty-first century as a high school education is today."[15] The quality goal, while perhaps more difficult to meet, appears to be a better approach than reverting to our past practice of emphasizing just quantity of schooling.

Research underscores the long-run importance of high achievement of our students and our future labor force. Higher achievement is associated both with greater individual productivity and earnings and with faster growth of the nation's economy. It no longer appears wise or even feasible to rely on more years of low-quality schooling.

Chapter 17

When Illegals Stop Crossing the Border

By Gary S. Becker

f large-scale illegal immigration from Mexico stops, will the United States need to increase legal immigration in order to bolster its economy?

For decades, the United States has been the destination of millions of illegal immigrants, many originally from Mexico. Public debates have therefore often centered on how to end large-scale illegal border crossing on the country's southern edge. Since 1990, these debates have been fueled by the fact that the number of illegal immigrants entering the country from the south was increasing rapidly.

Today, there are an estimated 11.2 million illegal immigrants in the United States, many from Mexico. But in recent years, the flow of illegal immigration has slowed significantly. So rather than increasing by hundreds of thousands each year, the number of illegal immigrants in the country appears to be leveling off. There are still illegal border crossings, but the volume is down to a trickle.

Some observers have attributed much of the decline from Mexico to tightened border security, stricter search laws against illegal immigrants enacted in Arizona and other border states, and greater enforcement against employers who hire illegal immigrants. And there is something to this argument. Over the past several years, the federal government has increased the number of Border Patrol agents, invested heavily in new technology, and stepped up scrutiny of American businesses. States have also passed laws aimed at illegal immigration.

But the main factors of this decline are likely economic and demographic, and therefore may last much longer than the current recession.

The great majority of immigrants all over the world, both legal and illegal, move for economic reasons. Few people want to leave the communities they are born into. What lures immigrants is often the chance to find jobs that pay significantly more than what they can earn in their home countries. The average illegal immigrant in the United States from Mexico appears to earn about three to four times what he would earn in Mexico. The lure of economic betterment is why virtually all the illegal (and legal) immigration is from poorer to richer countries. For this same reason, immigration increases when poorer countries are hit by recessions, financial crises, or internal conflicts that make life there dangerous and more uncertain.

Illegal immigration is also especially sensitive to recessions and other causes of weak job markets in richer, destination countries. Illegal immigrants are usually the first to be laid off, often because they are unskilled. In addition, illegal immigrants tend to have low seniority in the workplace, since they tend to be young, and employees with lower seniority are generally fired first in tough economic times. What's more, laid-off illegal immigrants usually do not qualify for unemployment compensation or other safety-net benefits.

Without safety-net benefits and facing long odds in landing a new job in a tough economy, many low-skilled illegal immigrants return home when they are laid off, even though that may mean they will bear the costs and risks of possible future illegal entry into the country. Similarly, in tough economic times, fewer people are likely to risk entering the country illegally because the odds are low that they will land a job. More than border security or enforcement laws inside the United States, the lack of economic opportunity for unskilled workers is likely why fewer people are attempting to enter the country illegally.

There is also another factor that could permanently reduce the flow of illegal immigration: demographics.

High unemployment in the United States is presumably temporary (although it has already persisted for several years). But over the past thirty years there has been a sharp decline in birthrates in Mexico. The total fertility rate—that is, the number of children born to the average woman over her lifetime—has declined to about two children today from about seven children in 1970. Despite being a much poorer country, Mexico's fertility rate is now about the same as the fertility rate in the United States. (This is a little surprising, because poorer countries typically have higher fertility rates than wealthier countries.)

A lower fertility rate means that, in the decades ahead, there will be fewer young people relative to the population than there have been in the past. And since illegal immigrants tend to be young people, there will almost certainly be fewer illegal immigrants from Mexico. Regardless of the economic opportunities available in the United States, lower fertility rates in Mexico will almost certainly mean lower immigration rates to the United States.

The very high fertility rates in Mexico in the 1970s and '80s produced many young Mexicans in the 2000s. This is an important determinant of why illegal immigration from Mexico peaked during 2000–2006. The young can more easily bear the hardships and risks of crossing illegally into the United States, and they can look forward to higher earnings for a longer period of time than older workers. Moreover, higher birthrates in the past led to a large number of illegal workers in the United States, and with lots of workers to choose from, employers are paying lower-skilled workers less than they could otherwise. The combination of these factors means that there is less economic opportunity in the United States for illegal immigrants than there once was, and fewer young people in Mexico to be tempted to emigrate north.

What's more, out-migration from poorer countries, especially of illegal immigrants, tends to fall rather sharply when job availability and incomes in their countries are improving at a good pace. This has been happening in Mexico for the past fifteen years. Since 2000 Mexico's per capita income has risen by about 40%. Job markets have become a little more open as well, and average years of schooling have increased significantly. Today, better-paying jobs in Mexico are more readily available than they had been in the past.

Most immigrants, especially illegal immigrants, prefer not to leave their own countries if economic prospects are reasonably good, even if their earnings would be considerably higher in richer countries. Individuals and young families prefer to stay with their parents, siblings, and friends, and with a culture they grew up with rather than becoming strangers in a new country. This is especially true for persons who would have to migrate illegally from Mexico, since they bear the physical and other risks of crossing the Mexican-U.S. border, have difficulty returning to see their families and friends, and can be sent back if discovered in the United States.

Low birthrates and growing incomes are likely to be part of the Mexican landscape for a long time. These forces should greatly reduce the long-run flow of illegal immigrants to the United States even after the American economy recovers from the financial crisis, and even without stepped-up enforcement measures aimed at illegal immigration. With greater economic opportunities in Mexico in the coming years, anyone who would like to emigrate to the United States will be better able to wait for visas and other permits to cross the border legally than they had been in the past.

This development could pose a challenge for the United States. Mexico isn't the only relatively poor country with declining birthrates and increasing economic opportunity. The same is true for other Latin American countries, as well as several Asian countries. The net result of this progress is that the United States could see a decline in new immigrants.

Immigration, especially legal immigration, is good for a country like the United States that has many opportunities for ambitious and hard-working men and women. Immigration increases a country's human capital. That is to say it increases the number of workers available to help businesses expand or innovators make that next big breakthrough. By increasing the size of a country's workforce, immigration can also increase a country's gross domestic product. And because many immigrants are young, a healthy inflow of them can provide the economic growth and the tax revenues that older and retired workers depend on.

So to spur its own economy and secure a better economic future, the United States may need to increase the number of immigrants who can enter the country legally.

There are several ways to do this, including simply increasing the number of visas given out annually to those wishing to come to the United States. One idea that I've raised is to openly sell the right to immigrate. Visas could be granted to those who can pay a set price.

Depending on how such a program was structured, it could attract talented individuals looking for greater economic opportunities than they have in other countries, and, even with a somewhat large price tag in the tens of thousands of dollars, could allow workers of modest means into the country. Payments for a loan on the price of a visa could be in line with what many college graduates pay for their student loans.

In any case, expanding legal immigration would be good for America, and it would also further reduce the number of illegal immigrants. When workers can more easily come to the United States legally, they have less reason to come illegally. After all, there are several advantages to legal immigration, such as the ability to conduct financial transactions that are essential in a modern economy.

An economy cannot grow on human capital alone. But without human capital, an economy is not going to develop, particularly in the modern world. Other steps can be taken to improve the country's human capital, such as education reform that raises student achievement. But education reform is a long-term project. Immigration reform has a great advantage over other changes that can increase human capital: It is something that can be done almost immediately. If the federal government changed the relevant laws and admitted highly skilled people into the country, the United States would see those new immigrants contributing to the economy within a year. That's a straightforward step toward greater prosperity, and one that will pay dividends for years to come.

Chapter 18

Immigration and Growth

By Pia M. Orrenius and Madeline Zavodny*

In 2000, as the United States was reaching the end of its longest economic expansion in history, Federal Reserve chairman Alan Greenspan noted that one reason the economy was booming was immigration.[1] Indeed, research has long shown a clear link between economic growth and immigration. Higher growth rates and rising wages are typically accompanied by more migration. In developed countries, such as the United States and Western European nations, migration is usually from abroad, but in emerging economies, such as China and India, migration consists mainly of residents moving, within the country, from rural to urban areas.

Economic opportunity clearly draws migrants, and more workers are a boon for employers. But how, exactly, does immigration contribute to economic growth? The answer is both straightforward and complex. Immigrants yield a number of economic benefits. They bring new skills, fill vital niches in the labor market, and move to where the jobs are; they contribute to innovation and new business creation.

In the end, however, only a more rapid increase in productivity will boost U.S. companies' international competitiveness and put the United States on a higher, sustainable growth path. And recent research suggests that to achieve such growth the United States needs high-skilled immigration, particularly in fields where scientific discovery and technological innovation are important. U.S. industry has long

---

* The views expressed in this chapter are those of the authors and do not reflect the views or position of the Federal Reserve Bank of Dallas or the Federal Reserve system.

relied on immigrant workers to complement native talent in science, technology, engineering, and math (STEM) fields, but over time, immigration policy has increasingly limited the number of foreign workers who can come here. In doing so, it has hurt the economy's ability to grow.

An immigration policy geared toward economic growth would favor skill-based immigration or employment-based immigration. Current U.S. immigration policy, in contrast, emphasizes family-based migration. While the ease of reuniting with family is certainly a draw for both high- and low-skilled immigrants, the priority placed on family migration means that fewer work- and skill-based immigrants—the forms of migration that correlate directly with higher rates of economic growth—are allowed to enter and stay permanently.

But before we delve into the details (and shortcomings) of American immigration policy, let's first sort through how immigration helps drive the economy and what types of immigrants the country needs to produce the innovations that will boost productivity and competitiveness and put the nation on a path to faster economic growth.

THE ECONOMIC GAINS FROM IMMIGRATION

Immigration influences the macro economy in a number of ways. First, immigration increases the labor force, making the economy larger. While foreign-born workers were only 16% of the workforce in 2010, they made up nearly half of U.S. labor force growth between 1996 and 2010. Immigrants have come to play a key role in labor force growth not only in the United States, but in many advanced nations where the native-born population is aging and labor force participation rates are declining.

Over the past twenty-five years, advanced economies with the fastest per capita output growth have also had the highest rates of immigration. In other words, the economies that grew the most typically experienced higher rates of immigration than countries that had economies that grew more slowly. The top right quadrant in Figure 1 contains these fast-growing, high-immigration countries, which include the Netherlands, Portugal, Ireland, Chile, Finland, Norway, and

Spain. Some of these nations in the past had experienced more out-migration than in-migration. So the fact that they became magnets that attracted immigrants (as opposed to losing their own population), while also experiencing significant economic growth during the past twenty-five years, is remarkable.

In contrast, the bottom left quadrant contains nations that grew at below-average rates and had below-average immigration, including Canada, Germany, Mexico, France, and others. The line shows the average relationship between economic growth and immigration. The United States lies very close to the line and to the origin of the graph, suggesting it experienced average growth and immigration when judged against the entire group of countries.

One benefit of having more immigration in an economy is that it leads to greater specialization, which means that when there are more immigrants, workers tend to choose the jobs for which they are better suited. This raises productivity and increases efficiency. Immigration

Figure 1: Economic Growth and Immigration in OECD Countries: 1985–2010

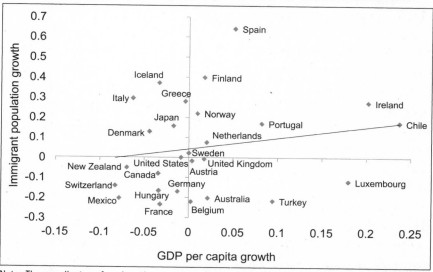

Note: The coordinates of each nation represent the deviation from median real per capita GDP growth (horizontal axis) and median immigrant population growth from 1985 to 2010 (Germany 1985–2009). OECD stands for Organisation for Economic Co-operation and Development.
Source: IMF, World Bank

increases specialization because immigrants have different skills than native workers, so when immigrants hold jobs for which natives are relatively ill-suited, natives can take jobs that they are relatively better suited for. Or, put another way, economists Giovanni Peri and Chad Sparber show that natives have a comparative advantage in communication-intensive jobs, probably due to their fluency in English, while immigrants have a comparative advantage in manual labor jobs.[2] Having more immigrant workers enables natives to move to jobs in which they are relatively more productive, and total output and income increase as a result. Most of the benefits accrue to immigrants via their earnings, but some of the gains flow to natives, whose average income rises. These gains to natives, sometimes called the "immigration surplus," are real, but they are relatively small, typically estimated at less than 0.5% of U.S. GDP annually given the level of immigration in recent decades.[3]

In addition to filling niches in the job market, there is another way that immigrants make an economy more efficient: They are more willing than native-born workers to move to regions or industries that are experiencing growth and rising wages. In other words, they go where the jobs are. A mobile workforce leads to something economists call "wage convergence," which is beneficial because it raises wages in depressed regions while taking pressure off wages in fast-growing regions. Economist George Borjas estimates that the efficiency gains accruing to natives from this convergence are nearly as big as the immigration surplus, around $5–10 billion per year for a $10 trillion economy.[4] In addition, bringing in foreign workers reduces growth bottlenecks, such as region- or industry-specific shortages of workers. The result is a more efficient economy with fewer resources sitting idle, lower unemployment, and higher productivity.

One way we can track how responsive foreign workers are to economic incentives is to look at where immigrants end up moving after coming to the United States. There is a handful of "gateway states," which serve as the initial landing spot for many immigrants. In the 1980s, demographers noted the high concentration of immigrants in certain states and cities, and there was much pessimism regarding immigrants' prospects for assimilation and progress if they remained concentrated in ethnic enclaves. But we saw in the 1990s that many immigrants picked up and moved to other states that had better economic opportunities. During that decade, three of the five traditional Mexican-destination states—Illinois, California, and Texas—experienced net out-migration of Mexican immigrants.[5] Mexicans and other immigrants moved to low-immigration states in the South and mountain regions of the country that were experiencing faster economic growth. By 2000, one-quarter of Mexican-born immigrants resided outside the five traditional gateway states, up from only one-tenth a decade earlier.[6]

A plot of job growth and immigration by state shows that states that experienced higher employment growth typically had higher rates of immigration (the top right quadrant of Figure 2). States that grew at above-average rates during 1990–2009 were predominately in the South and West, while states that grew at below-average rates were mainly in the Midwest and Northeast (the bottom left quadrant). Fast-growing states typically had faster immigration, although the lack of immigration in some rapidly growing states, such as North Dakota and Alaska, suggests those regions had a hard time attracting foreign workers.

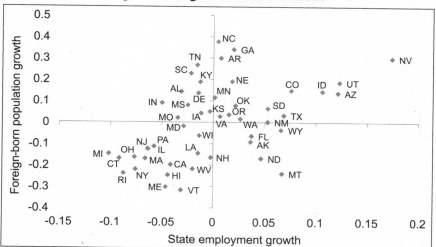

Figure 2: Immigrants Go Where Jobs Are

Note: Coordinates indicate deviation from average foreign-born population growth (vertical axis) and from average state nonfarm payroll growth (horizontal axis) from 1990 to 2009.

Source: 1990 Census; 2009 American Community Survey; BLS

Low worker mobility has traditionally been a major concern in Western Europe, where social programs and government assistance stifle the incentive that displaced workers have to move. A study by the German Institute of Employment Research reports that in a sample of unemployed Germans, 63% said they would "by no means" be willing to move for a job.[7] As in the United States, immigrants in Europe are more mobile than natives.[8] Free labor movement among the EU nations and additions to the EU, such as the joining of the Accession 8 nations in 2004, has increased labor mobility considerably there.

GROWTH-LIMITING POLICIES

The gains to immigration occur as the labor market adjusts to the introduction of new workers with different skills. Laws and regulations that prevent prices and wages from changing will slow this adjustment and reduce the gains from immigration. Natives' gains from immigration can even become net losses if immigration results in increased unemployment, which can happen if wages and prices are inflexible. Specifically, rules governing hiring; restrictions on firing; price and wage controls; occupational certification or licensing requirements; and restrictions on business start-ups all hamper the entry of new workers into the labor market. This can result in unemployment, underemployment, or job-skill mismatches that lower efficiency rather than raise it. Economists Joshua Angrist and Adriana Kugler conclude that job losses in the wake of emigration from the Balkans in the 1990s were significantly worse in EU countries with more regulated markets than in those with less regulation.[9] Research that Pia Orrenius conducted with Genevieve Solomon shows that immigrants have substantially higher unemployment rates and lower labor force participation rates than do natives in nations with more restrictive labor markets.[10]

OTHER ECONOMIC EFFECTS

Immigration can also affect the capital stock, which further increases gains from migration and the immigration surplus. In a standard economic model, as the number of workers increases, the relative return to capital rises, attracting investment that further boosts the capital stock and increases output. Some immigrants, such as entrepreneurs and investors, also bring capital with them in the form of savings, which is an additional boost to the U.S. economy.

Immigration may also lead to additional efficiency gains if there are economies of scale, which means that production becomes cheaper per unit as more units are produced. Economist Julian Simon describes economies of scale as occurring in a number of different ways when the population increases: Production rises and fixed costs per unit fall; larger markets allow for a better division of labor and more specialization; higher production volume leads to more learning-by-doing; and a bigger population makes public projects worthwhile and encourages more investment in infrastructure.[11] All of these scale effects should create efficiency gains, that is, more output per unit of input. However, there is little empirical evidence quantifying these gains vis-à-vis immigration.

If immigration has external effects that are not captured in market transactions, then the immigration surplus can be smaller or larger than the estimates noted above. Negative externalities that reduce the immigration surplus include congestion and pollution costs associated with population growth. Positive externalities that increase the immigration surplus include innovation and business creation, which are more likely when immigrants are high-skilled, as we discuss next.

IMMIGRATION AND PRODUCTIVITY GROWTH

So far, this chapter has focused on static effects of immigration on the macro economy. More specialization and hence greater efficiency are one-time gains that boost output but do not change the long-run rate of growth. The chapters in this volume are concerned with putting the U.S. economy on a higher, sustained growth path, which is a more difficult task because it requires increasing productivity growth. In the long run, increases in output per capita come from productivity growth, which is a result of technological progress.[12]

New research both on long-run economic growth and the contributions of immigrants, particularly high-skilled immigrants, suggests there is a strong connection between the two. According to recent work in macroeconomics, technological change is endogenous (it comes from within) and stems from profit-motivated investment in research and development that generates new innovations, which in turn permanently raise productivity.[13] Hence continued innovation drives productivity growth. Research has shown that adding high-skilled immigration to an endogenous growth model substantially increases innovation, boosts the immigration surplus, and leads to a higher long-run growth rate of the economy.[14]

As these economic models suggest, if immigrants are innovative, immigration can actually boost productivity growth. Recent research provides convincing empirical evidence that high-skilled immigrants play an important role in innovation.[15] Highly educated immigrants receive patents at more than twice the rate of highly educated natives. The difference has been linked to immigrants' overrepresentation in STEM fields and the growing number of immigrants entering on employment-based and student visas. There is also evidence of positive spillovers on natives, meaning that immigrants not only raise innovation directly but also boost overall patent activity, perhaps by attracting additional resources and boosting specialization.

ENTREPRENEURSHIP

As Joseph Schumpeter noted, innovation and entrepreneurship are often linked, and they both contribute to economic development.[16] Immigrants also raise economic growth via their entrepreneurial activities. Entrepreneurship facilitates the incorporation of new ideas, boosting innovation and technological progress. It also creates jobs. Research indicates that entrepreneurship among high-skilled immigrants has been instrumental in the growth of the high-tech sector. AnnaLee Saxenian concludes that immigrant entrepreneurs were an important part of the growth and success of Silicon Valley in the 1990s.[17] Vivek Wadhwa and others report higher self-employment rates among immigrants employed in science and engineering than among U.S. natives in that sector; in fact, 25% of U.S. high-tech start-ups between 1995 and 2005 had an immigrant founder.[18]

Immigrants are typically more entrepreneurial than natives in the United States, although differences in self-employment rates at a point in time are typically small. Business ownership rates in the 2000 Census were 9.7% and 9.5% for immigrants and natives, respectively.[19] The self-employment rate for immigrants had risen to 11.3% by 2010, perhaps due to the recession, while the rate for natives was 9.1%.[20]

The small differences at a point in time mask large differences in entrepreneurial activity, however. Immigrants are much more likely to enter and exit self-employment. They are nearly 30% more likely to start a business than natives.[21] This fact is surprising given that immigrants have less wealth and worse English skills, and lack institutional knowledge and access to credit.

However, there are several possible explanations. Enclave economies and networks may help immigrants overcome barriers to self-employment.[22] Self-employment may also be a reaction to labor market discrimination, particularly for immigrants who are racial or ethnic minorities. While immigrants are more likely to start a business than natives, their businesses may also be more likely to fail. Relatively high failure rates among Hispanic immigrant business owners stem from differences in wealth, access to credit, education, experience, industry composition, language ability, and legal status.[23] Easing some of these barriers to immigrants' entrepreneurial success may stimulate economic growth.

ADDITIONAL BENEFITS OF HIGH-SKILLED IMMIGRATION

In addition to the direct effects of high-skilled immigration on the economy and economic growth, there are indirect effects, including fiscal impact. High-skilled immigrants, by virtue of their education and income levels, pay substantially more in taxes than they consume in publicly provided services.[24] Low-skilled immigrants, in contrast, are a net fiscal drain on the government as a result of their low wages, large families, and lack of employer-provided health insurance coverage. The overall economic effect of immigrants' fiscal impact is probably not large since the economic gains from immigration and the positive fiscal contributions of high-education immigrants offset the fiscal drain of low-education immigrants. However, due to the local nature of most education and health-care spending, federal policies that redistribute tax revenue to cities and towns with large numbers of low-skilled immigrants may be necessary.

Most studies show that immigration has had a small but significant negative effect on the wages of low-skilled natives while high-skilled immigration has not had an adverse impact on high-skilled natives' wages.[25] Although the labor market impact is a distributive consequence of immigration, not a growth-related effect, it has implications for the well-being of low-wage native workers and therefore for immigration policy and the prospects for immigration reform. In other words, low-skilled immigrants may drive down wages for low-skilled native workers. But highly skilled immigrants tend not to drive down the wages of native workers. The implication of this is, of course, that the U.S. economy and American workers have a lot more to gain from increasing the number of skilled workers allowed into the country than they do from admitting a higher number of less-skilled workers.

U.S. IMMIGRATION POLICY AND THE NEED FOR REFORM

Creating a pro-growth immigration policy requires prioritizing work- and skill-based immigration. While current U.S. policy does reserve some places for such immigrants, it primarily admits family-based immigrants. In a typical year, family-based immigrants are 65% of new legal permanent residents. Humanitarian immigrants make up another 15%. Two smaller categories, including the diversity visa lottery for immigrants from countries with low rates of U.S. migration, comprise 6% of permanent resident admissions, which leaves 14% for employment-based immigrants and their families. Once spouses and children are subtracted, the United States admits only about 79,000 workers in employment-based preference categories in a typical year, or 7% of permanent resident admissions.

No other major developed economy gives such a low priority to work-based immigration. The United States is a statistical outlier among OECD nations, allocating the smallest share of permanent resident visas to work-based immigrants (Table 1). Even Japan, which has a low number of immigrants, gives a larger percentage of its visas to work-based immigrants than the U.S. does.

Table 1: Where Do Immigrant Visas Go in Each Country?

Country	Total Number (Thousands)	Work (Percent)	Family (Percent)	Humanitarian (Percent)	Other (Percent)
Korea	195	81	17	0	2
Switzerland	139	80	14	5	2
Spain	392	79	20	0	1
Italy	425	65	31	3	1
Germany	228	59	22	16	2
United Kingdom	347	58	31	1	10
Australia	206	42	51	6	1
France	168	34	52	7	8
Canada	247	25	62	13	0
United States	1107	7	73	15	5

Note: Only includes OECD countries; work includes free movement migrants; percents may not add up to 100 due to rounding.

Source: 2010 OECD International Migration Outlook

Under U.S. law, employment-based (EB) immigration is made up almost entirely of high-skilled workers. Only 5,000 permanent resident visas ("green cards") in the EB-3 category are reserved for low-skilled workers. Employers who want legally to hire low-skilled foreign workers can apply for temporary work visas under seasonal work-based visa programs like H-2A and H-2B. Together, these programs admit about 117,000 low-skilled workers in a typical year. With demand for such workers far outstripping the supply of work visas, most low-skilled workers come illegally.

In contrast to low-skilled workers, high-skilled workers tend to enter the country legally. But they are increasingly entering on temporary, not permanent, visas. The United States has created several temporary work visa programs in the past two decades to admit high-skilled workers. The best known is the H-1B program, which admits about 131,000 workers in a typical year, many of them skilled Indians going to work in the information technology sector.[26] Another important temporary job-based measure is the Trade NAFTA (TN) visa, which admits an additional 72,000 professionals, mostly from Canada. The L1 program admits multinational corporations' intracompany transferees (about 74,000 annually), while the O1 program provides visas for a small number of workers of "extraordinary ability." Together these temporary visa programs brought in only about 62,000 workers in 1992, but 267,000 in 2009.

As admissions under temporary visas have grown, two problems have arisen. First, caps on popular visa programs, such as the H-1B, have not been raised despite the fact that the government runs out of the private-sector allotment almost every fiscal year. The caps result in high-skilled immigrants being turned away and U.S. corporations scrambling to find qualified workers (typically in the STEM fields). An oft-cited example of the consequences of these policies is Seattle-based Microsoft's Vancouver, British Columbia, office, set up in order to hire foreign workers in Canada when U.S. laws do not permit them to be hired here. A second problem stemming from the growth in temporary visa usage is that there has been no corresponding effort by policy makers to increase the number of permanent resident visas so that the high-skilled temporary workers can stay in the United States permanently.

The mismatch between temporary and permanent visa quotas has led to long queues for green cards in the employment-based program. The State Department calculates "priority dates" for processing applications from immigrants from different countries. These dates are simply the dates for which applications were approved by the Department of Homeland Security and were then sent on to the State Department for processing, so the earlier the date, the longer immigrants have been waiting for their visa paperwork to be processed. As of October 2011, in the EB-3 category, the priority date for immigrants from India was July 2002, and from China it was August 2004. So Indians in the EB-3 category who are just now being issued green cards have waited nine years since their applications were approved.

Priority dates do not reveal anything about the length of the current queue, however. To learn that, sociologist Guillermina Jasso and others took advantage of a one-time release of information on the number of applications pending in order to estimate the size and length of the employment-based queue.[27] Their study estimated there were 1.1 million people in the United States in the employment-based green card queue in fiscal year 2006 who were approved for legal permanent residence but waiting for a visa to become available so they could adjust status. Under average processing times, it would take more than ten years to clear such a queue. An additional 127,000 persons were waiting abroad.

The binding caps on employment-based admissions are only part of the problem. There are also country caps that limit immigration from a single country to only 7% of total admissions across capped categories each year. This restriction slows immigration from India, China, and the Philippines—all important sources of skilled migrants—as well as from Mexico. Labor certification is another hurdle. Employers who petition for green cards for their workers must first receive labor certification, which requires that employers attempt to recruit native workers in order to demonstrate to the government that no qualified U.S. workers are available at the prevailing wage. The stated goal is to protect U.S. workers from large or sudden increases in the inflow of foreign workers. But, given the presence of binding caps on work-based immigration, the jobs for U.S. workers that labor certification seems likely to save or create are for immigration lawyers.

LOW-SKILLED IMMIGRATION

As noted above, compared to other industrialized democracies, the United States gives a small role to employment- and skill-based immigration. Another important difference from other large immigrant-receiving countries is, until recently, large inflows of unauthorized immigrants. Not only does the United States have more immigrants than any country in the world, but it also has the largest number of unauthorized immigrants. Their estimated population is 11 million, and unauthorized workers are believed to number about 8 million, comprising more than 5% of the U.S. labor force.[28]

Persistent labor demand, weak interior enforcement, and proximity to Mexico are the main reasons that there is so much unauthorized immigration into the United States. The availability of jobs is the main driver of illegal immigration. Border Patrol apprehensions are strongly correlated with job growth.[29] The limited number of permanent and temporary visas for low-skilled workers and the lengthy queues for those with relatives who can sponsor them for a family-based permanent visa have made illegal entry the preferred alternative for millions.

IMMIGRATION REFORM

Expanding employment-based immigration would offer a host of benefits. First, raising the caps on work-based immigration would boost high-skilled immigration. The economic benefits are significant, as we have shown. There are reasons to increase the number of work visas for low-skilled immigrants as well, such as diverting some of the stream of unauthorized immigrants into legal channels. Simplifying the onerous regulations for H-2A and H-2B visas could accomplish the same goal.

Another benefit of more work-based immigration would be more procyclical immigration. Employment-based immigration is demand driven, which means it declines when the U.S. labor market weakens. The high-tech boom of the late 1990s and the housing and financial boom of the mid-2000s produced rapid expansion in temporary visas, while the 2001 recession, the subsequent jobless recovery, and the recession that began in late 2007 were all periods of declines. While temporary work-based visas respond to the business cycle, the total number of green cards issued does not. Green card issuance barely budged in 2008 and 2009, during the worst recession in seventy years, despite the loss of 8 million jobs and a steep rise in unemployment. Binding quotas that lead to lengthy queues have made permanent visas largely immune to the business cycle; while the number of new applications moves with the business cycle, prospective immigrants whose applications were approved years ago are admitted regardless of current economic conditions.

In addition to increasing the number of work-based visas, the economy would benefit from moving to a more market-oriented way of distributing visas. Auctioning off work-based visas would better ensure that the highest-productivity workers were able to enter the United States than does the current first-come, first-served system.[30] A point system that prioritized potential immigrants based on skill and having an offer of employment would also be more efficient than the current system.

THE COST OF DOING NOTHING

Developments in other countries make adoption of a pro-growth immigration policy an economic imperative for the United States. Other industrialized nations have realized the myriad economic benefits that skilled immigrants can offer. The United Kingdom and Germany are among the nations that have adopted policies aimed at attracting skilled immigrants in recent years, while Canada has been doing it for decades. At the same time, faster economic growth in emerging markets is luring immigrants back home and reducing the incentive for others to leave. The share of Chinese students educated abroad—most of them in the critical STEM fields—and returning to China to work has doubled since 2001.

■ ■ ■

Immigration is the stepchild of globalization. Whereas international trade and capital flows have grown significantly in the post–World War II era, migration has been severely restricted. Only 3% of the world's population is made up of international migrants. This lack of mobility has led to enormous international differences in pay for workers with similar skills. These pay differences are a huge incentive for workers to come to the United States and other industrialized nations. They also represent a tremendous opportunity for governments to attract the best and brightest.

Millions of high-skilled workers want to come to the United States, and U.S. employers want to hire them. Immigration policy is standing in the way, allocating a tiny fraction of permanent resident slots to work-based immigrants and instead reserving green cards for family- and humanitarian-based immigrants who generally don't have the human or physical capital of highly educated immigrants. While family and humanitarian migration must continue to hold a key place in U.S. immigration policy, new priorities are necessary in order to leverage immigration to achieve higher economic growth.

Immigrants, representing about one in every six workers, fuel the U.S. economy. Because of accelerated immigration and slowing U.S. population growth, foreign-born workers have accounted for almost half of labor force growth since the mid-1990s. Both high- and low-skilled immigrants offer economic benefits. Both tend to complement the native workforce, bringing brains or brawn to locations and occupations where there is a need. Nonetheless, the disproportionate number of low-skilled immigrants in recent decades has imposed fiscal costs and likely harmed competing native workers.

High-skilled workers come with more benefits and fewer costs than low-skilled workers. Their skills are important to the growth of some of the nation's most globally competitive industries and to research and development. In addition, many high-skilled immigrants work in industries that produce tradable goods or services, meaning companies can employ their workers at home or abroad. Google can hire programmers to work in Mountain View, California, or in Guangzhou, China, or any of the other fifty non-U.S. cities in which it currently operates. If it cannot get visas for its workers, it can just employ them overseas. For all these reasons, the United States has a lot to gain from rewriting immigration policy to focus more on high-skilled and employment-based immigration.

Chapter 19

How Technology Can Lead a Boom

By Floyd Kvamme

I'm not an economist. I am a technologist. But I know that the world's GDP is growing at more than 4%, so I am confident that a competitive America can grow at such a fast rate as well. I also know that the technology industries can play a major role in that growth.

I've had the pleasure of being involved in the rise of the technology industry from a perch in Silicon Valley for the past fifty years. I've seen an optimistic industry take shape and grow. Indeed, growth has always been a tech industry theme, and a target of only 4% growth would not have gone over well in any Valley boardroom. In Silicon Valley we targeted double-digit growth rates each year and expected half or more of our revenue to come from international customers.

But even with this history, Silicon Valley can't escape the current stagnating economy. As this book went to press, the Valley's unemployment rate ran above 10% and technology firms struggled to expand. The optimistic view of those facts is that today Silicon Valley has a lot of unrealized potential. The tech industry that is centered in this corner of California can contribute more to GDP growth than it is now and can once again steer more of its rewards to American workers. To do that, however, the federal government needs to take a number of steps.

America is the fount of innovation, and innovation has been the engine of GDP growth for more than two centuries. We continue to innovate. Our venture capital industry is envied across the globe. Our universities draw students from every corner of the world, and those students come here to participate in the American dream by learning to innovate and learning how to start their own companies. Our system continues to provide the seeds for new companies to grow and thereby continues to lead the world in innovation.

However, we often don't reap the fruits of that innovation through manufacturing activity, particularly advanced manufacturing. The reason is that our political leaders have adopted policies that make the United States uncompetitive or encourage our innovators to take the funds necessary to produce their innovations and invest them overseas. Our innovators increasingly turn to countries with friendlier capital formation practices—countries where there are lower tax rates and more sensible regulations or where energy is cheaper and more plentiful. Investment is best measured by its return on capital employed (ROCE), and as I'll illustrate, the United States isn't doing all it can to ensure that investors will get a good ROCE. In many cases, our policies deprive innovators of the capital they need to grow their businesses or sustain the growth they've achieved in the past. It's hard to imagine how we could achieve a target of 4% growth without reversing such policies.

■ ■ ■

To consider which policies are harming growth and how to fix them, let's go back to the beginning of the modern technology industry.

Microelectronics and the modern technology on which it is based is a product of the American university system. In the 1940s and '50s, the predominant place where this technology was being developed was the Massachusetts Institute of Technology (MIT) in Cambridge, Massachusetts, and Stanford University in Palo Alto, California. The Palo Alto/Silicon Valley story starts with the transistor—a replacement for the hot glass vacuum tube that a few of us remember jockeying in our television sets to keep programs on the tube.

The transistor—invented in the venerated Bell Laboratories— sparked interest in multiple universities. But it was Stanford that landed one of the inventors of the transistor, William Shockley. He set up his company—Shockley Labs—there in order to exploit the invention. Transistors of those days were sensitive things, requiring careful handling in the manufacturing process to ensure that the end product was reliable. As a consequence, that process was labor-intensive.

We now know that the transistor was transitional. In 1957, it was discovered that more than a single transistor could be built on a silicon chip and the integrated circuit, or microchip, was born. The microchip was a revolutionary invention. Computers and many other systems could be built with it, and it was far more reliable than its vacuum tube predecessor.

At the time, the Cold War was raging, and American technology was booming. The Russians launched Sputnik that year, touching off a space and technology race. We poured more resources into scientific research and in the years ahead grew determined to get to the moon before the Russians. Meanwhile, transistors were finding their way into everything from simple handheld consumer radios to the Polaris and Poseidon missile systems. But it was the Apollo mission that offered the first sizable application of the integrated circuit. Government, through its contractors and their subcontractors, became a customer for the new technology and thereby provided a lot of funding that sparked additional innovations.

During the 1960s, military and aerospace applications accounted for almost half of the revenue of many semiconductor companies. Government procurement demanded that the end products be built in the United States, a requirement that gave America an early leg up in manufacturing using this newly minted technology. Government dominance as a customer for the industry began to wane in the late 1960s, and federal procurement procedures also became more onerous. By the early 1970s, government business was not the driver it had been earlier, though it was still important for much of the decade.

From the start, producing silicon wafers used for microchips was labor-intensive, and packaging those little chips was even more labor-intensive. As demand for low-cost transistors grew, technology companies realized they needed to cut their labor costs in order to compete. One way to do that was to outsource the assembly of microchips to Asian countries.

Hong Kong got its first microchip assembly factory in 1959. Other

Asian countries followed. Initially, the finished products were shipped back to the United States for testing before being sent to customers. The combination of U.S.-based wafer fabrication and Southeast Asian assembly allowed American producers to be competitive with the Japanese, who were aggressively courting the microcircuit market but refused to assemble their microchips outside Japan.

Anxious to land manufacturing sites, several Asian countries started offering attractive incentives, including tax holidays on profits and tax breaks for job training and other costs. These incentives enabled technology companies to lower their costs even further.

It didn't take long before American technology companies figured out that they could lower their tax bills significantly by shifting their facilities overseas. The rate and structure of the corporate income tax provided a strong incentive to move manufacturing offshore. U.S. companies paid American taxes on what they produced inside the United States and on the profits they repatriated back to the States. But they paid taxes—in addition to tariffs—only on the value added to components that they shipped overseas for assembly and then shipped back.

And thanks to the textile industry, tariffs on the value-added component of a finished microchip were a lot cheaper than corporate tax rates. (The tariff rules known as 806/807 were originally drafted for textile mills to ship cloth and threads overseas, where they were turned into finished garments and then shipped back.) Semiconductor companies used these rules, shipped their chips and other materials to Asia for assembly, and then shipped the completed transistors or microcircuits back to the United States. By the mid-1970s, the industry employed more than two hundred thousand people in Asia.

The value added by this process was always being disputed by one arm or another of the government. The U.S. Customs authorities wanted to place a large value on the overseas assembly portion of the process because technology companies paid a tariff based on that valuation. The Internal Revenue Service, however, wanted overseas assembly to carry a low value because then a larger share of the total value of each microchip would be subject to U.S. taxes. Logically, U.S. companies favored the Customs approach for a simple reason: Tariff rates of 5–6% were only a fifth or sixth of U.S. tax rates.

The result of this bifurcation between tariff rates and tax rates is that U.S. policies created a perverse incentive for American companies to produce more of their goods overseas than here at home. As a result, American companies began to accumulate a large volume of corporate cash in foreign countries. What's more, American companies began using their overseas capital to expand overseas rather than repatriating that money and subjecting it to U.S. taxes. While the justification for this strategy has changed (as I will describe later), the fact that most technology companies hold most of their cash in foreign entities is not new and continues to be true today.

In the 1960s, the capital costs to build a world-class wafer fabrication plant were relatively low. My recollection is that when a group of us started National Semiconductor in 1967, a fully functioning wafer fabrication plant cost about $1 million. With labor costs then accounting for a large percentage of the cost of producing a microchip, companies would control expenses during downturns by reducing their workforce.

As demand for microchips grew, the process for producing them became more automated. This lowered labor costs, improved reliability, and otherwise allowed technology companies to become more competitive, but higher capital expenditures were needed. One estimate that I made in the 1970s was that our industry was split about 50/50 between capital costs and labor costs. Today, more than 70% of the expense of wafer fabrication is capital-related and only 4–6% is labor-related (the balance being materials and regulatory compliance).

I use the example of the semiconductor industry because that is my background, but the same is true in many other industries. When manufactured products first enter the market, they require a tremendous amount of human labor to produce. Over time, as demand for the product increases, the manufacturing process is automated and costs fall. This is true for high-tech companies, and it's true for more traditional manufacturers as well, including automakers. The bottom line is that mature and maturing industries use automation to control costs and provide reliable product.

This is an important fact to consider when thinking about economic growth. As companies move toward automation, capital costs become increasingly important. As labor costs fall, high taxes on capital give mature and maturing industries increasingly compelling reasons to shift to more friendly tax environments. To see what I mean, ask yourself why some years ago Dell built an advanced "lights out" factory in China that was completely automated. With no employees at the factory, Dell could not have been seeking cheaper labor rates in China. Rather, the move was driven by considerations of after-tax return on capital.

As the semiconductor industry became more capital-intensive decades ago, we thought long and hard about bringing some of our manufacturing back to the United States. We were operating in many places where communist incursion was a distinct possibility—Thailand, Malaysia, and Indonesia—and were worried about political instability. But the numbers for moving the manufacturing facilities back to the United States just didn't add up. The tax rate on profits was very attractive in these foreign locations. Sending profits to the United States (using current tax rates as an example) meant paying 35% or more of that capital gain to the federal government. Investing the capital overseas meant we would have 90% or 100% of our money (after paying local taxes) to spend, but investing it in the United States meant that we would have only 65% or less of that capital to invest.

Given those numbers, it's not hard to see why the industry decided to keep its manufacturing operations in Asia (and, subsequently, in other low-tax foreign locations). As manufacturing became even more capital-intensive, the after-tax ROCE calculation ruled the day. Over time, the industry moved the entire manufacturing process—from wafer fabrication to assembly and even microchip testing—to Asia. So what began as a move to lower assembly costs over time shifted to a strategy for getting a lower tax rate on capital.

As an example of how powerful incentives embedded in our tax policies can be, consider a report published by the President's Council of Advisors on Science and Technology in 2007. That report looked at a $4 billion project to build a new semiconductor wafer fabrication plant. The company involved compared building the plant in China to building it in the United States. After careful review, the company realized the difference in the after-tax ROCE over ten years was a stark $1.3 billion in China's favor. And it wasn't labor costs that made the difference; labor accounts for just 4% of the cost of producing wafers. The difference was driven by Chinese tax and regulatory policy.

Many have argued that the semiconductor industry's move to Asia doesn't matter. What matters is that consumers can now pay less for technology products. I might be inclined to agree with this sentiment if not for some of the facts involved. If the chief driver of moving manufacturing facilities overseas were lower labor costs or cheaper materials, then I could agree that China and other countries have a comparative advantage in high-tech manufacturing. The drivers here, however, aren't labor or material costs. China and other Asian countries don't have a natural comparative advantage over the United States. Rather they have an invented comparative advantage. These countries have seen that they can be more competitive in world markets through their taxing policies. It seems to me that rigging one's tax policies to advantage your manufacturing base is not unlike the maligned practice of currency exchange rate manipulation. Meanwhile, a nation's consumers benefit from the success of the economy in which they live. If the economy of a country—like the United States—is not competitive in world markets, its consumers will suffer in the long term through lower employment and lower value created by the workforce.

MANUFACTURING MATTERS

In the late 1980s, Stephen S. Cohen and John Zysman published a book, *Manufacturing Matters,* touching off a heated debate about world trade and its impact on individual nations.[1] The authors argued that the manufacturing era was not over and that manufacturing still counts in a modern age. As I said, I'm not an economist, but after having helped manage a fast-moving technology company, I know that manufacturing matters a great deal to a country's well-being. Here's why:

First, in the nascent days of a new technology, most manufacturing is labor-intensive. So the emergence of new technologies can produce jobs for American workers. As the product matures, companies will increasingly turn to automation to control their costs. The automation process actually yields extensive knowledge to the engineering team, which can use that knowledge to improve the next generation of products (or an existing version of the product). It's possible for an engineering team to acquire this knowledge from a factory that is being automated across the ocean, but it's much easier for the team to acquire that knowledge if the factory being automated is located down the street.

Second, as a company reduces the number of workers it employs at a factory being automated, that automated factory can become very profitable. The return on investment that the automated factory produces allows a company to grow. So automation can lead to higher profits, which in turn can be invested in new ventures, technologies, and innovations. All lead to the creation of new jobs.

What happens to job creation as automation moves in? The simple answer is that it goes down on the product being automated. But that is not the whole story. The building and maintenance of these factories offer employment to Americans. The feeder plants to automated factories and the distribution networks that are used to bring products to market also employ many people and contribute to value. So even a "lights out" factory contributes to a community's well-being and to its country's GDP.

The number of manufacturing jobs in America has fallen from more than 30% of the labor force a half-century ago to only about 12% of the labor force today. Some of those manufacturing jobs have moved to China and other countries. But not all of them. Many were simply eliminated through automation. Over the past couple of decades, reports suggest as many as 30 million manufacturing jobs have disappeared in the world. Even China has lost manufacturing jobs.

At the same time, new kinds of jobs are emerging. Good ones can be found in the factories that make the precision equipment necessary for automated manufacturing plants. Even today, American companies provide much of the precision machinery that is deployed in automated factories around the world. What we need are public policies that make it profitable for many more factories using products from those precision equipment makers to be located in the United States. This would bring the manufacturing value added back to the United States, which would expand our GDP. We can't tolerate the misleading "we can't compete because of labor rate" argument any longer. Labor is only a small portion of the cost that makes a country competitive, and we can do a great deal to address the other drivers that compel companies to move facilities overseas. Let's look at the actions we can take.

THE NEED FOR LOW-COST ENERGY

In most automated facilities today, the cost of energy, mostly electricity, exceeds the cost of all direct labor. Unfortunately, the United States is allowing its aging power grid to languish, while other countries upgrade and expand theirs. China, for example, has more than doubled its electricity supply over the past decade, and that new capacity is coming from modern power plants with modern efficiency standards, giving a major economic advantage to Chinese factories. Americans have missed the importance of electricity competitiveness for two reasons:

First, U.S. industry has been particularly successful at becoming more energy-efficient. Advances in electronic controls as well as controls for lighting, heating, and air-conditioning all ensure that power is not wasted. In 2004 the Energy Information Agency (EIA) of the Department of Energy estimated that energy requirements in the United States would grow about 1.7% per annum from approximately 100 quads (100 quadrillion BTUs) to 150 quads by 2030. Recently, the EIA has revised that growth down to say that only 110 quads would be required in 2030. Currently, the United States is still consuming only about 100 quads of energy a year. Our energy consumption has been flat to down since 2004, so we haven't yet felt the pinch that will come once rising energy demand outstrips supply.

The second reason this concern is not front and center for most policy makers is that competing nations have only recently been building their energy infrastructure; its impact has not yet been realized. When new modern generators are fully on line in China, energy costs in that country could continue to fall. That would give the Chinese a substantial competitive advantage in attracting manufacturing installations. Similarly, other nations are also scrambling to bring new, efficient energy sources on line so that they can compete for the factories of the future.

WHAT IS A PRACTICAL PLAN FOR COMPETITIVE ENERGY?

Today, our energy needs are bifurcated into transportation and electricity. Oil serves mostly our transportation needs. (About 75% of the oil we consume is used for transportation—most of the rest is used as an ingredient in some three hundred thousand products ranging from asphalt to plastics to lipsticks.) Oil, much of it imported, is a big driver in our transportation costs, but there are a few developments worth noting. First, the amount of imported oil we consume has been falling for the past several years, from 12.5 million barrels a day in 2005 to 9.4 million in 2010.

The main reasons for the drop are new oil discoveries in the United States—notably, the Bakken fields in the Dakotas—and the introduction of a large volume of biofuels into the market. Last year, ethanol replaced the need for more than 350 million barrels of oil; it accounted for 1% of our gasoline usage in 2001 and over 8% today, saving Americans about $35 billion at current oil prices in our balance of payments for oil imports. Anytime oil exceeds about $75 per barrel, ethanol is cheaper than gasoline.

Biofuels, like domestic oil production, create jobs, lower transportation fuel cost, and decrease cash outflows to foreign suppliers while making gasoline burn more cleanly. And biofuels don't rob from the food supply, as some claim. Ethanol factories use almost 40% of our corn supply today but extract only the sugars; the grain is sold as cattle feed, just as it would have been without an ethanol plant. This corn retains every bit of protein and fiber that beef, pork, and poultry producers rely on. Media commentators who claim we "burn" food for fuel are just wrong. There is also new research under way that is looking at how to use biofuels to replace the need for oil in plastics, rubber, and many other products. Encouraging this research will help our economy if it leads to manufacturing these products in the United States.

Until the electric car displaces the need for oil, producing more domestic oil and using biofuels to replace foreign oil imports will boost our GDP and provide meaningful jobs to thousands of American workers.

As for electricity, according to the latest data, our needs are primarily met by coal (51%), nuclear (21%), natural gas (17%), and hydro (6%). Oil plays almost no role in providing power to our wall plugs. Solar, wind, geothermal, and other "green" generation technologies are growing rapidly but from a very small base. It is very hard to imagine a scenario that has these newer "green" technologies supplying even 20% of our needs by 2030, but it's a goal worth pursuing.

Currently about 40% of the energy we consume goes toward electricity production. But that could change in the future. New uses for electricity, such as charging electric vehicles and producing fresh water by desalination, will dramatically increase our demand for electricity. Manufacturing should augment that demand even more.

To prepare for coming changes in electricity markets (and to replace the worn-out electricity generation equipment), we must build modern electricity capacity and do it at competitive costs. At the moment, our best option is some combination of coal, natural gas, and nuclear systems. If we assume that future coal and natural gas plants will be required to capture carbon emissions—which seems likely—then we can see that nuclear energy could be very cost-competitive. For example, the Department of Energy factors in the cost of capturing carbon and then estimates the total cost per kilowatt hour for coal at 12.9 cents; for natural gas, 11.3 cents; for nuclear, 11.9 cents.

So costs are about the same at 12 cents per kWh. But the Operating and Maintenance (O&M) portion of the cost (which includes the important cost of fuel) for these three generation types is very different. For coal, the Energy Department estimates O&M at 2.6 cents per kWh; for natural gas, 6.3 cents; and for nuclear, just nine-tenths of a cent. The bottom line is that once a plant is built, fuel costs vary widely.

We know that coal is plentiful in the United States, but carbon capture requirements add about 3 cents per kWh to its cost; if this requirement persists, coal may be our most expensive alternative. Natural gas provides the lowest construction cost but is highly influenced by the cost of natural gas in the future; the good news here is that the recent discovery of large quantities of natural gas within our borders should hold prices in check, but the political battle over modern gas recovery technology creates a risk.

Nuclear, however, could become a lot more cost-effective over time. It's true that the earthquake and tsunami that hit Japan in March 2011 also delivered a body blow to the nuclear industry. Fewer people trust nuclear energy now than before. But Fukushima also tells us how nuclear power can be safe. First, the nuclear power plants in Japan survived the earthquake. The real problems began when the tidal wave that followed knocked out the electric power and generators that served the plants. The entire catastrophe could have been averted if the nuclear power plants' generators were shielded from the tidal wave.

Certainly this tragedy is not going to encourage use of nuclear power. We can only hope that the public will respond over time to nuclear's realities. First, from a safety point of view, America's 104 nuclear plants, while old, have never caused a single fatality. Second, modern systems are "passive," meaning that they don't require power, as Fukushima did, to flood the reactor in the event of an accident. Further, modern systems are now of a fixed design, which means that building them shouldn't be as expensive as it has been in the past. Also, more than 90% of the construction costs of a coal or nuclear power plant are related to the cost of steel and concrete. A nuclear plant uses 50% less of these two materials than a coal plant does. To date, most new "Gen 3" nuclear plants are being built in Asia, but twenty-one such plants are under consideration in the United States (mostly in the Southeast). I hope they get built.

In any case, in order to grow at 4% or more, the United States needs low-cost energy. It is hard to imagine a scenario where coal— with carbon-capturing mandates—can deliver. If natural gas pricing doesn't rise appreciably, it could supply power more cheaply than coal, but I worry that fuel prices will spike. Nuclear plants provide the best long-run promise for power generation at low operating costs.

EDUCATING THE AMERICAN PUBLIC ON CAPITAL FORMATION AND CORPORATE TAX POLICY

In my years as the head of a nine-thousand-person division at National Semiconductor, I had lunch with ten to twenty frontline production workers each week. All questions were permitted and honestly answered; this was family. Most of these employees were blue-collar. To me they were the backbone of America. Each had a unique story.

The principal lesson I learned from my colleagues at these lunches was that general knowledge of how the American capitalism system works is a complete mystery. The simple fact is that we do a great disservice to our citizens by not teaching them how our economic system works, and especially how capital formation is the source of growth.

In the tech industry, cash has always been king. When a new venture is started, payment in the start-up's equity is frequently offered to service providers to preserve cash; your suppliers become your partners. This cash preservation mode of operating continues as the company grows. Young companies rarely offer dividends. They hoard cash to be ready for the unforeseen obstacles and opportunities that come along.

In fact, until only a few years ago, tech companies that paid dividends were considered firms that had run out of new ideas on how to grow. Capital formation usually came from retained earnings since companies tried not to dilute their equity by excessive equity offerings except when absolutely necessary. A rule of thumb in Silicon Valley is that cash on the balance sheet should equal a minimum of one quarter's worth of revenue. This capital is used to underwrite the large research and development budgets of the average tech company and to fund the cash requirements inherent in a fast-growing enterprise.

In those employee lunches at National Semiconductor, questions frequently arose about who got the profits that we publicly announced; some colleagues even implied that they thought management divided the pot after each reporting period. I always had to explain the simple truth: Our profits funded future growth, new buildings, and more jobs.

In those explanations it would often become clear how destructive taxes can be. When taxes consume 35% or more of profits, then they also consume a third of the money we need to keep growing and to continue to create new jobs. I could see why managers of tech companies adopted the belief that taxing authorities should be avoided if at all possible, particularly when the shareholders have received no dividend payments for their investments. Remember, in Silicon Valley, the practice until recently was that every employee was a shareholder (a practice, alas, killed by regulation of the Sarbanes-Oxley law). CFOs, as a result, are constantly pressured to find ways to preserve cash and lower tax liabilities. Offshore operations have frequently been the answer.

I'm sure some of our domestic employees didn't like the fact that we had factories overseas, but we tried to make them understand that the reason was competitiveness. Since capital is the seed from which enterprises grow, it is hard to defend tax rates that dramatically decrease capital formation. By its tax policies, the U.S. government, in particular, is reducing the capital available to fund both GDP and job growth. Jobs are dependent on a company being competitive; if their government is harming their company's competitiveness, employees should know it.

■ ■ ■

There is plenty of reason to believe that the United States can grow at 4% annually over a sustained period of time. After all, over the past decade world per capita purchasing power has grown by almost 50%, and demand continues to rise. The world needs American technology and American products, so there is a strong and growing market opportunity. The question is this: How do we take advantage of that opportunity?

By looking at the tech industry, I can say what we need is to spark new innovation that will enable us to grow and create an environment where even more innovation will occur. Innovation has always led to growth in the tech sector. Why? Because innovative products and services open up new opportunities for consumers, creating new markets and new profits. In some cases these innovations are based entirely on new science (think of biosciences and nanotechnology). In other cases, these innovations are new versions of existing products or services such as personal computers, the Internet, cellphones, etc. And in still other cases, these innovations are new ways to work that lead us to be more productive, and thus higher-paid, workers.

Of course, innovations can also be disruptive. The "Rust Belt"— that band of territory that's full of boarded-up old factories and shuttered manufacturing plants in the Midwest and Northeast—is the result of innovations. Over the past several decades, electronics technology has been replacing the springs, levers, stepping motors, and gears that were a previous generation's way of doing logic functions by mechanical means. This transition has had a high human cost.

Such transitions will likely continue to occur, but they don't have to be as disruptive as in the past. To ensure that we don't leave our workers unemployed, the United States needs to maintain a lead in each area of discovery, and its workforce must be ready to adapt to new technology. What we require is a flexible workforce, where workers can shift to better jobs as they emerge. Silicon Valley has been particularly good at adapting to new technologies in this way.

Government support of research and development activities within our colleges and universities has led to significant technological innovations. Therefore, if we wish to enact policies that will lead to growth, the government should continue to support basic research primarily in our institutions of higher learning.

But supporting research alone isn't enough. American industry has the money and the human capital to unleash new waves of innovation. What it needs are policies that make this country more competitive with foreign nations. U.S. firms need to be able to find investment opportunities here that offer after-tax returns on capital employed that are competitive with opportunities abroad. The government can help create those opportunities by supporting policies that give us cheaper, more reliable sources of energy; more sensible regulations; expanded trading opportunities; and a reformed tax code.

I have already explained how taxes drive jobs overseas. To reverse that, I'd like to see the corporate tax rate fall to 15% or 18%. This suggested rate is lower than some are proposing and is lower than some of our competitors, but I consider it necessary to offset the tremendous lead that Asia has achieved in advanced manufacturing and infrastructure in recent decades. America has fallen behind; it must offer incentives to recover lost ground.

Some are calling for the United States to adopt a "territorial tax system" that would tax only profits made within American territories. This type of tax system is now common among our trading partners. Creating such a system could do a lot of good for the United States, but if it were enacted before our domestic tax rates were lowered, it would trigger an even larger shift of advanced manufacturing jobs out of the country.

Finally on taxes, we need to think carefully about how to repatriate profits parked overseas. In years past, the federal government has sought to bring that money to the United States over a short-term "holiday," with an 85% exclusion. My friends in Silicon Valley will hate me for writing this, but that program sends the wrong message and will not create jobs. Let's repatriate money parked overseas, but let's also tie that policy to lowering the overall corporate tax rate and the possible adoption of a territorial system. American companies need American-based cash to pay dividends, to enter into M&A transactions, and for other uses. Repatriating without fixing the root cause of why the cash is maintained offshore in the first place will not change behavior and will not lead to domestic job creation.

We need expanded trade opportunities because we live in a shrinking world. If you are not now competing internationally, your competitors, abroad and at home, will crush you. Alternatively, going head-to-head with your fiercest competitor on his home turf will prepare you for the hard realities involved in competing on the global stage. Europe built a wall around its technology innovations in the 1970s and hurt its growth for years thereafter; Japan would not open up its markets to foreign investment in the 1970s and '80s, and it is no longer the factor it was earlier. These examples convince me that walling oneself off from the realities of the global market does not work. In fact, it can make you weaker.

Similarly, imposing trade barriers on, say, China would only succeed at shutting off access to one of the world's fastest-growing markets— not a smart move for Americans who wish to sell their goods abroad. Chiding China for the fact that many of our manufactured products come from its factories is also silly. The Chinese have outcompeted us; it's not their fault, but ours. If we become competitive, I am confident we will outpace them.

Many Americans may not realize it, but our regulatory measures are archaic, and they are holding us back. We need to overhaul federal regulations that make it too cumbersome or costly to run a public company or access capital. And we should enact reforms that wipe out duplicative regulations. There are many areas where regulations come from federal, state, regional, county, and city ordinances. They are all slightly different, and keeping up with them is enough of a nightmare to drive investors to a location where the regulations are easier to understand and comply with. Getting the federal government out of state business and states out of county business, and so on, would be a godsend. And a strong patent system that defends American innovation is mandatory.

On energy, I have three broad suggestions. First, we should expand our use of biofuels as a way to encourage energy innovation in this country. To the extent that we develop domestic energy sources, we'll be cultivating new jobs, new sources of innovation, and new opportunities in the United States. Congress has passed legislation making several reforms to ethanol policy, saving the federal government money and likely leading to a greater use of biofuels in the years ahead. This is an important step toward promoting growth through energy policy. Second, the United States should set a goal of bringing a minimum of thirty-six new nuclear plants on line by 2025. This will ensure that at least 20% of our electricity comes from nuclear energy. And third, we need to continue to promote the creation of "green" energy sources. If we factor in the cost of sequestering carbon, wind and geothermal energy sources are today nearly competitive with coal. What I like about wind and geothermal is that their fuel expense is negligible; they could provide us with a future supply of energy with a low variable cost. We should also support solar energy where its cost is nearly competitive.

■ ■ ■

Innovation is part of the American DNA. The tech industry doesn't need government support in order to innovate in ways that will raise our standard of living, provide us with new products, and probably surprise even the most forward-thinking among us. But if we are to see a significant jump in our GDP, we will need innovation in our public policies that allows us once again to become much more competitive in global markets.

America is capable of competing in today's international markets.

We can solve our unemployment problems by creating new high-productivity jobs and by growing at world rates. It is always easy to solve a financial problem by increasing the "top line," but we must not take our eyes off the necessity of cutting government spending. When the government spends less, it will be easier to reform the tax code and take the other steps necessary to make it simpler to find lucrative investment opportunities right here in the United States. Growth and lower spending should both be our goals. If so, we can probably reach a sustained growth rate in America of 4%, or better.

Chapter 20

Growth Lessons from Calvin Coolidge

By Amity Shlaes

Impossible.

That's our basic assumption about the United States achieving a balanced budget, low tax rates, and a smaller government in the future. Strong economic growth over a sustained period? That seems the most elusive goal of all.

One reason we're so pessimistic is that we can't even imagine a president who could achieve such a thing. But there was such a president: Calvin Coolidge, who served between 1923 and 1929. Though today Coolidge is hardly discussed, he was Ronald Reagan's favorite president. There's a reason for that: Coolidge achieved nearly all that we aspire to today. He is therefore worth getting to know.

This story starts with basic details: Coolidge was a New Englander, a Vermonter, a governor of Massachusetts, and a vice president. He became president when, in August 1923, Warren Harding died in office. Coolidge stayed in the White House, winning his own election in 1924, until 1929.

To read the standard texts is to take away the idea that Coolidge was a laconic, unremarkable man, a former governor whose role in history was to keep the chair in the White House warm between the Roosevelts. Most Americans know little of him besides his nickname, "Silent Cal." Indeed, there were many jokes about his taciturn demeanor. There is a favorite story of him as a New Englander at a dinner party. A lady next to him bet that she could get him to say three words. At the end he said, "You lose." Other jokes are more hostile. Commenting on him, Alice Roosevelt Longworth said, "He looked as though he had been weaned on a pickle."

Along with the jokes, there was commentary, which was even nastier, from the outset of his administration. Though incoming presidents usually receive a polite greeting from press and public, Calvin did not. Here is what Oswald Garrison Villard, the editor of *The Nation*, wrote about Coolidge to welcome him into office in the summer of 1923: "And now the presidency sinks low indeed. We doubt if ever before it has fallen into the hands of a man so cold, so narrow, so reactionary, so uninspiring, so unenlightened, or one who has done less to earn it, than Calvin Coolidge."

The hostility continued unabated and even increased after Coolidge died, persisting through the decades until we get the caricature of today. Why even mention all this? First of all, because the clichés are inaccurate. Coolidge was, in fact, a talker: There are almost two thousand pages of him chatting in his off-the-record press conferences. Second, when Coolidge was silent (and that was often), there was a productivity to his silences. Third, we know that when other people are *that* nasty there is usually a force behind the nastiness that goes beyond the people involved.

In this case that force was envy. First it was prospective envy: The Progressives knew Coolidge would serve well. Then it was contemporary envy of something in the process of being achieved. Coolidge's record was *too good*, both as governor and vice president and then as president from 1923 to 1929. He was too popular to bear. In the 1924 presidential election, there were three significant parties: Democrats, Progressives (who got 16.6%), and Coolidge's party, the Republicans. Coolidge won by a majority, not a plurality.

It might be worthwhile, then, to sketch out several things, starting with the reason that Coolidge's presidency elicited envy. The second item to consider is the thinking behind the Coolidge policy and what it has to do with economic freedom, and economic growth.

In the 1920s, there were troubled areas of the American economy: Farming, where average income was almost always below the national average, was the main one. Foreclosures on farms rose throughout the decade. The Ku Klux Klan enjoyed a troubling amount of power in the

South. Another problem area was banks, some five thousand of which failed. In the later 1920s, the stock market rose too rapidly. A euphoric annual increase of more than 50% (the Dow Jones index rocketed from 200 to 381) followed in the summer of 1928. Some Americans bought stock on margin and some drank too much champagne, just as the literature has it.

The rest of the story of the 1920s represents positives. Real gross domestic product grew at an average of 3.48%. Coolidge sustained the high growth of his prececessor, Warren Harding. Nor was growth all taking place in Jay Gatsby's tax bracket. Regular people benefited, too. People acquired Model Ts and radios and refrigerators and vacuum cleaners. Houses were wired for power and telephone. In 1923, some 20% of households had telephones; by 1929 that figure was 40%. Before our entry into World War I, just 30% of manufacturing used electricity; by 1929, the proportion was 70%.

The productivity gains at factories in the 1920s came along with another gift: shorter hours. At the beginning of the decade, firms were just starting to cut the average week from fifty hours to forty or forty-five. Suddenly people found themselves working only five days a week. In 1922, the *New York Times* reported that "nearly all employees used their free Saturday for study or recreation and that very few sought other kinds of paying work." Pay kept up, too. Between 1923 and 1929, the average real weekly wage for the unskilled worker in 1929 dollars rose from $22.37 to $24.40. The average wage for skilled and semiskilled workers taken together rose from $30.93 to $32.60. Union membership actually went down. That was in part because people did not see a need for unions.[1]

Even in Progressives' own terms, Coolidge did well. Today we're often compelled by others to judge eras by their distribution tables, especially tax distribution tables that chart which quintile of earners pays what share of the income tax. Progressives want the rich to pay more. That happened in the 1920s. Before Coolidge, bottom earners didn't pay the income tax, but those just above, earning $3,000 to $5,000 a year, shouldered a full 15% of the tax burden in 1920, while those at the top, millionaires earning above $500,000, contributed just 4.25%. By 1929, the figures had reversed. The taxpayers at the bottom of the system paid less than 1% of the taxes and those with $500,000–$1 million in income paid a 10.6% share. Those who had income over $1 million a year paid 19% of the taxes. As for unemployment, it averaged below 5% in all but one year.

All this was achieved even as the federal government was becoming a smaller part of the economy. The federal government shrank from 4.35% of gross domestic product in 1923 to 3.68% in 1929. At the same time, Washington was running a surplus every year. Economists often refer to the Phillips Curve, which holds that policy makers have to pick their poison: inflation or unemployment. The 1970s disproved that rule by supplying both poisons, and the 1920s represent a happy inverse, disproving the curve by featuring low unemployment and little inflation. In other words, the 1920s was not a pretty good decade. It was a stupendous decade.

How did Coolidge achieve this? The short answer: free-market policy; getting the government out of the way when he could. At times he seemed like the Little Dutch Boy, putting his finger in the dike to stop the Progressive waters.

This work started with the energy President Coolidge poured into maintaining a stable environment for the economy and the individual by reducing uncertainty. Warren Harding, Coolidge's predecessor, specifically combated uncertainty by calling for a "return to normalcy," getting back to the average humdrum after World War I. In his inaugural address, Harding said that "any wild experiment will only add to the confusion. Our best assurance lies in the efficient administration of our proven system." When Harding died, Coolidge remained committed to the policy of normalcy.

Coolidge believed and taught that government had to stay out of the way for the private sector to grow, which he interpreted to mean that Washington had to keep the budget under control. Coolidge did that, and in a fashion that puts subsequent Republicans to shame. In fact, credit here is also due to Woodrow Wilson and Harding, who together reduced the federal budget from $6.4 billion in 1920 to $3.1 billion in 1923. Coolidge's feat was to cut yet again in the five years of his stewardship.

Coolidge also loudly affirmed the importance of the private sector. One of Coolidge's lines is, in fact, remembered—albeit also by the mockers: "The business of America is business." This reassured business that Coolidge was serious about keeping the government out of the private sector's way, which is never easy. The utilities industry was the equivalent of the Internet today: the most promising industry on the rise. Naturally, it was coveted by government. There was a concerted effort to involve the federal government in the production of electricity through the expansion of a government dam, the Wilson Dam at Muscle Shoals, Alabama. Coolidge vetoed the attempt. There were other useful vetoes as well: for a veterans bonus, for farm subsidies. This last veto was notable because Coolidge was the son of a farmer. Coolidge talked progressive from time to time about labor price, but on his watch there was no big union legislation.

That a seasoned politician might achieve so much seems paradoxical because of the modern premium on being an outsider: Today we tend to believe that only the novice, the revolutionary, can bring necessary political change. The reality was that Coolidge was able to do all he did precisely because he was an experienced politician, with long years in the Massachusetts legislature and as president of its state senate. Remarkably, Coolidge managed the budget himself and struck out spending routinely. His mastery in using experience in government to achieve the philosophical end of limiting government is well known thanks to one relatively friendly journalist, Walter Lippmann. He had the president's modus operandi down:

> The White House is extremely sensitive to the first symptoms of any desire on the part of Congress or of the executive departments to do something.
>
> The skill with which Mr. Coolidge applies a wet blanket is technically marvelous. . . . There has never been Mr. Coolidge's equal in the art of deflating interest. The naïve statesman . . . imagines that it is desirable to interest the people in their government . . . that indignation at evil is useful. . . .
>
> Mr. Coolidge is more sophisticated. He has discovered the value

of diverting attention from the government and with an exquisite subtlety that amounts to genius, he has used dullness and boredom as political devices.

One test of Coolidge's convictions came with the Katrina of his era, the 1927 flood of the Mississippi. Its dramatic consequences included walls of water more than twenty feet high and hundreds of thousands of displaced people. Coolidge confronted the same dilemma as President George W. Bush after him: whether to react as a military leader would and run down as commander in chief or to pause and respect federalism. Coolidge did the latter. He did not see it as the role of Washington to lead the rescue. Private philanthropy should take the lead. The government's job was secondary, to help the Red Cross do the work, maybe through coordination, maybe with supplemental funds.

Tax rates were another determinant of the growth in the 1920s. Remember the outcome: The rich paid a greater share of the taxes and there was more tax revenue and strong growth all around. To get there, however, required enormous legislative effort. In this area, Coolidge had an ally, also mocked: Secretary of the Treasury Andrew Mellon. Mellon was the cabinet member Coolidge liked most, perhaps because they were both taciturn and selected their words carefully. People joked about their silence, too: It was said that Mellon and Coolidge conversed in pauses.

The pair set a dramatic goal: to reduce the tax burden on individual enterprise and to curtail the tax breaks that diverted capital to less productive areas of the economy. The top marginal rate of the income tax was 77% when the war ended. Presidents Wilson and Harding cut that top rate to 73% and then 58%. Many considered those reductions sufficient. Coolidge disagreed: "If we had a tax whereby on the first working day the government took five percent, the second day ten percent, the third day thirty, the fourth day forty, the fifth day fifty, the sixth day sixty, how many of you would continue to work on the last days of the week? It is the same with capital."

When Coolidge came into office, he and Mellon pushed that rate down again, to 46% and then 25% in 1925. Their reforms were cuts across the board, so that the bottom rates on the schedule also came down, from 6% or 4%, to 2%. That 25% is a level we have not seen since. The top marginal rate went back up into the 60% range after the Depression began. Coolidge and Mellon both believed that low taxes were a good idea for reasons beyond utility or maximizing incentives on a graphed curve. They believed low rates were morally better. Coolidge's statement at the time: "The collection of any taxes which are not absolutely required . . . is only a species of legalized larceny." In other words, Coolidge did not merely cut taxes because it was efficient. He did so because it was the right thing to do.

A final feature of the Coolidge method was his humility. He not only had the ability to delegate, but he believed he ought to, out of respect for the structure of the executive branch. Coolidge generally didn't run Treasury policy; Mellon did. Nor did he run foreign policy; he relied on the Department of State or his friend, Ambassador Dwight Morrow. When the time came to run for a second elected term in 1928, Coolidge declined with an admonition that could have been written by Lord Acton: "The chances of having wise and faithful public service are increased by a change in the presidential office after a moderate length of time."

Coolidge practiced humility in his dealings with other men. He revered the contract. He cared much about civility, about mutual respect. *The Nation* might attack him, but it is hard to find in all of Coolidge's work an ad hominem attack anywhere. He also showed humility before his God. He believed that there were some areas where the spiritual had authority that should not be assailed. Teachers and documentaries often repeat that Coolidge quotation "The business of America is business," at the cost of giving a complete picture. Coolidge followed that famous line with "The ideal of America is idealism." He repeatedly made clear that there were precincts government and law could not enter. This approach was captured in remarks at the naming of a statue of Bishop Francis Asbury in October 1924. Coolidge said that "the government of a country never gets ahead of the religion of a country. There is no way by which we can substitute the authority of law for the virtue of man."

Once you realize the extent of his achievements and the depths of

Coolidge's philosophy, you see why some people resented him. They were envious. Who could argue against a president who presided over increases in the real wage even as union membership dropped? The only way to beat Coolidge was to misrepresent and marginalize him. You can hear it very clearly in the words of *The Nation*'s commentary. Villard continues his complaining about Coolidge's ascent to the presidency: "Every reactionary may today rejoice; in Calvin Coolidge he realizes his ideal, and every liberal may be correspondingly downcast."

This brings us to the final question: If Coolidge and the 1920s were a success, and the 1920s did roar, how could history manage to drown out that roar so well? One reason is the Great Depression. Here is the current schoolbook logic. If the Great Depression was exceptionally great—great enough to last a decade—then the error that caused the Great Depression had to be commensurately great and cover an entire decade. If Roosevelt is to be great, he must be preceded by demons.

Coolidge is also forgotten because of modern economic theory, based on the work of the British economist John Maynard Keynes. Keynesian vocabulary is our vernacular. But Keynesianism lacks the words to describe what happened in the 1920s. Under Keynesian rules, a recession where budget cuts and increases in the interest rate do not halt recovery is indeed an impossibility. In the 1920s, the Coolidge economy gave the country high growth, but the Keynesians could never explain why. So instead they pretended the 1920s were all fluff and champagne bubbles. It is not paranoid therefore to say that these days Calvin Coolidge is not "Silent Cal" so much as he is "Silenced Cal." And this itself is a silent tragedy. Budget reduction, tax cuts, and the gold standard are worth reconsidering as potential remedies to today's ill. They are strategies that could allow the U.S. economy to grow at 4% or more. Free-market philosophy didn't lose out in the United States because it failed. It lost out because it succeeded too well.

Chapter 21

The Moral Imperative of a Free Economy

By Michael Novak

The first moral obligation is to think clearly.
—BLAISE PASCAL

Indispensable to both the democratic republic and the creative economy are certain crucial moral and cultural institutions, such as the churches, the poets, the historians, the scientists—all those charged with the life of the soul and the habits of the heart in any republic. It is difficult to find critics in our time who do not recognize the massive decline that has occurred in one after another of these institutions. Think of the role of writers and preachers at the time of the American Founding, and even up through the Civil War. Our literature has been noble, and our churches have been serious, both about the deepening and purification of the soul and about the general improvement of the lot of all humankind.

Without such cultural institutions, where would the prairie fire of the drive and resolve for independence have originated and been stoked? From whence the fires of abolition and an end to slavery, apart from other resources of the human spirit, at Princeton and in Joshua Chamberlain's Maine? As Harvard's Mary Ann Glendon has made clear in her book, *The Tower and the Forum*, the republic of letters and the republic of political advancement tend to feed each other.

But today, many of our mainline churches have lost their moral starch and intellectual depth. In the various fields of social action, many of our activists have conducted themselves more as sentimental sloganeers than as hard and critical thinkers. It seems obligatory to estimate that intellectually and morally our universities are not what they were; nor are our churches; nor are our editorialists.

It is astonishing how many of these sentimentalists and sloganeers have gathered around the faded, ill-used, and badly thought-out banners of "social justice" and the "common good." For some hundred years, generation by generation, these tattered flags have been flown, nearly always bringing empirical disaster in their train. At the very least, one would wish to find their employers today cautious and critical.

Our repetitive revolutionaries declare themselves the advocates for those who are poor or for those who are otherwise feeling economic distress (such as, say, middle-class homeowners who are behind on their mortgages). However, these advocates tend to confuse their intentions and their noble ideals with state spending and taxation. One can reliably draw their fire simply by suggesting that the federal budget for welfare or other entitlement programs should be rethought or even cut. The advocates will quickly assert that this new policy proposal violates principles of social justice and harms the common good. They take raw spending as a measure of helping the poor.

But what's the evidence that social welfare programs actually help in the long run those who receive benefits? Do we not have available for anyone interested in seeing it abundant evidence that many kinds of social spending hurt those they are intended to help?

Feeling sentiments of moral superiority over those who judge reality differently is not the same as achieving real improvements in the lives of the needy. Not to think clearly about such matters is a moral fault.

Consider, for a moment, the plight of unwed mothers. Never as in the past fifty years has so much spending been authorized to assist these households. Yet as one *New York Times* headline from 2009 reminds us, "Out-of-Wedlock Birthrates Are Soaring, U.S. Reports." In fact, the number of out-of-wedlock children, white and black, keeps swelling. The prognosis for these children is, according to unarguable government records, bleak. Such children are far more likely to be born with medical problems and to grow up without the guidance and discipline of a father (especially needed by young males). They are also likely to be uninterested in schoolwork, drop out of school, be unable to hold a job, become involved in crime, be wounded or killed in neighborhood strife, fail to raise two-parent families themselves, and stay on welfare for generation after generation. Are these the consequences that those of us who at first supported the War on Poverty intended?

Let me put this tongue-in-cheek for a moment. According to a secret plan, the federal government wiped out poverty in America by the end of 2008—but out of modesty refused to let anybody know. That year the federal government spent enough money on all sixty-nine of its means-tested programs to provide every poor and near-poor person in the United States with $7,700. That meant that every family of four received at least $30,800 income that year, far above the poverty line. Poverty was eliminated overnight.

Documentation for these expenditures has been assembled by Robert Rector of the Heritage Foundation, among others. The truth is that the federal government reaches this achievement every year. It gives away—just on means-tested programs alone—far more per person than is strictly called for to eliminate poverty.

However, since the 1960s the proportion of the poor has changed remarkably little, despite all that vast spending. In fact, a higher proportion of people raised themselves out of poverty (mainly with the help of their own intact families) in the decades before the Great Society than in those afterward.

It is true that after the Great Society, the condition of the elderly has improved far beyond where Hubert Humphrey and John F. Kennedy hoped during the campaign of 1960, and far beyond the great stretches of poverty across America, not least in rural regions, to which Michael Harrington's electrifying book *The Other America* awakened the whole nation. In 1960, the largest cohort of the poor was elderly (those over the age of sixty-five). That is no longer the case, even though today more Americans are living longer (and better) lives. The increased life span and the increased financial means of the elderly is a great achievement, of course.

But the condition of America's younger cohorts has dramatically worsened. Today the largest (and fastest-growing) proportion of the poor is found in households of unwed mothers with children and no fathers present. Our age displays the most wholesale abandonment of pregnant women by males in Western history.

Did the design of well-intentioned programs have anything to do with that? Do some programs hurt the poor, more than they help?

It is not self-evident that more spending is the same as social justice and the achievement of the common good. It is not self-evident that the state is an appropriate instrument of humanitarian intentions, especially considering that it has vigorously attempted to address the issue of the poor for decades while making so little progress. It is one thing to long for the common good and to work for it—and it is a whole other thing to achieve the common good, through effective, practical instruments.

The argument in America today is not whether the chains of poverty should be broken for every poor man, woman, and child in America. In all justice and charity, those chains must be broken.

The argument concerns the most effective means for achieving that goal. Is statism—the belief that in government there is a solution to the problem—the effective answer? Or is the state too ineffective, too counterproductive in its clumsy procedures, too involved in generating new patterns of political self-interest (for instance, state poverty programs seem to benefit their middle-class dispensers much more than the poor they are putatively aimed at), too expensive, too out of touch with the way human things actually work, to deliver on its vast promises?

Pope John Paul II had an answer to the question concluded in paragraph 48 of his encyclical *Centesimus Annus* of 1991:

> . . . In recent years the range of such intervention has vastly expanded, to the point of creating a new type of State, the so-called "Welfare State." This has happened in some countries in order to respond better to many needs and demands, by remedying forms of poverty and deprivation unworthy of the human person. However, excesses and abuses, especially in recent years, have provoked very harsh criticisms of the Welfare State. . . . Malfunctions and defects . . . are the result of an inadequate understanding of the tasks proper to the State. . . .
>
> [T]he [Welfare] State leads to a loss of human energies and an inordinate increase of public agencies, which are dominated more by bureaucratic ways of thinking than by concern for serving their clients, and which are accompanied by an enormous increase in spending. . . .

The pope had learned from bitter personal experience in Poland that the communist state was not the answer. He also learned in Italy, and especially in Sicily, how corrupt, corrupting, and ineffective the state could be at liberating the poor from poverty and at encouraging appropriate familial independence.

Pope John Paul II saw the illnesses of statism spreading elsewhere in the West, too, not least its disturbing increase in out-of-wedlock births and its loss of the strengths the intact family had demonstrated throughout history. Often, when no other institution could be counted on, the family had held human life together. The family often was stronger and more enduring than the state.

Again, the argument in America and elsewhere should no longer be whether the best road to progress is via the state (the left's position) or the individual (the right's position, of old). The argument should be which intermediate institutions and associations are better suited, and more effective, than the state in achieving social justice and the common good. The new best hope seems to be the growth of a strong and vigorous civil society, with all its personal and associational energies. Civil society, the new argument runs, is a better social instrument than the state in achieving social justice and the common good. It will be better at raising the poor out of poverty.

In which direction does the evidence point? What are the best, most critical arguments on both sides? The first moral imperative is to think clearly, and with evidence. And if we do think clearly and follow the evidence, the argument need not be ideological. The argument must be about concrete results. It cannot be about feelings or intentions.

REMEMBERING SOME HISTORY

The partisans of social justice and the common good of the past fifty years, it is fair to say, did not foresee the consequences of their compassionate (but not well-designed) methods. They did not predict that juvenile delinquency (which in 1960 John F. Kennedy quaintly spoke of reducing) would become in the next forty years a sixfold increase in violent youth crime. Nor did those of us who supported President Kennedy and President Johnson anticipate the serious multiplication of fathers who would take no responsibility for children. Nor did we predict the unprecedented decline of young families (white and black, rural and urban) into the ranks of the disoriented and dependent poor.

During the administration of Barack Obama, with especial vigor, the partisans of the religious left have argued that they help the poor when they increase federal spending for the poor. They pretend that feeling compassion and spending more money actually helps, rather than hurts, the poor. Where is their evidence?

Government records show that the problems of families receiving benefits from the state are not chiefly financial. More devastatingly, most suffer not from monetary poverty but from illnesses, disorders, and careless habits that for the last twenty years have been classified by social scientists as "dependency." The victims of dependency do not support themselves, their elderly parents, or their own children. They rely on others, and continue that way for decade after decade. In this condition, many persons who take in far more money from the state than do much poorer immigrant families (and more than millions of native families) continue generation after generation in this dependency. Meanwhile, millions of well-ordered immigrant and native families work their way out of poverty during an amazingly short span of years. And the disabilities of dependency now affect the white poor in far greater numbers than the black poor.

Yet these are not the worst of the intellectual errors committed by those who value their own sentiments more than reality-based reasoning. Those who empower a leviathan government will all too soon be forced to dance to the tunes that government plays. Federal administrators are already telling Catholic Charities whom to hire and what secular creedal statements to make their guidelines. Bureaucrats are also telling doctors who cannot conscientiously carry out abortions that they must do so, as a professional responsibility, punishing those who do not hold to the changing but current secular morality.

Wise Christian churches are already ruing the role they played in uncritically accepting concepts of "social justice" and "common good" that invited the state into their business. Social justice and the common good do not flow best from the state. These churches have realized, quite poignantly, that religious liberty in particular has had no greater enemy than the unchecked state.

In these matters, the history of the years since the end of World War II shows that we have not thought clearly enough about ends and means. Nor have we thought deeply enough about unintended consequences. Nor have we thought about the dangers that are embedded in every sweet intention and good deed. We have missed the point of the original meanings of social justice and the common good, which are critical tools, not enablers of sentimental feelings.

SOCIAL JUSTICE IS NOT WHAT LEFT OR RIGHT THINKS IT IS

In *The Mirage of Social Justice*, Friedrich von Hayek applied a critical brush to this often sentimentally (sometimes cynically) used battle cry, social justice. The term, he noted, was first used in the Catholic Church and gradually made canonical by Leo XIII in 1891 and Pius XI forty years later. In short, social justice is an ideal first articulated by the Catholic Church, with its tradition of using words carefully.

Even as John Stuart Mill was still swooning over the happy possibilities of socialism, Leo XIII was warning of at least nine crippling moral properties of socialism, each one of which, in fact, manifested itself over the next hundred years. (Pope John Paul II, who lived under socialism, unemotionally pointed this out in 1991.)

In any case, Pope Leo XIII was looking for an alternative to socialism. He wanted a different social path, not the increasingly powerful central state that he saw growing all around him. He foresaw the dangers of this new state to religious freedom, to the daily life of the Church, to the family, and to the traditional human associations of the European countryside and towns. He saw the dangers to private property, and thus to creativity in every sphere, including the economy and the arts.

Pope Leo XIII earned the sobriquet "the Pope of Associations," precisely because he saw the necessity of a social means of individuals and families organizing themselves, independent of the state, and checking state power. Leo XIII was no statist; statism was his nightmare.

Although Hayek's footnotes show that he was aware of this history, he concentrated his fire on a development he saw chiefly in Europe during the 1920s and beyond: the fascination with the state as a force for good (forgetting its propensities for great evils). Hayek noted that social justice was first conceived by Leo XIII as a *virtue* inhering in individual persons, a power to act, a firm habit of acting well. But he also noted, correctly, that by the 1920s the communists and the fascists saw the potential fruits for their side in this same battle cry.

Hayek's critique of Catholics and other Christians using the term is that most of them slowly fell away from speaking of social justice as a virtue inhering in persons. More and more they spoke of programs launched and paid for by the state. Well, now, Hayek pointedly asked, is social justice achieved as a virtue, or is it achieved by a state program? If by the latter, show me the evidence that states act from altruism, not for self-interest and self-aggrandizement. And show me evidence that government actions are effective at achieving their stated purposes.

Whatever the issue, Hayek ventured, *more* is always what the state demands. Government social programs are not motivated and formed by moral virtue but by state interests, and the stronger the state the less likely there will be any quotient of virtue.

In short, as a moral battle cry, social justice is impotent. It is a battle cry for more state power and more money. Judge it by its fruits. Seek out its unintended consequences. Look for its rampant abuses. Sentiment is not enough. For many, social justice has in fact become a mirage. Yes, Hayek exaggerated, but the challenge he laid down was clear.

Now the irony is that Hayek himself was one of the greatest practitioners in our time of the virtue that Leo XIII was intellectually groping for at the end of the 19th century, and trying quite desperately to promote. Hayek spent decade after decade, when he was not working out the key concepts in his books and essays, forming new associations all around the world: the Mont Pelerin Society (of scholars of law, economics, legislation, philosophy, and religion, committed to political and personal freedom), the international network of Atlas Societies, and hundreds of cooperative study groups around the world.

Hayek's photo hangs like that of a patron saint in think tanks in

London, Chile, Argentina, Slovakia, the Czech Republic, Germany, and most probably by now in India and China. Hayek developed to a high pitch of excellence the virtue of inspiring social action through associations that are independent of government. He tried to counter the cravings of government by creating checks and balances against government authority and action. For Hayek, free people and their associations were a fresh source of the initiative, creativity, and personal responsibility that by their very existence remove the justification for vigorous social welfare policies.

And please note, this new modern virtue of social justice (not singled out in earlier centuries but eagerly praised by Leo XIII) is properly called social in two senses. First, its goal is social—to improve one's social community, whether local (digging a new village well, putting up a school, building new homes) or national. Examples of the latter are forming political associations across the whole spectrum of persuasions, from Occupy Wall Street to the Tea Party, from the left-wing Students for a Democratic Society of the 1960s to the conservative Young America's Foundation of the 1970s, from the National Organization for Women to the National Right to Life Committee. There are many voluntary associations of international scope, too, such as Human Rights Watch, Chambers of Commerce, Amnesty International, and a multiplicity of others. The world is teeming with voluntary associations.

And by the way, partisan loyalties of any kind tend not to be permanent—they are always under personal review. Critical intelligence leads many to change their minds. One of the most interesting features of a free society is how many free persons, learning from experience, do change sides. Moreover, many leaders of business support the left—that is, a large state whose aim is motherly and helping. And many people nourished by the left learn by careful thinking to discern the left's illusions about the would-be humanitarian state.

The free society is founded on the free competition of ideas, and therefore of ideas organized, thought through, presented, and promoted through associations. Associations embody ideas, give them social force. The competition among associations forms healthy checks and balances. As James Madison put it, natural rights are not defended by words on paper, by parchment barriers, but by the virtues and associations of a free people.

The key to a real human rights revolution is the fresh articulation of powerful ideas necessary to liberty, then free people taking up the responsibility to make those ideas a reality. There is nothing more powerful than free people working through free associations to fight for ideas. Rights do not become real by someone putting words down on paper, but by free people acting together in the great political act of social persuasion.

THE COMMON GOOD IS NOT A LICENSE FOR STATISM

Moralists also like to use the "common good" as a club to bludgeon those who question the loss of their liberty to the state. Liberty, these moralists imply, is selfish. Unless corralled by the state, individuals will kick up like wild mustangs and take advantage of others.

What is needed, they say, is an impartial umpire, a fair distributor of goods. They tend to imagine the state in maternal, caring, sweet, expansive, disinterested terms. They tend to regard the private sector, especially the business sector, as greedy, rapacious, one-sided, and unconcerned about what the public needs. They think of themselves as sensitive, and their political opponents as insensitive.

In fact, if there is any real meaning in *left* and *right* today, it tends to be found in the intellectual argument over which set of institutions best achieves the "common good." Often today, this argument is couched not precisely in terms of the common good, but rather in these terms: Which policy better helps the poorest, the neediest, and the most vulnerable in our society? A policy that enlarges the state, or a policy of limited government that draws its energy from multiple associations in a free civil society?

If you argue, for example, that raising the minimum wage does not really help the poor, you run the risk of being cast as taking a just wage from a poor kid in the city, to give it in tax breaks to rich plutocrats who fly private jets.

If you argue that current welfare designs have gravely worsened the conditions of young parents with children (predominantly single mothers), you are likely to be cast as, well, it used to be as racist. You can hardly be called a racist any longer. The growing raw number and greater proportion of persons living in such households are now white. But if you continue to argue the facts against the current methods of providing welfare, there is a good chance you will be disparaged as heartless.

The government makes laws and regulations about almost everything, tying Lilliputian silken strings around every part of our lives, in one way or another, under the mantle of the common good.

This nation has slowly, unresistingly, as though through the spread of an odorless, invisible gas, become an enervated America, as Alexis de Tocqueville predicted it would in the 19th century. We now experience a new soft tyranny, so strictly and minutely constricting our freedoms that we Americans are only a shadow of our former selves. Quoting from Tocqueville's *Democracy in America*:

> I see an innumerable multitude of men, alike and equal, constantly circling around in pursuit of the petty and banal pleasures with which they glut their souls. . . . Over this kind of men stands an immense, protective power which is alone responsible for securing their enjoyment and watching over their fate. That power is absolute, thoughtful of detail, orderly, provident, and gentle. . . . It provides for their security, foresees and supplies their necessities, facilitates their pleasures, manages their principal concerns, directs their industry, makes rules for their testaments, and divides their inheritances. Why should it not entirely relieve them from the trouble of thinking and all the cares of living? . . . It covers the whole of social life with a network of petty, complicated rules that are both minute and uniform, through which even men of the greatest originality and the most vigorous temperament cannot force their heads above the crowd. It does not break men's will, but softens, bends, and guides it; it seldom enjoins, but often inhibits, action; it does not destroy anything, but prevents much being born; . . . it

hinders, restrains, enervates, stifles, and stultifies so much that in the end each nation is no more than a flock of timid and hardworking animals with the government as its shepherd.

We all live now—one almost wishes to be hyperbolic—on a giant government plantation. Overburdened by debt (more than $14 trillion), the federal government is no longer able to meet even the promises it has made. Yet it keeps making new ones. It is a horrible irony that most of the damage has been done through appeals to the common good.

My experiences as ambassador to the U.N. Human Rights Commission in 1981 and 1982, and at the Bern Round of the Helsinki Talks in 1985, illuminated for me as never before how easily the slogan the "common good" can be made the enemy of the rights of the human person.

At Bern, suave Soviet officials drew the issue to the fore: Yes, some of our citizens have (unwisely) married foreigners, they said. But how on earth could the Soviets ever allow such persons to live with their new spouses outside the Soviet Union? After all, had not the Soviet state educated them, housed them, fed them? They now had a huge bill to pay back. The common good of the Soviet people counts heavier than the emotions or wishes of unwise individuals. Soviet adults cannot be allowed to move just because they would choose to do so. They cannot join a spouse languishing far away. The common good trumps individual rights, familial love, and marital obligation.

Those who want more of an uncritically defined common good should watch out, lest that cry become an enemy of the rights and freedoms of human persons. Those rights and freedoms are a crucial part of the human common good, as Catholic social teaching carefully promulgates. From the Second Vatican Council, this definition: "The common good of society consists in the sum total of those conditions of social life which enable men to achieve a fuller measure of perfection with greater ease. It consists especially in safeguarding the rights and duties of the human person."[1]

A CONCLUDING REFLECTION

Claiming to speak for social justice and the common good does not by itself achieve the results one wishes for. Social justice is not always achieved through the state. The common good is not always well protected by government policies. In these matters, clear thinking is urgently needed. What works? What results are actually achieved?

Besides the state, there is another social alternative: the free associations of a vital civil society. This was the emphasis of Leo XIII as he pushed against the extreme powers of the socialist vision of the state.

The radical argument here is not ideological. It is simply empirical, a matter of carefully measuring which policies and practices, based on broad experience, best serve the needs of the most vulnerable in our societies. It is important that we open our eyes and ears to the evidence and the best arguments of those who answer this question differently. And then summon up our reasons for deciding as we do.

As we summon those reasons, the question we seek to answer will be critical. If we accept without further inquiry that the common good requires us to give up our liberties and enlarge the state, we could continue to allow those with noble intentions to carve a hole in the center of our civil society. If the goal is to serve the poor, raise living standards, create jobs, and create a growing economy, then our answers need to assess honestly how to accomplish those things. Uncritically accepting a misguided version of the common good won't serve society's interests, even if it does serve the interests of a few powerful factions within society.

INTRODUCTION: We Can Do It

1. Source: Bureau of Economic Analysis, 1946–2011, based on chained 2005 dollars.
2. The graph in Figure 1 of Lucas's chapter actually shows GDP per capita, or per person, but the powerful trend line is the same.
3. At this writing, the CBO's most recent budget and economic outlook was completed in August 2011, at http://www.cbo.gov/ftpdocs/123xx/doc12316/08-24-BudgetEconUpdate.pdf.
4. John Maynard Keynes, *The General Theory of Employment, Interest and Money* (1935), Book 4, Chapter 12, Section 7, p. 161. The book is online and free at: http://www.marxists.org/reference/subject/economics/keynes/general-theory.
5. For the conference proceedings, including video and transcripts, go to http://www.bushcenter.com/economic-growth/4percent-project.
6. http://www.bushcenter.com/downloads/theInstitute/economicGrowth/4percentProject/TheBusinessLeadersRoundtable.pdf.
7. www.bea.gov/national/xls/gdpchg.xls.
8. http://www.econ.yale.edu/smith/econ116a/keynes1.pdf.
9. http://www.gpoaccess.gov/eop/tables11.html. See Table B-79.
10. *New York Times*, "How the U.S. Lost Out on iPhone Work," is important and received a good deal of attention, but, in my opinion, it focused less on taxes than it should have: http://www.nytimes.com/2012/01/22/business/apple-america-and-a-squeezed-middle-class.html?_r=4&pagewanted=all.
11. http://www.nytimes.com/2012/01/22/business/apple-america-and-a-squeezed-middle-class.html?_r=4&pagewanted=all.

CHAPTER ONE: Why We Grow

1. Robert E. Lucas Jr., "The Industrial Revolution: Past and Future," The Region, Federal Reserve Bank of Minneapolis, May 2004, http://www.minneapolisfed.org/publications_papers/pub_display.cfm?id=3333.
2. Donald J. Boudreaux, "Corruption's Cost, Beyond Blagojevich," *Christian Science Monitor*, December 23, 2008, http://mercatus.org/media_clipping/corruptions-cost-beyond-blagojevich.

CHAPTER TWO: Incentives

1   Six drivers put the country on the fast track: a great leap in technology centered on the microchip, globalization of epic proportions, strong consumer spending, an explosion of debt and easy credit, low inflation, and smaller government, especially in the form of lower taxes and less regulation. For a discussion of these drivers, see "Six Themes for the Decade Ahead," a six-part editorial series by W. Michael Cox and Richard Alm in *Investor's Business Daily*, June 28, 2010, to July 6, 2010.

2   The Organisation for Economic Co-operation and Development's latest study of thirty-four countries ranked American fifteen-year-olds 27th in math, 17th in science, and 13th in reading.

3   For more information on education and the economy, see W. Michael Cox and Richard Alm, "What D'Ya Know? Lifetime Learning in Pursuit of the American Dream," Federal Reserve Bank of Dallas annual report, 2004.

4   Education could benefit from the kind of progress on cost and quality that we've routinely seen in the private sector. Take telecommunications, for example. In the mid-1980s, cellphones the size and weight of a brick cost $4,000—and all they did was transmit voice calls. Today it costs just $40 for a phone that fits in your pocket, takes pictures, and surfs the Internet.

5   For a discussion of the success of market initiatives in education, see Lisa Snell, "Annual Privatization Report: Education," Reason Foundation, February 2011. A pertinent paragraph: "Researchers from Mathematica Policy Research, Inc., Florida State University, Michigan State University and RAND analyzed data on four to five cohorts of eighth graders in Florida and Chicago as they moved to high school and beyond. The students who attended public charter schools were 7 to 15 percentage points more likely than the regular high school students to graduate and 8 to 10 percentage points more likely to attend a two- or four-year college. Baltimore has 27 charter schools, and in 2009–2010 charter schools recorded a 5 percentage-point lead in the number of students who showed proficiency in math and reading when compared with traditional schools, test results show."

6   The top federal income tax rate was 35% in 2011, encountered at $379,151. Top-bracket earners pay an additional 12% in Massachusetts, 11% in Hawaii and Oregon, and 10.8% in New Jersey.

7   In addition to benefits paid by states from the Federal Unemployment Trust Fund, the federal government maintains programs for railroad unemployment, trade readjustment allowances under the Trade Act of 1974, unemployment benefits under the Airline Deregulation Act of 1978, and unemployment assistance under the Disaster Relief Act Amendments of 1974.

8   State labor laws heavily influence the strength and spread of unions. All but two of the twenty-five states with the highest membership rates allow contracts that require workers to join unions and pay dues. The other twenty-five states have taken a different tack, enacting laws that prohibit mandatory union membership. Among the twenty states with the lowest unionization rates, only Colorado doesn't impose these right-to-work laws.

9   Average annual returns are calculated using the inflation-adjusted data of Ibbotson Associates, which assumed an initial investment in 1925 with all dividends reinvested.

10 http://www.eia.gov/forecasts/aeo/pdf/0383%282011%29.pdf.

11 "The opening up of new markets, foreign or domestic, and the organizational development from the craft shop to such concerns as U.S. Steel illustrate the same process of industrial mutation—if I may use that biological term—that incessantly revolutionizes the economic structure from within, incessantly destroying the old one, incessantly creating a new one. This process of Creative Destruction is the essential fact about capitalism." Joseph Schumpeter, *Capitalism, Socialism and Democracy*, p. 83.

12 "This term . . . cover[s] . . . displacement of workmen by machinery . . . [and by] industries that introduce new production functions. Questionnaires devised to find out from workmen reasons for their dismissal can, therefore, never bring out the phenomenon we mean and will always yield results that understate it." Joseph Schumpeter, *Business Cycles: A Theoretical, Historical, and Statistical Analysis of the Capitalist Process*, p. 514.

13 The country's goods exports exceeded $1.8 trillion in 2010—good enough to rank the U.S. third in the world behind China and Germany. In services exports, the U.S. ranks number one by a large margin, eclipsing the total of the next two countries in the rankings, Britain and Germany.

14 The returns on innovation rise with market size. The pharmaceutical industry offers a particularly telling example with so-called orphan diseases. They afflict fewer than two hundred thousand Americans—not enough to create adequate incentive for spending the time and money needed to bring new drugs to market. A global market for these drugs, however, offers enough potential customers to justify R&D costs.

15 The Tax Foundation analyzed IRS data on what companies actually paid after credits and deductions and found an average effective federal corporate tax rate of 26% between 1994 and 2008. Another Tax Foundation report reviews research showing U.S. effective rates are well above the world average. The top U.S. statutory rate is 39.5%. Japan's rate reflects a 5% reduction scheduled for April 2011, but it was postponed to help finance tsunami recovery efforts. Philip Dittmer, "U.S. Companies Suffer High Effect Tax Rates by International Standards," Tax Foundation Special Report, September 2011.

16 U.S. Census Bureau, "Place of Birth of the Foreign-Born: 2009," American Community Survey Briefs, October 2010. The foreign-born share of the U.S. population has been rising in recent decades—4.7% in 1970, 6.2% in 1980, 7.9% in 1990, 11.1% in 2000.

17 Many Americans worry that immigrants strain government budgets. Educated immigrants, however, are less likely than native-born Americans to require public assistance. The college-educated immigrants' reliance on government benefits declines the longer they reside in the United States.

18 The first immigration law was the Chinese Exclusion Act of 1882, which

"was conceived in ignorance, was falsely presented to the public, and had consequences undreamt of by its creators." Those words come from Roger Daniels, an expert on immigration. For a primer on the history of U.S. immigration policy, see Roger Daniels, *Guarding the Golden Door* (New York: Hill & Wang, 2004).

19   The United States issued 482,052 immigrant visas in 2010, according to the Department of State. Employment-based preferences accounted for only 12,701 of them.

20   Pia Orrenius and Madeline Zavodny propose an auction system that would use market mechanisms to channel immigration slots to companies and industries with the greatest need for foreign labor. See *Beside the Golden Door: U.S. Immigration Reform in a New Era of Globalization* (Washington, DC: AEI Press, 2010).

21   In *The Rise and Decline of Nations* (1982), economist Mancur Olson argued that rent-seeking behaviors build up over time, protecting the status quo and thwarting the forces of economic change. As a result, economies become saddled with inefficiencies, growth slows, and nations decline.

22   W. Michael Cox and Richard Alm, "Looking for the 'New' New World," O'Neil Center for Global Markets and Freedom, annual report, 2010. In the regression analysis, six factors proved statistically significant. The two others are better schools and climate.

CHAPTER THREE: The History and Future of Economic Growth

1   Edward C. Prescott, "Why Do Americans Work So Much More Than Europeans?" *Federal Reserve Bank of Minneapolis Quarterly Review* 28 (2004): 2–13.

2   Harold L. Cole and Lee E. Ohanian, "The Great Depression in the United States from a Neoclassical Perspective," *Federal Reserve Bank of Minneapolis Quarterly Review* 23 (1999): 2–24.

3   Shlaes, Amity. *The Forgotten Man: A New History of the Great Depression* (New York: HarperCollins, 2007).

CHAPTER FOUR: More Time on the Job

1   U.S. GDP per capita in 2010 was $47,199: http://data.worldbank.org/indicator/NY.GDP.PCAP.CD. GDP per capita for the European Union was $33,500: https://www.cia.gov/library/publications/the-world-factbook/geos/ee.html.

2   http://www.heldrich.rutgers.edu/sites/default/files/content/Work_Trends_May_2011.pdf.

CHAPTER FIVE: At Home in the Great Recession

1   The net flow of mortgage funds is the change in total mortgage credit outstanding. It is approximately equal to new mortgage originations (including home equity loans) minus mortgage prepayments and mortgage principal payments. The net flow of consumer credit is the change in consumer credit

outstanding. The declines reported for the recessions between the 1953–54 recession and the 1990–91 recession are all reductions in the growth of credit to households, not actual declines in credit to households, as in the 2007–09 recession and its aftermath. These data are taken from the Federal Reserve Flow of Funds, Table F.100, lines 42 and 43.

2   Among the past seventeen downturns in the United States, from 1920–21 through 2007–09, there were only two in which residential construction, households' consumption of durable goods, and their consumption of non-durable goods and services all increased. These were the 1923–24 and the 2001 recessions, and both were anomalous in that mortgage credit grew sharply during them. From 1923 to 1924, the total amount of mortgage credit outstanding grew 13.7%; during the 2001 recession mortgage credit outstanding grew 8.6%.

3   Between 1947 and 2011 there were only two periods when spending on new housing units fell by 10% or more without a recession following soon afterward. Those periods were 1950–51 and 1964–66. In 1950–51, expenditure on new housing units declined sharply and remained at its lower level without a recession following soon afterward. Durables fell too during the same period, but defense expenditure increased 90% more than the decline in housing plus durables expenditures. From early 1964 to early 1966, expenditure on new housing units declined, but households' durable goods consumption increased sharply so that the sum of households' expenditure on new housing units and consumer durables rose from the first quarter of 1964 to the first quarter of 1966. During 1966, the sum of housing and durable goods declined, but defense expenditures increased slightly more than housing and durables declined, while a recession was narrowly averted.

4   For brevity we refer to personal consumption of services and nondurable goods (NIPA Table 1.1.5, lines 5 and 6) as "consumption" (C), households' durable goods expenditures (NIPA Table 1.1.5, line 4) as "durables" (D), nonresidential fixed investment (NIPA Table 1.1.5, line 9) as "investment" (I), and expenditure on new single-family and multifamily housing units (from NIPA Table 5.4.5, line 36, and Table 5.3.5, line 19) as "housing" (H). (Many researchers take NIPA Table 1.1.5, line 12 as their measure of residential construction, but that category includes brokers' commissions on real estate sales.) All series are converted from nominal to real figures by dividing by GDP deflators. GDP deflators are calculated by dividing NIPA Table 1.1.5, line 1 by Table 1.1.6, line 1.

5   By far the largest component of these private expenditures is C. Moreover, C is also the most stable component. Consequently, housing expenditures make up an important part of those components of private product—H, D, and I—that are the most volatile.

6   National Income and Product Accounts and macroeconomic accounts of economic cycles treat housing as an investment, but housing expenditures have a strong impact on economic cycles that differs systematically from the impact of nonresidential (primarily business) investment. Regardless of

whether these expenditures are investment or consumption, they are determined by households, and their expenditure decisions have a different temporal pattern than firms' investments. Therefore, we use "housing" or "housing expenditure" to indicate expenditures on new single-family and multifamily residences, rather than "housing investment."

7   The mortgage interest rate used in this comparison is from series MORTG in the Federal Reserve Economic Data (FRED) compiled by the St. Louis Federal Reserve Bank. The quarterly net flow of mortgage lending series in the Flow of Funds table F.218 begins in Q1 1952. The net flow of mortgage funds as a percentage of GDP fell more in Q2 1980 than in any other quarter in the series up to that point.

8   The current account deficit figures are from the Federal Reserve Flow of Funds, Table F.107, line 63.

9   Bernanke's paper "Monetary Policy and the Housing Bubble," presented at the American Economic Association annual meeting, is available at http://www.federalreserve.gov/newsevents/speech/bernanke20100103a.pdf.

10   Nominal Case-Shiller house price indices increased 72% in Las Vegas during this two-year period, 62% in Phoenix, 56% in Los Angeles, 47% in San Diego, and 43% in San Francisco.

11   All dollar amounts in this section and in the remainder of the chapter are inflation-adjusted to 2005 dollars unless otherwise noted.

12   These figures are calculated from the Q3 2006 and Q2 2007 National Delinquency Survey from the Mortgage Bankers Association. The increases in these three states were the largest in the United States during that period.

13   Households' residential assets are from the Flow of Funds, Table B.100, line 4. Residential mortgage debt is from the Flow of Funds, Table L.218, line 2.

14   As we've seen in several other recessions—1974, 1980, and 2008—inflation peaked during the middle of the recession. This is common. Inflation also peaked in the middle of the 1969–70 recession and in the middle of the 1990–91 recession. For the other recessions since the one in 1957–58 it has always peaked just before the recession began. Inflation peaked at 3.73% in March 1957, five months before the recession began; in the middle of the recession ten months later, inflation was still at 3.62%. After the recession ended, inflation fell below 0.5% in Q1 1959, then rose until it reached a new peak in Q2 1960, during the 1960–61 recession. Inflation peaked just before the 2001 recession in Q3 2000 at 3.5%, but in the first quarter of the recession it was still at 3.4%. The 1981–82 recession is the only one since 1957–58 in which inflation didn't peak during or just before the recession. Even in that case, if we consider the double-dip recessions as one recession interrupted by a brief monetary stimulus from May to September 1980, then the course of inflation between 1978 and 1983 followed the standard pattern.

15   The figure on Treasury security acquisition of the Federal Reserve comes from line 3 in Table 1 of the November 18, 2010, and July 7, 2011, H.4.1

releases from the Federal Reserve. The figures on bank lending come from line 9 on page 2 of the H.8 release from the Federal Reserve.

16 Figure 1 in "The Aftermath of Financial Crises," by Carmen M. Reinhart and Kenneth S. Rogoff, published in the *American Economic Review* in 2009, shows that house prices fell 50% in Finland and 19% in Thailand during the period associated with their financial crises. Figure 2 in the same paper shows that equity prices fell about 83% in Thailand and 62% in Finland during the periods associated with their financial crises.

17 We saw its opposite occur in the aftermath of the stimulus of 2008–2009, which ushered in an increase in the U.S. current account deficit and worked against an increase in domestic demand and employment.

CHAPTER SIX: Spending, Taxes, and Certainty

1 Carmen M. Reinhart and Kenneth S. Rogoff, "The Aftermath of Financial Crisis," NBER Working Paper Series, 2009, http://www.nber.org/papers/w14656.

2 Ibid., p. 9.

3 Carmen M. Reinhart and Kenneth S. Rogoff, "Growth in a Time of Debt," NBER Working Paper Series, 2010, http://www.nber.org/papers/w15639.

4 See John Irons and Josh Bivens, "Government Debt and Economic Growth: Overreaching Claims of Debt 'Threshold' Suffer from Theoretical and Empirical Flaws," Economic Policy Institute Briefing Paper #271, July 26, 2010, http://www.epi.org/page/-/pdf/BP271.pdf.

5 For example, Yeva Nersisyan and L. Randall Wray, "Does Excessive Sovereign Debt Really Hurt Growth? A Critique of This Time Is Different, by Reinhart and Rogoff," Levy Economics Institute Working Paper 603 (2010).

6 Manmohan S. Kumar and Jaejoon Woo, "Public Debt and Growth," IMF Working Paper WP/1, no. 174 (2010), http://www.imf.org/external/pubs/ft/wp/2010/wp10174.pdf.

7 Mehmet Caner, Thomas Grennes, and Fritzi Koehler-Geib, "Finding the Tipping Point—When Sovereign Debt Turns Bad," World Bank Conference on Debt Management, 2010, http://ssrn.com/abstract=1612407.

8 Ibid.

9 According to the definition by the OECD, fiscal consolidation is a policy aimed at reducing government deficits and debt accumulation.

10 Many papers from the peer-reviewed literature confirm these results. Alesina and Perotti (1996) report that successful consolidations were 64% expenditure cuts and 37% revenue increases. Unsuccessful consolidations were 34% expenditure cuts and 66% revenue increases. Alesina and Ardagna (1998) report that successful consolidations were 62% expenditure cuts and 38% revenue increases. Unsuccessful consolidations were –79% expenditure cuts and 178% revenue increases. Alesina and Ardagna (2009) report that successful consolidations were 135% expenditure cuts and –35% revenue increases. Unsuccessful consolidations were 34% expenditure cuts and

66% revenue increases. Von Hagen and Strauch (2001) report that successful consolidations were 52% expenditure cuts and 48% revenue increases. Unsuccessful consolidations were 12% expenditure cuts and 88% revenue increases. Zaghini (1999) reports that successful consolidations were 77% expenditure cuts and 23% revenue increases. Unsuccessful consolidations were 2% expenditure cuts and 98% revenue increases. McDermott and Wescott (1996) found that expenditure-based consolidations have a 41% chance of success, whereas revenue-based consolidations have a 16% chance of success.

11   Alberto Alesina and Roberto Perotti, "Fiscal Adjustments in OECD Countries: Composition and Macroeconomic Effects," *IMF Staff Papers* 44, no. 2 (1997): 210–48, http://www.jstor.org/stable/3867543.

12   For example, see Alberto Alesina and Silvia Ardagna, "Large Changes in Fiscal Policy: Taxes Versus Spending," NBER Working Paper w15438 (2009); Alberto Alesina and Silvia Ardagna, "Tales of Fiscal Adjustment," *Economic Policy* 13, no. 27 (1998): 489–545; Alberto Alesina and Roberto Perotti, "Fiscal Adjustments in OECD Countries: Composition and Macroeconomic Effects," NBER Working Paper 5730 (1996).

13   Daniel Leigh, Pete Devries, Charles Freedman, Jaime Guajardo, and Andrea Pescatori, "Will It Hurt? Macroeconomic Effects of Fiscal Consolidation," *World Economic Outlook: Recovery, Risk, and Rebalancing*, 2010.

14   Andreas Bergh and Magnus Henrekson, "Government Size and Growth: A Survey and Interpretation of the Evidence." Working Paper Series 858, Research Institute of Industrial Economics, 2011.

15   Andreas Bergh and Martin Karlsson, "Government Size and Growth: Accounting for Economic Freedom and Globalization," *Public Choice* 142, no. 1 (2010): 195–213.

16   Diego Romero-Ávila and Rolf Strauch, "Public Finances and Long-term Growth in Europe—Evidence from a Panel Data Analysis," *European Journal of Political Economy* 24 (2008): 172–91.

17   Antonio Afonso and Davide Furceri, "Government Size, Composition, Volatility and Economic Growth," ECB Working Paper No. 849, January 2008. Available at SSRN: http://ssrn.com/abstract=1077767.

18   Stefan Fölster and Magnus Henrekson, "Growth Effects of Government Expenditure and Taxation in Rich Countries," *European Economic Review* 45 (2001): 1501–20.

19   Alan J. Auerbach and Kevin A. Hassett, ed., *Toward Fundamental Tax Reform* (Washington, DC: AEI Press, 2005).

20   Victor R. Fuchs, Alan B. Krueger, and James B. Poterba, "Economists' Views about Parameters, Values, and Policy: Survey Results in Labor and Public Finance," *Journal of Economic Literature* 36, no. 3 [n.d.]: 1387–1425.

21   Paul Pecorino, "The Growth Rate Effects of Tax Reform," *Oxford Economic Papers* 46, no. 3 (1994): 492–501.

22   David Altig, Alan J. Auerbach, Laurence J. Kotlikoff, Kent A. Smetters, and

Jan Walliser, "Simulating Fundamental Tax Reform in the United States," *American Economic Review* 91, no. 3 (2001): 574–95.

23   Jens M. Arnold, "Do Tax Structures Affect Aggregate Economic Growth? Empirical Evidence from a Panel of OECD Countries," *OECD Economics Department Working Papers* 643 (2008), http://dx.doi.org/10.1787/236001777843.

24   Michael Devereux and Rachel Griffith, "The Taxation of Discrete Investment Choices," Institute for Fiscal Studies, Working Paper Series W98, no. 16, 1999.

25   Kevin A. Hassett and Aparna Mathur, "Report Card on Effective Corporate Tax Rates: United States Gets an F," *AEI Tax Policy Outlook*, February 2011, http://www.aei.org/outlook/101024.

26   Kevin S. Markle and Douglas A. Shackelford, "Cross-Country Comparisons of Corporate Income Taxes," NBER Working Paper Series (n.d.), http://www.nber.org/papers/w16839.pdf.

27   Avinash K. Dixit and Robert S. Pindyck, *Investment Under Uncertainty*. Princeton, NJ: Princeton University Press, 1994.

28   Simon Gilchrist, Jae W. Sim, and Egon Zakrajsek, "Uncertainty, Financial Friction and Investment Dynamics," National Bureau of Economic Research, 2010.

29   Joshua Aizenman and Nancy Marion, "Policy Uncertainty, Persistence and Growth," NBER Working Papers Series (1991), http://www.nber.org/papers/w3848.

30   Scott R. Baker, Nicholas Bloom, and Stevin J. Davis, "Measuring Economic Policy Uncertainty," October 10, 2011, http://www.stanford.edu/~nbloom/PolicyUncertainty.pdf.

31   Jesús Fernández-Villaverde, Pablo Guerrón-Quintana, Keith Kuester, and Juan Rubio-Ramírez, "Fiscal Volatility Shocks and Economic Activity," NBER Working Paper Series, 2011, http://www.nber.org/papers/w17317.

CHAPTER NINE: Entrepreneurs and Creative Destruction

1   Nicolai J. Foss and Peter G. Klein, *Organizing Entrepreneurial Judgment: A New Approach to the Firm* (Cambridge: Cambridge University Press, 2012).

2   Joseph A. Schumpeter, *The Theory of Economic Development* (Cambridge, MA: Harvard University Press, 1934).

3   Ludwig von Mises, *Human Action: A Treatise on Economics* (New Haven, CT: Yale University Press, 1949).

4   Peter G. Klein, "Opportunity Discovery, Entrepreneurial Action, and Economic Organization," *Strategic Entrepreneurship Journal* 2 (2008): 175–90; Michaël Bikard and Scott Stern, Review of Landes et al., "The Invention of Enterprise: Entrepreneurship from Ancient Mesopotamia to Modern Times," *Journal of Economic Literature* 49, no. 1 (2011): 164–68.

5   John L. Chapman, "What Is Entrepreneurship? Steve Jobs and Herman Cain Define It," *Thinking Things Over* 1, no. 12 (2011).

6   Israel M. Kirzner, *Competition and Entrepreneurship* (Chicago: University of Chicago Press, 1973).

7   Frank H. Knight, *Risk, Uncertainty, and Profit* (New York: August M. Kelley, 1912).

8   Ludwig M. Lachmann, *Capital and Its Structure* (Kansas City, MO: Sheed Andrews & McMeel, 1978 [1956]), p. 16.

9   Ludwig von Mises, "Economic Calculation in the Socialist Commonwealth" [1920], in F. A. Hayek, ed., *Collectivist Economic Planning* (London: Routledge, 1935).

10   Ludwig von Mises, "Profit and Loss," in Mises, *Planning for Freedom* (South Holland, IL: Libertarian Press, 1952), p. 110.

11   Peter G. Klein, "Economic Calculation and the Limits of Organization," *Review of Austrian Economics* 9, no. 2 (1996): 51–77.

12   Peter G. Klein, Joseph T. Mahoney, Anita M. McGahan, and Christos N. Pitelis, "Toward a Theory of Public Entrepreneurship," *European Management Review* 7 (2010): 1–15.

13   Wilhelm Roepke, *Civitas Humana: A Humane Order of Society* (London: William Hodge, 1948).

14   Robert A. Higgs, "Regime Uncertainty: Why the Great Depression Lasted So Long and Why Prosperity Resumed after the War," *Independent Review* 1, no. 4 (1997): 561–90; Scott R. Baker, Nicholas Bloom, and Steven J. Davis, "Measuring Economic Policy Uncertainty," Working paper, Chicago Booth School of Business, 2011.

15   Ludwig von Mises, *The Theory of Money and Credit* (New Haven, CT: Yale University Press, 1953); F. A. Hayek, *Prices and Production* (London: Routledge, 1931). See also Murray N. Rothbard, *America's Great Depression* (Princeton, NJ: Van Nostrand, 1963); Roger W. Garrison, *Time and Money: The Macroeconomics of Capital Structure* (London: Routledge, 2000); and Rajshree Agarnal, Jay B. Barney, Nicolai Foss, and Peter G. Klein, "Heterogeneous Resources and the Financial Crisis: Implications of Strategic Management Theory," *Strategic Organization* 7, no. 4 (2009): 467–84.

16   Michael Aarstol, "Inflation, Inflation Uncertainty, and Relative Price Variability," *Southern Economic Journal* 66, no. 2 (1999): 414–23.

17   Mises, "Profit and Loss," p. 109.

18   Agarwal et al., "Heterogeneous Resources and the Financial Crisis," p. 476.

19   Ibid., pp. 474–75.

20   Mises, *Human Action,* p. 253.

21   Ibid., p. 582.

22   John L. Chapman and Peter G. Klein, "Value Creation in Middle-Market Buyouts: A Transaction-Level Analysis," in Douglas J. Cumming, ed., *Private Equity: Fund Types, Risks and Returns, and Regulation* (Hoboken, NJ: Wiley, 2010), pp. 229–55.

23   S. F. Kreft and Russell S. Sobel, "Public Policy, Entrepreneurship, and Economic Freedom," *Cato Journal* 25 (2005): 595–616; Christian Bjørn-

skov and Nicolai J. Foss, "Economic Freedom and Entrepreneurial Activity: Some Cross-Country Evidence," *Public Choice* 134 (2008): 307–28; K. Nyström, "The Institutions of Economic Freedom and Entrepreneurship: Evidence from Panel Data, *Public Choice* 136 (2009): 269–82.

CHAPTER TEN: Baseball's Answer to Growth

1   John Haltiwanger, Ron Jarmin, and Javier Miranda, "Jobs Created from Business Startups in the United States," Kauffman Foundation, January 2009, http://www.kauffman.org/uploadedFiles/BDS_Jobs_Created_011209b.pdf.

2   Dane Stangler and Robert E. Litan, "Where Will the Jobs Come From?" Kauffman Foundation, November 2009, http://www.kauffman.org/uploadedFiles/where_will_the_jobs_come_from.pdf.

3   Tim Kane, "The Importance of Startups in Job Creation and Job Destruction," Kauffman Foundation, July 2010, http://www.kauffman.org/uploadedFiles/firm_formation_importance_of_startups.pdf.

4   Michael Horrell and Robert E. Litan, "After Inception: How Enduring Is Job Creation by Startups?" Kauffman Foundation, July 2010, http://www.kauffman.org/uploadedFiles/firm-formation-inception-8-2-10.pdf.

5   See p. 145 of *Economic Report of the President*.

6   Dane Stangler, "The Economic Future Just Happened," Kauffman Foundation, June 2009, http://www.kauffman.org/uploadedFiles/the-economic-future-just-happened.pdf.

7   Dane Stangler and Paul Kedrosky, "Neutralism and Entrepreneurship: The Structural Dynamics of Startups, Young Firms, and Job Creation," Kauffman Foundation, September 2010, http://www.kauffman.org/uploadedFiles/firm-formation-neutralism.pdf.

8   Horrell and Litan, "After Inception: How Enduring Is Job Creation by Startups?"

9   This calculation sums all net new employment gains from 1980 to 2007 (46 million) and divides by total 2007 employment of 146 million as shown in the 2008 *Economic Report of the President*. The percentage of cumulative net new jobs created is a proxy for the percentage of output generated in 2007 by firms that did not exist before 1980.

10   For more on the distinction between start-ups and existing companies with respect to innovation, see William J. Baumol, *The Free-Market Innovation Machine: Analyzing the Growth Miracle of Capitalism* (Princeton, NJ: Princeton University Press, 2002); William J. Baumol, *The Microtheory of Innovative Entrepreneurship* (Princeton, NJ: Princeton University Press, 2010); William J. Baumol, Robert E. Litan, and Carl J. Schramm, *Good Capitalism, Bad Capitalism, and the Economics of Growth and Prosperity* (New Haven, CT: Yale University Press, 2010).

11   Robert E. Litan, "Inventive Billion Dollar Firms: A Faster Way to Grow," Kauffman Foundation, December 2010, http://www.kauffman.org/uploadedFiles/billion_dollar_firms.pdf. The same idea is also fleshed out in

Robert E. Litan and Carl J. Schramm (2012, forthcoming), *Better Capitalism: An Entrepreneurial Agenda for a More Rapidly Growing American Economy.*

12   William D. Nordhaus, "Schumpeterian Profits and the Alchemist Fallacy Revised," Yale Working Papers on Economic Applications and Policy, Discussion Paper No. 6 (April 2, 2005), http://www.econ.yale.edu/ddp/ddp00/ddp0006.pdf.

13   See Robert E. Litan, "Inventive Billion Dollar Firms: A Faster Way to Grow," Kauffman Foundation, December 2010, http://www.kauffman .org/uploadedFiles/billion_dollar_firms.pdf, and chapter 2 of Litan and Schramm, *Better Capitalism.*

14   This 500,000 businesses refers to a fairly constant number of employer businesses launched annually from 1977 to 2005. See Dane Stangler and Paul Kedrosky, "Exploring Firm Formation: Why Is the Number of New Firms Constant?" Kauffman Foundation, January 2010, http://www.kauffman .org/uploadedFiles/exploring_firm_formation_1-13-10.pdf.

15   The KIEA is compiled by Professor Robert Fairlie of the University of California, Santa Cruz, and is available at http://www.kauffman.org/KIEA. The KIEA differs from our studies that use census data that excludes nonemployer businesses.

16   See AnnaLee Saxenian, *Silicon Valley's New Immigrant Entrepreneurs* (San Francisco: Public Policy Institute of California, 2009); and Vivek Wadhwa, AnnaLee Saxenian, Richard Freeman, Gary Gereffi, and Alex Salkever, "America's Loss Is the World's Gain: America's New Immigrant Entrepreneurs, Part IV," Kauffman Foundation, April 2009, http://www.kauffman .org/uploadedFiles/americas_loss.pdf.

17   See Stuart Anderson, "The Impact of the Children of Immigrants on Scientific Achievement in America," National Foundation for American Policy, May 2010, http://www.nfap.com/pdf/Children_of_Immigrants_in_ Science_and_Math_NFAP_Policy_Brief_May_2011.pdf.

18   See Chapter 2 and appendix tables 02-13, 02-27, and 02-28 from National Science Board, *Science and Engineering Indicators 2010* (Arlington, VA: National Science Foundation, 2010).

19   Fred Block and Matthew Keller, "Where Do Innovations Come From? Transformations in the U.S. National Innovation System, 1970–2006," Information Technology and Innovation Foundation, July 2008, http://www .itif.org/files/Where_do_innovations_come_from.pdf.

20   Jonathan Cole, *The Great American University: Its Rise to Preeminence, Its Indispensable National Role, Why It Must Be Protected* (New York: PublicAffairs, 2009).

21   Jay Ritter, "Initial Public Offerings: Tables Updated Through 2010," June 1, 2011, http://bear.warrington.ufl.edu/ritter/IPOs2010Statistics060111.pdf.

22   CRA International, "Sarbanes Oxley Section 404 Costs and Implementation Issues: Spring 2006 Survey Update," April 2006, www.compliance week.com/s/documents/cra_survey.pdf.

23   Office of the Chief Accountant, U.S. Securities and Exchange Commission,

"Study and Recommendations on Section 404(b) of the Sarbanes-Oxley Act of 2002 for Issuers with Public Float Between $75 and $250 Million," April 2011, http://www.sec.gov/news/studies/2011/404bfloat-study.pdf.

24   After this chapter had been completed, Congress passed by a large bipartisan majority vote the JOBS Act, which not only largely exempted young public companies with market capitalization below $1 billion from SOX, but also contained a number of other provisions that should reduce the costs of financing start-ups and growing privately held companies.

25   Harold Bradley and Robert E. Litan, "Choking the Recovery: Why New Growth Companies Aren't Going Public and Unrecognized Risks of Future Market Disruptions," Kauffman Foundation, November 2010, http://www.kauffman.org/uploadedFiles/etf_study_11-8-10.pdf.

26   At the time this chapter went to press, the Senate was considering the JOBS Act, passed by a large bipartisan majority in the House, that would relax a number of the securities-law-related hurdles to companies raising money and going public. One of those provisions is an "on-ramp" amendment to Sarbanes-Oxley that would reduce burdens under that Act for many companies in the first five years after going public.

CHAPTER ELEVEN: The Role of Intangibles

1   William Easterly, *The White Man's Burden: Why the West's Efforts to Aid the Rest Have Done So Much Ill and So Little Good* (New York: Penguin Press, 2006).

2   From Kirk Hamilton et al., *Where Is the Wealth of Nations? Measuring Capital for the 21st Century* (Washington, DC: World Bank, 2006).

3   From Simeon Djankov, Florencio Lopez de Silanes, Rafael La Porta, and Andrei Shleifer, "The Regulation of Entry," World Bank Policy Research Paper No. WPS2661, http://econ.worldbank.org/external/default/main?pagePK=64165259&piPK=64165421&menuPK=64166093&theSitePK=469372&entityID=000094946_01091104014189.

4   From Friedrich Schneider, "Size and Measurement of the Informal Economy in 110 Countries Around the World," World Bank Policy Research Paper, July 2002, http://rru.worldbank.org/Documents/PapersLinks/informal_economy.pdf.

CHAPTER TWELVE: The Virtuous Cycle

1   Chapter draws significantly on previous work by the author, in particular, Minniti (2008), Minniti and Lévesque (2010), and Minniti (2006).

2   In 1998, for example, the OECD launched the program Fostering Entrepreneurship, while the European Union released the report "Fostering Entrepreneurship: Priorities for the Future." Kim and Nugent (1999) documented that, following a change of the country's constitution, Korean public policy shifted from supporting large conglomerate firms (chaebol) prior to 1970, to promoting small business and new start-ups during the 1980s and '90s. Also, in the last few years, the governments of Australia, Finland, Germany,

Ireland, Israel, Italy, the United Kingdom, and several other countries have launched a series of initiatives designed to create science and industrial parks, enhance entrepreneurship, and promote entrepreneurship as a source of employment. Finally, the OECD, the World Bank, and the IMF have all produced reports and launched programs related to entrepreneurship.

3   R. Solow, "Technical Change and the Aggregate Production Function," *Review of Economics and Statistics* 39, no. 3 (1957): 312–20; R. Solow, "A Contribution to the Theory of Economic Growth," *Quarterly Journal of Economics* 70, no. 1 (1956): 65–94.

4   P. M. Romer, "Endogenous Technological Change," *Journal of Political Economy* 98 (1990): 571–602.

5   P. M. Romer, "Increasing Returns and Long-run Growth," *Journal of Political Economy* 94, no. 5 (1986): 1002–1037.

6   M. Minniti and M. Lévesque, "Entrepreneurial Types and Economic Growth," *Journal of Business Venturing* (2010).

7   E. P. Lazear, "Entrepreneurship," *Journal of Labor Economics* 23, no. 4 (2005): 649–80.

8   See Z. Acs, P. Arenius, M. Hay, and M. Minniti, *2004 Global Entrepreneurship Monitor* (London: London Business School; Babson Park, MA: Babson College, 2005). Also see Z. J. Acs, D. B. Audretsch, P. Braunerhjelm, and B. Carlsson, "The Knowledge Spillover Theory of Entrepreneurship," working paper, Case Western Reserve University, 2005.

9   C. Michelacci, "Low Returns in R&D Due to the Lack of Entrepreneurial Skills," *Economic Journal* 113 (2003): 207–25.

10   Minniti and Lévesque, "Entrepreneurial Types and Economic Growth."

11   See I. M. Kirzner, *Competition and Entrepreneurship* (Chicago: University of Chicago Press, 1973). Also see S. Shane and S. Venkataraman, "The Promise of Entrepreneurship as a Field of Research," *Academy of Management Review* 25, no. 1 (2000): 217–26.

12   G. Gancia and F. Zilibotti, "Horizontal Innovation in the Theory of Growth and Development," in P. Aghion and S. Durlauf, eds., *Handbook of Economic Growth*, vol. 1A (Amsterdam: Elsevier, 2005), pp. 111–66.

13   See R. K. Goel and R. Ram, "Research and Development Expenditures and Economic Growth: A Cross-country Study," *Economic Development and Cultural Change* 42, no. 2 (1994): 403–12. Also see G. Gong and W. Keller, "Convergence and Polarization in the Global Income Levels: A Review of Recent Results on the Role of International Technology Diffusion," *Research Policy* 32, no. 6 (2003): 1055–79.

14   Acs et al., *Global Entrepreneurship Monitor 2004*, Executive Report.

15   The figure is from Bosma and Levie (2010), p. 23. The sources of data are the Adult Population Survey of the Global Entrepreneurship Monitor (GEM) project for 2009, and the World Economic Outlook indicator of the IMF from October 2009. The countries depicted in the figure are Algeria, Argentina, Belgium, Bosnia and Herzegovina, Brazil, Chile, China, Colombia, Croatia, Denmark, Dominican Republic, Ecuador, Fin-

land, France, Germany, Greece, Guatemala, Hong Kong, Hungary, Iceland, Iran, Israel, Italy, Jamaica, Japan, Jordan, Korea, Latvia, Lebanon, Malaysia, Morocco, Netherlands, Norway, Panama, Peru, Romania, Russia, Saudi Arabia, Serbia, Slovenia, South Africa, Spain, Switzerland, Syria, Tonga, Tunisia, Uganda, United Arab Emirates, United Kingdom, United States, Uruguay, Venezuela, Yemen, West Bank, and Gaza Strip.

16   S. Wennekers and R. Thurik, "Linking Entrepreneurship and Economic Growth," *Small Business Economics Journal* 13, no. 1 (1999): 27–56.

17   A. J. van Stel and D. J. Storey, "The Link Between Firm Births and Job Creation: Is There a Upas Tree Effect?" *Regional Studies* 38, no. 8 (2004): 893–917.

18   L. P. Dana, "A Contrast of Argentina and Uruguay: The Effects of Government Policy on Entrepreneurship," *Journal of Small Business Management* 35, no. 2 (1997): 99–104.

19   G. A. Giamartino, "Will Small Business Be the Answer for Developing Economies?" *Journal of Small Business Management* 29, no. 1 (1991): 91–94.

20   A. Oxenfeldt, *New Firms and Free Enterprise* (Washington, DC: American Council on Public Affairs, 1943).

21   See David M. Blau, "A Time Series Analysis of Self-Employment in the United States," *Journal of Political Economy* 95, no. 3 (1987): 445–67. See also David S. Evans and Linda Leighton, "Small Business Formation by Unemployed and Employed Workers," *Small Business Economics* 2, no. 4 (1990): 319–30.

22   See Paul A. Geroski, "Entry, Innovation, and Productivity Growth," *Review of Economics and Statistics* 71 (1989): 572–78. See also F. Pfeiffer and F. Reize, "Business Start-ups by the Unemployed—An Econometric Analysis Based on Firm Data," *Labour Economics* 7, no. 5 (2000): 629–63.

23   For a survey of existing research, see R. Thurik, M. Carree, A. van Stel, and D. Audretsch, "Does Self-Employment Reduce Unemployment?" *Journal of Business Venturing* (2008).

24   D. G. Blanchflower, "Self-Employment in OECD Countries," *Labour Economics* 7 (2000): 471–505.

25   Martin Carree, André van Stel, Roy Thurik, and Sander Wennekers, "Economic Development and Business Ownership: An Analysis Using Data of 23 OECD Countries in the Period 1976–1996," *Small Business Economics* 19, no. 3 (2002): 271–90.

26   Thurik et al., "Does Self-Employment Reduce Unemployment?"

27   D. C. North, "Institutions," *Journal of Economic Perspectives* 5, no. 1 (1991): 97–115.

28   P. J. Boettke and C. Coyne, "Entrepreneurial Behavior and Institutions," in M. Minniti, ed., *Entrepreneurship: The Engine of Growth*, vol. 1, Praeger Perspectives (Westport, CT: Greenwood, 2007).

29   For a review see M. Minniti, "The Role of Government on Entrepreneurial Activity: Productive, Unproductive, or Destructive?" *Entrepreneurship Theory and Practice* 32, no. 5 (2008): 779–90.

30   Van Stel and Storey, "Firm Births and Job Creation," 893–917.

31   B. A. Gilbert, D. B. Audretsch, and P. P. McDougall, "The Emergence of Entrepreneurship Policy," *Small Business Economics* 22, no. 3/4 (2004): 313–23.

32   See J. McMillan and C. Woodruff, "The Central Role of Entrepreneurs in Transition Economies," *Journal of Economic Perspectives* 16, no. 3 (2002): 153–70. Also see R. Aidis, S. Estrin, and T. Mickiewicz, "Institutions and Entrepreneurship Development in Russia: A Comparative Perspective," *Journal of Business Venturing* (2008).

33   See D. B. Audretsch and M. Keilbach, "Entrepreneurship and Regional Growth: An Evolutionary Interpretation," *Journal of Evolutionary Economics* 14, no. 5 (2004): 605–16. Also see D. B. Audretsch and M. Keilbach, *Entrepreneurship Capital—Determinants and Impact,* Tech. Rep. No. 4905 (London: CEPR, 2005).

34   Paul A. Geroski, "Entry, Innovation, and Productivity Growth," *Review of Economics and Statistics* 71 (1989): 572–78.

35   R. Koppl, "Computable Entrepreneurship," *Entrepreneurship Theory and Practice* (2008).

36   W. J. Baumol, *The Free-Market Innovation Machine: Analyzing the Growth Miracle of Capitalism* (Princeton, NJ: Princeton University Press, 2002).

CHAPTER THIRTEEN: Growth Needs Trade

1   The Smoot-Hawley tariff, also known as the Tariff Act of 1930, was sponsored by U.S. senator Reed Smoot of Utah and U.S. representative Willis C. Hawley of Oregon. It was signed into law on June 17, 1930. The original intent of the law was to protect farmers against agricultural imports, but interest group politics quickly led to tariff protections for all sectors of the economy.

2   *CIA World Factbook: Chile.*

3   ASEAN includes Brunei, Cambodia, Indonesia, Laos, Malaysia, Myanmar, the Philippines, Singapore, Thailand, and Vietnam.

4   U.S. Census Bureau Foreign Trade Data.

5   John Murphy, "Locked Out and Left Behind: The Consequences of U.S. Inaction on Trade," June 28, 2010.

6   U.S. Department of Commerce, "Exports Support American Jobs," 2010.

7   International Trade Administration, "Do Jobs in Export Industries Still Pay More? And Why?" July 2010.

8   International Trade Administration, "Weekly Earnings in Export-Intensive U.S. Services Industries," March 2011.

9   U.S. Department of Commerce, "Exports Support American Jobs," 2010.

10   Census data.

11   USDA, "National Export Initiative: Importance of U.S. Agricultural Exports," February 2010.

12   U.S. Department of Commerce, "Exports Support American Jobs," 2010.

13   U.S. Chamber of Commerce, "Opening Markets, Creating Jobs: Estimated U.S. Employment Effects of Trade with FTA Partners," May 2010.

14   Ibid.

15   Jordan, Chile, Singapore, Australia, Bahrain, Morocco, El Salvador, Honduras, Nicaragua, Guatemala, Dominican Republic, Costa Rica, Oman, and Peru.

16   CATO, "Free Trade Bulletin: As Promised, Free Trade Agreements Deliver More Trade: Manufacturing Exports Receive an Extra Boost," No. 45, June 7, 2011.

17   U.S. Census Bureau Foreign Trade Data.

18   CATO, "Free Trade Bulletin."

19   Building America's Future Educational Fund, "Building America's Future: Falling Apart and Falling Behind," Transportation Infrastructure Report, 2011.

20   "U.S. Ports Unready for Larger Panama Canal, Say Officials," *Dredging Today.com*, May 16, 2011.

21   I. M. Destler, *American Trade Politics*, 4th ed. (Washington, DC: Institute for International Economics, 2005).

22   2011 Trade Policy Agenda and 2010 Annual Report of the President of the United States on the Trade Agreements Program.

CHAPTER FOURTEEN: Market-Friendly Energy

1   Gene Whitney et al., *U.S. Fossil Fuel Resources: Technology, Reporting, and Summary* (Washington, DC: Congressional Research Service, 2010).

CHAPTER FIFTEEN: Social Security Reform and Economic Growth

1   CBO, *Alternative Budget Policies*, May 19, 2008, http://www.cbo.gov/ftpdocs/92xx/doc9216/05-19-LongtermBudget_Letter-to-Ryan.pdf.

2   See Robert Barro and Charles Redlick, "Macroeconomic Effects of Government Purchases and Taxes," Working Paper No. 22, Mercatus Center at George Mason University, Arlington, VA, 2010.

3   Christina D. Romer and David H. Romer, "The Macroeconomic Effects of Tax Changes: Estimates Based on a New Measure of Fiscal Shocks," *American Economic Review*, June 2010, http://elsa.berkeley.edu/~dromer/papers/RomerandRomerAERJune2010.pdf.

4   Alberto Alesina and Silvia Ardagna, "Large Changes in Fiscal Policy: Taxes Versus Spending," Discussion Paper No. 2180, Harvard Institute of Economic Research, Cambridge, MA, 2009.

5   Carmen Reinhart and Kenneth Rogoff, "Growth in a Time of Debt," NBER Working Paper No. 15639, January 2010.

6   Stephen Cecchetti, M. S. Mohanty, and Fabrizio Zampolli, "The Real Effects of Debt," Bank for International Settlements, September 2011.

7   For the purposes of this discussion, the term *debt* refers to *debt held by the public*, the largest of the categories of the United States' *gross debt*. This

debt represents the amount owed to persons and entities outside the United States federal government.

8   World Economic Forum, *Global Competitiveness Report,* and Matt Mitchell and Jakina Debnam, *Crowding Out,* Mercatus Working Paper. This crowding-out effect persists even given the existence of international financial transactions.

9   Gregory Mankiw, *Principles of Economics* (Mason, OH: South-Western Cengage Learning, 2008).

10   Joseph Schumpeter, *Capitalism, Socialism and Democracy* (New York: Harper, 1942); Robert Solow, "A Contribution to the Theory of Economic Growth," *Quarterly Journal of Economics* (1956): 65–94; Trevor W. Swan, "Economic Growth and Capital Accumulation," *Economic Record* (1956): 334–61.

11   *New Palgrave Dictionary of Economics,* 2nd ed., s.v. "Crowding Out." The importance of capital accumulation for economic growth has been emphasized across the literature examining developed countries. Examples include Xavier Sala-i-Martin, Gernot Doppelhofer, and Ronald I. Miller, "Determinants of Long-Term Growth: A Bayesian Averaging of Classical Estimates (BACE) Approach," *American Economic Review*; and Horst Siebert in *Debt and Capital Accumulation,* Weltwirtschaftliches Archiv. Also, Urquhart finds a strong relationship between capital accumulation and economic growth in Canada in "Capital Accumulation, Technological Change, and Economic Growth," *Canadian Journal of Economics and Political Science/ Revue canadienne d'Economique et de Science politique* 25, no. 4 (November 1959): 411–30. See also Peter Howitt and Philippe Aghion, "Capital Accumulation and Innovation as Complementary Factors in Long-Run Growth," *Journal of Economic Growth* 3, no. 2 (June 1998): 111–30; Paul Davidson, "Portfolio Balance, Capital Accumulation, and Economic Growth," *Econometrica* 36, no. 2 (April 1968). In the case where domestic borrowing is primarily financed through international capital inflows, the federal demand for loanable funds may not compete directly with domestic demand for lending, so in the short run interest rates may not increase and domestic production may not decline. However, national income will nonetheless ultimately decrease as the nation must eventually repay its foreign debts. William Gale, "Budget Deficits," in *The New Palgrave Dictionary of Economics*.

12   The effect of macroeconomic stability on economic growth is documented in World Economic Forum, *Global Competitiveness Report*.

13   Congressional Budget Office, Monthly Budget Review, Fiscal Year 2011, October 7, 2011, http://www.cbo.gov/ftpdocs/124xx/doc12461/2011_10_07_MBR.pdf.

14   CBO, "The Budget and Economic Outlook: An Update," August 2011.

15   Ibid.

16   Unlike the "extended baseline scenario," the alternative fiscal scenario incorporates various changes to current law that are widely expected, many of which simply extend current policies.

17 CBO's Long-Term Budget Outlook, June 2011.

18 Ibid.

19 Emma Aguila, "Personal Retirement Accounts and Saving," *American Economic Journal: Economic Policy* (November 2011). Also see CBO, "Social Security and Private Saving: A Review of the Empirical Evidence," July 1998.

20 See Shoven and Nataraj, "Are Trust Fund Surpluses Spent or Saved?" NBER 2003, and Smetters, "Is the Social Security Trust Fund Worth Anything?" NBER 2003.

21 Carlos Sales-Sarrapy, Fernando Solís-Soberón, and Alejandro Villagómez-Amezcua, "Pension System Reform: The Mexican Case," in *Privatizing Social Security,* ed. Martin Feldstein (Chicago: University of Chicago Press, 1998), referenced in Aguila, "Personal Retirement Accounts and Saving."

22 Jose Pinera, "Liberating Workers: The World Pension Revolution," Cato Letters, 2001, http://www.cato.org/pubs/catosletters/cl-15.pdf.

23 Andrew G. Biggs and Glenn R. Springstead, "Alternative Measures of Replacement Rates for Social Security Benefits," *Social Security Bulletin* 68, no. 2 (2008).

24 An aged beneficiary unit can be either a married couple living together or a nonmarried person, also including persons who are separated or married but not living together.

25 U.S. Social Security Administration, Fast Facts & Figures, August 2010, "Relative Importance of Social Security, 2008," accessed March 20, 2011, http://www.ssa.gov/policy/docs/chartbooks/fast_facts/2010/fast_facts10.html#agedpop.

26 http://www.cbo.gov/ftpdocs/60xx/doc6044/12-22-Diamond-Orszag.pdf.

27 http://www.cbo.gov/ftpdocs/56xx/doc5666/07-21-CraigLetterUpdated.pdf.

28 Gayle Reznik, David Weaver, and Andrew Biggs, "Social Security and Marginal Returns to Work Near Retirement," April 2009, Social Security Administration, http://www.aei.org/docLib/Issue%20Paper%20No%202009-02.pdf.

29 http://www.ssa.gov/OACT/NOTES/ran7/index.html.

30 See Jeffrey B. Liebman, Erzo F. P. Luttmer, and David G. Seif, "Labor Supply Responses to Marginal Social Security Benefits: Evidence from Discontinuities," December 2, 2008, http://www.nber.org/~luttmer/ssbenefitlink.pdf.

31 See report of the Committee on Economic Security, 1935, www.ssa.gov/history/reports/ces/ces5.html.

32 http://www.bls.gov/mlr/1999/12/art1full.pdf.

33 Ibid.

34 http://www.ssa.gov/history/reports/crsleghist2.html. The option was created for women in the 1956 amendments and for men in the 1961 amendments.

35 http://www.bls.gov/mlr/1999/12/art1full.pdf.

36 http://ssa.gov/pubs/10069.html#howmuch.

37 http://www.ssa.gov/policy/docs/statcomps/supplement/2010/6b.html.

38 Ibid.

39 http://www.socialsecurity.gov/pubs/10147.pdf.

40 Blahous, "Social Security and Work," *National Affairs*, Winter 2010.

41 http://www.nber.org/programs/ag/rrc/NB06-06%20Goda,%20 Shoven,%20Slavov%20FINAL.pdf.

42 See Testimony of Charles Blahous before the Subcommittee on Social Security of the U.S. House of Representatives Committee on Ways and Means, July 8, 2011.

43 http://www.nber.org/programs/ag/rrc/NB06-06%20Goda,%20 Shoven,%20Slavov%20FINAL.pdf.

44 This is complicated somewhat by the fact that benefits after initial claim are adjusted for growth in the Consumer Price Index, but is nevertheless true as a zeroth-order approximation.

45 http://www.cbo.gov/ftpdocs/120xx/doc12085/03-10-ReducingTheDeficit .pdf, p. 63.

46 http://www.cbo.gov/ftpdocs/56xx/doc5666/07-21-CraigLetterUpdated .pdf.

47 http://www.cbo.gov/ftpdocs/60xx/doc6044/12-22-Diamond-Orszag.pdf.

48 Butrica et al., http://www.urban.org/uploadedpdf/411121_DoesWorkPay .pdf.

49 http://www.actuary.org/pdf/socialsecurity/Social_Sec_Retirement_Age_ IB_FINAL_10_7_10_2.pdf, http://www.aei.org/outlook/100999, http:// www.urban.org/publications/901411.html.

50 http://www.aei.org/outlook/100999.

51 http://www.ssa.gov/OACT/TR/2011/lr5a3.htmll; http://www.ssa.gov/ OACT/TR/2011/lr5a3.html.

52 http://www.socialsecurity.gov/pubs/10147.pdf.

53 http://www.ssa.gov/policy/docs/statcomps/supplement/2010/6b.html.

54 Testimony of Charles Blahous before the Subcommittee on Social Security of the U.S. House of Representatives Committee on Ways and Means, July 8, 2011.

55 http://www.ssa.gov/OACT/NOTES/ran7/index.html.

56 http://www.ssa.gov/OACT/solvency/Warshawsky_20080917.pdf.

57 http://www.nber.org/programs/ag/rrc/NB06-06%20Goda,%20 Shoven,%20Slavov%20FINAL.pdf.

58 For details on provisions that would increase system progressivity while preserving work incentives, see Blahous, *Social Security: The Unfinished Work*, chapter 13.

59 Liebman, Luttner, and Self, "Labor Supply Responses to Marginal Social Security Benefits."

60 Examples include the personal income tax exemption for dependent children, the Child Tax Credit, and the Earned Income Tax Credit.

61 See for example H.R. 242 in the 107th Congress, establishing Social Security "KidSave" accounts: http://www.opencongress.org/bill/110-h242/show.

62   It is worth noting that other variables affecting the future number of workers, such as immigration, have a comparatively smaller effect.

63   Michele Boldrin, Mariacristina De Nardi, and Larry E. Jones, "Fertility and Social Security," NBER Working Paper No. 11146, February 2005.

64   Isaac Ehrlich and Jinyoung Kim, "Has Social Security Influenced Family Formation and Fertility in OECD Countries?" NBER Working Paper 12869, January 2007.

65   As one example, see Jason Furman, "Coping with Demographic Uncertainty," September 2007.

CHAPTER SIXTEEN: Education Quality and Economic Growth

1   National Commission on Excellence in Education, *A Nation at Risk: The Imperative for Educational Reform* (Washington, DC: U.S. Government Printing Office, 1983).

2   Robert J. Barro and Xavier Sala-i-Martin, *Economic Growth,* 2nd ed. (Cambridge, MA: MIT Press, 2004).

William Easterly, *The Elusive Quest for Growth: An Economists' Adventures and Misadventures in the Tropics* (Cambridge, MA: MIT Press, 2002).

Barro and Sala-i-Martin (2004) review recent analyses. Some have questioned the precise role of schooling in growth. Easterly (2002), for example, notes that education without other facilitating factors such as functioning institutions for markets and legal systems may not have much impact. He argues that World Bank investments in schooling for less developed countries that do not ensure that the other attributes of modern economies are in place have been quite unproductive. As discussed later in the chapter, schooling clearly interacts with other factors, and these other factors have been important in supporting U.S. growth. Nonetheless, school quality and the cognitive skills of the population remain extremely important.

3   Eric A. Hanushek and Ludger Woessmann, "Do Better Schools Lead to More Growth? Cognitive Skills, Economic Outcomes, and Causation," NBER Working Paper 14633, National Bureau of Economic Research, Cambridge, MA, January 2009.

4   Eric A. Hanushek and Dennis D. Kimko, "Schooling, Labor Force Quality, and the Growth of Nations," *American Economic Review* 90, no. 5 (December 2000): 1184–1208.

5   Ibid.; Eric A. Hanushek and Ludger Woessmann, "The Role of Cognitive Skills in Economic Development," *Journal of Economic Literature* 46, no. 3 (September 2008): 607–68.

The initial work in Hanushek and Kimko (2000) has now been expanded in a number of directions; see Hanushek and Woessmann (2008).

6   The present value gives added weight to economic gains closer to today compared with those in the future. It is easiest to interpret the present value as the amount of money that, invested at an assumed return of 3% per year, could produce the projected GDP pattern over time.

7   See, for example, Krueger (1974); World Bank (1993); Parente and Prescott (1994, 1999).

Anne O. Krueger, "The Political Economy of the Rent Seeking Society," *American Economic Review* 64, no. 3 (June 1974): 291–303.

World Bank, *The East Asian Miracle: Economic Growth and Public Policy* (New York: Oxford University Press, 1993).

Stephen L. Parente and Edward C. Prescott, "Barriers to Technology Adoption and Development," *Journal of Political Economy* 102, no. 2 (April 1994): 298–321.

Stephen L. Parente and Edward C. Prescott, "Monopoly Rights: A Barrier to Riches," *American Economic Review* 89, no. 5' (December 1999): 1216–33.

8   Claudia Goldin and Lawrence F. Katz, *The Race Between Education and Technology* (Cambridge, MA: Harvard University Press, 2008).

9   National Commission on Excellence in Education (1983).

10   See the various analyses in Peterson (2003).

Paul E. Peterson, ed., *Our Schools and Our Future: Are We Still at Risk?* (Stanford, CA: Hoover Institution Press).

11   Hanushek (2003). The other general finding that goes along with this is that class size has little consistent impact on student achievement, even though class size reduction has been extremely popular over this period.

Eric A. Hanushek, "The Failure of Input-Based Schooling Policies," *Economic Journal* 113, no. 485 (February 2003): F64–F98.

12   Eric A. Hanushek and Steven G. Rivkin, "Teacher Quality," in Eric A. Hanushek and Finis Welch, eds., *Handbook of the Economics of Education* (Amsterdam: North Holland, 2006): 1051–78.

13   Early academic research includes Hanushek (1971), Murnane (1975), and Armor et al. (1976). Policy interest rose with the introduction of the ideas directly into state evaluations (Sanders and Horn, 1994).

Eric A. Hanushek, "Teacher Characteristics and Gains in Student Achievement: Estimation Using Micro Data," *American Economic Review* 60, no. 2 (May 1971): 280–88.

Richard J. Murnane, *Impact of School Resources on the Learning of Inner City Children* (Cambridge, MA: Ballinger, 1975).

David J. Armor, Patricia Conry-Oseguera, Millicent Cox, Niceima King, Lorraine McDonnell, Anthony Pascal, Edward Pauly, and Gail Zellman, *Analysis of the School Preferred Reading Program in Selected Los Angeles Minority Schools* (Santa Monica, CA: Rand Corp., 1976).

William L. Sanders and Sandra P. Horn, "The Tennessee Value-Added Assessment System (TVAAS): Mixed-model Methodology in Educational Assessment," *Journal of Personnel Evaluation in Education* 8 (1994): 299–311.

14   For a detailed analysis of the impact of teacher effectiveness, see Hanushek (2011).

Eric A. Hanushek and Ludger Woessmann, "How Much Do Educational Outcomes Matter in OECD Countries?" *Economic Policy* no. 67 (July 2011): 1–65.

15   William J. Clinton, State of the Union Address, Washington, DC, 1997.

CHAPTER EIGHTEEN: Immigration and Growth

1   Alan Greenspan, remarks before the Economic Club of New York, January 13, 2000, http://www.federalreserve.gov/boarddocs/speeches/2000/200001132.htm.

2   Giovanni Peri and Chad Sparber, "Task Specialization, Immigration, and Wages," *American Economic Journal: Applied Economics* 1 (2009): 135–69.

3   George J. Borjas, "The Economic Benefits from Immigration," *Journal of Economic Perspectives* 9 (1995): 3–22; Council of Economic Advisers, "Immigration's Economic Impact," Executive Office of the President, Washington, DC, 2007, http://georgewbush-whitehouse.archives.gov/cea/cea_immigration_062007.html.

4   George J. Borjas, "Does Immigration Grease the Wheels of the Labor Market?" *Brookings Papers on Economic Activity* (2001): 69–119.

5   Frank D. Bean, Jennifer Van Hook, James Bachmeier, and Mark A. Leach, "Internal Migration in the Young Adult Foreign-Born Population of the United States, 1995–2000," U.S. Bureau of the Census and Sabre Systems Statistical and Demographic Analyses, Immigration Studies White Papers, Washington, DC, 2007.

6   Mark A. Leach and Frank D. Bean, "The Structure and Dynamics of Mexican Migration to New Destinations in the United States," in Douglas S. Massey, ed., *New Faces in New Places: The Changing Geography of American Immigration* (New York: Russell Sage Foundation, 2008), pp. 51–74.

7   Herbert Brücker, Gil S. Epstein, Barry McCormick, Gilles Saint-Paul, Alessandra Venturini, and Klaus Zimmerman, "Managing Migration in the European Welfare State," in Tito Boeri, Gordon Hanson, and Barry McCormick, eds., *Immigration Policy and the Welfare System* (Oxford: Oxford University Press, 2002), pp. 1–151.

8   Matthias Schündeln, "Are Immigrants More Mobile than Natives? Evidence from Germany," IZA Discussion Paper No. 3226, 2007.

9   Joshua D. Angrist and Adriana D. Kugler, "Protective or Counter-Productive? Labour Market Institutions and the Effect of Immigration on EU Natives," *Economic Journal* 113 (2003): F302–F331.

10   Pia M. Orrenius and Genevieve Solomon, "How Labor Market Policies Shape Immigrants' Opportunities," Federal Reserve Bank of Dallas, *Economic Letter* 1 (2006): 7.

11   Julian L. Simon, *The Economic Consequences of Immigration* (Oxford: Basil Blackwell, 1989).

12   Robert M. Solow, "Technical Change and the Aggregate Production Function," *Review of Economics and Statistics* 39 (1957): 312–20.

13   Philippe Aghion and Peter Howitt, "A Model of Growth Through Creative Destruction," *Econometrica* 60 (1992): 323–51; Paul M. Romer,

"Endogenous Technological Change," *Journal of Political Economy* 98 (1990): S71–S102.

14   Stephen Drinkwater, Paul Levine, Emanuela Lotti, and Joseph Pearlman, "The Immigration Surplus Revisited in a General Equilibrium Model with Endogenous Growth," *Journal of Regional Science* 47 (2007): 569–601.

15   Gnanaraj Chellaraj, Keith E. Maskus, and Aaditya Mattoo, "The Contribution of International Graduate Students to U.S. Innovation," *Review of International Economics* 16 (2008): 444–62; Jennifer Hunt, "Which Immigrants Are Most Innovative and Entrepreneurial? Distinctions by Entry Visa," *Journal of Labor Economics* 29 (2011): 417–57; Jennifer Hunt and Marjolaine Gauthier-Loiselle, "How Much Does Immigration Boost Innovation?" *American Economic Journal: Macroeconomics* 2 (2010) 31–56; William R. Kerr and William F. Lincoln, "The Supply Side of Innovation: H-1B Visa Reforms and U.S. Ethnic Invention," *Journal of Labor Economics* 28 (2010): 473–508.

16   Joseph Schumpeter, *The Theory of Economic Development* (Cambridge, MA: Harvard University Press, 1934).

17   AnnaLee Saxenian, *Silicon Valley's New Immigrant Entrepreneurs* (San Francisco: Public Policy Institute of California, 1999).

18   Vivek Wadhwa, AnnaLee Saxenian, Ben Rissing, and Gary Gereffi, "America's New Immigrant Entrepreneurs," Duke Science, Technology and Innovation Paper No. 23, 2007, http://people.ischool.berkeley.edu/~anno/Papers/Americas_new_immigrant_entrepreneurs_I.pdf.

19   Robert W. Fairlie, "Estimating the Contribution of Immigrant Business Owners to the U.S. Economy," Small Business Administration, Washington, DC, 2008.

20   Pia M. Orrenius and Madeline Zavodny, "From Brawn to Brains: How Immigration Works for America," *Federal Reserve Bank of Dallas 2010 Annual Report* (Dallas: Federal Reserve Bank of Dallas, 2011).

21   Robert W. Fairlie, "Estimating the Contribution of Immigrant Business Owners to the U.S. Economy," Small Business Administration, Washington, DC: Government Printing Office, 2008.

22   George J. Borjas, *Friends or Strangers: The Impact of Immigrants on the U.S. Economy* (New York: Basic Books, 1990).

23   Fairlie, "Estimating the Contribution"; Magnus Löfström and Chunbei Wang, "Mexican-American Self-Employment: A Dynamic Analysis of Business Ownership," *Research in Labor Economics* 29 (2009): 197–227.

24   James P. Smith and Barry Edmonston, *The New Americans: Economic, Demographic and Fiscal Effects of Immigration* (Washington, DC: National Academies Press, 1997).

25   Gianmarco I. P. Ottaviano and Giovanni Peri, "Rethinking the Effect of Immigration on Wages," *Journal of the European Economic Association* (2012): 152–97; Pia M. Orrenius and Madeline Zavodny, "Does Immigration Affect Wages? A Look at Occupation-Level Evidence," *Labour Economics* 14 (2007): 757–73.

26   Although the official H-1B cap is 85,000 visas (65,000 plus 20,000 for holders of U.S. advanced degrees), the nonprofit sector is exempt from the cap.

27   Guillermina Jasso, Vivek Wadhwa, Gary Gereffi, Ben Rissing, and Richard Freeman, "How Many Highly Skilled Foreign-Born Are Waiting in Line for U.S. Legal Permanent Residence?" *International Migration Review* 44 (2010): 477–98.

28   Jeffrey S. Passel and D'Vera Cohn, "Unauthorized Immigrant Population: National and State Trends, 2010," Pew Hispanic Center, Washington, DC, 2011, http://pewhispanic.org/files/reports/133.pdf.

29   Pia M. Orrenius, "U.S. Immigration and Economic Growth: Putting Policy on Hold," Federal Reserve Bank of Dallas, *Southwest Economy* 6 (November/December 2003).

30   Pia M. Orrenius and Madeline Zavodny, *Beside the Golden Door: U.S. Immigration Reform in a New Era of Globalization* (Washington, DC: AEI Press, 2010).

CHAPTER NINETEEN: How Technology Can Lead a Boom

1   Stephen S. Cohen and John Zysman, *Manufacturing Matters* (New York: Basic Books, 1987).

CHAPTER TWENTY: Growth Lessons from Calvin Coolidge

1   http://eh.net/encyclopedia/article/Smiley.1920s.final.

CHAPTER TWENTY-ONE: The Moral Imperative of a Free Economy

1   Paul VI, *Dignitatis Humanae,* December 7, 1965, n. 6, http://www.vatican.va/archive/hist_councils/ii_vatican_council/documents/vat-ii_decl_19651207_dignitatis-humanae_en.html.

Index